IN FOR A
PENNY

IN FOR A
POUND

IN FOR A PENNY

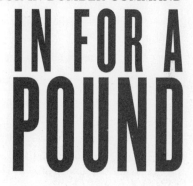

THE ADVENTURES AND MISADVENTURES
OF A WIRELESS OPERATOR IN BOMBER COMMAND

IN FOR A POUND

HOWARD HEWER

ANCHOR CANADA

National Library of Canada Cataloguing in Publication

Hewer, Howard
In for a penny, in for a pound : the adventures and misadventures
of a wireless operator in Bomber Command / Howard Hewer.

Includes bibliographical references and index.
ISBN 0-385-66077-4

1. Hewer, Howard. 2. Great Britain. Royal Air Force. Bomber
Command—Biography. 3. Flight radio operators—Canada--Biography.
4. World War, 1939-1945—Personal narratives, Canadian.
I. Title.

D811.H427 2004   940.54'4971'092   C2004-900724-6

Every reasonable effort has been made to obtain reprint permissions.
The publisher will gladly receive any information that will help rectify,
in subsequent editions, any inadvertent omissions.

The photo on page i shows a pair of Wellington IIs of 148 Sqn above the Nile Delta.

Cover photograph: courtesy of the author
Cover design: CS Richardson
Printed and bound in Canada

Published in Canada by
Anchor Canada, a division of
Random House of Canada Limited

Visit Random House of Canada Limited's website: www.randomhouse.ca

TRANS 10 9 8 7 6 5 4 3 2 1

*To my wife, Doris, and
to our son Robert and daughter Margaret,
and to those comrades with whom I trained and
flew who did not return*

REQUIEM FOR AN AIR GUNNER

My brief, sweet life is over, my eyes no longer see,
No summer walks — no Christmas trees — no pretty girls for me,
I've got the chop, I've had it, my nightly ops are done,
Yet in another hundred years, I'll still be twenty-one.

— R.W. Gilbert

CONTENTS

Foreword by G/C Kenneth McDonald, OBE, DFC, RAF (Ret'd)   xi
Preface   xiii
Introduction by F/L William H. Dixon, RCAF (Ret'd)   xvii
List of Maps and Illustrations   xxi

PART I: IN FOR A PENNY
1 First Steps into War   3
2 Wireless School in the West   11
3 Gunnery School and Real Warplanes   19
4 On the High Seas with HMS *Rodney*   23
5 London and the Blitz — First Loss of Innocence   28
6 Yatesbury Wireless School — Collision of Cultures   35
7 Operational Training: The "Wimpy"   39

PART II: IN FOR A POUND

8 Operational — "The Glamour Period Is Over" 53
9 Unto the Breach — Final Erosion of Innocence 66
10 Blooded Members of the Club 77
11 Adventures on Squadron Leave 82
12 Long Night to Berlin 90
13 Fear, Courage, and LMF 97
14 The End of the Beginning — A New Captain and Crew 101
15 Off to a Different War — Gibraltar, Malta, and Egypt 111

PART III: THE REMAINING FIFTEEN SHILLINGS

16 The Land of the Pharaohs 127
17 Kabrit — Into the Desert War 134
18 In Support of Eighth Army 144
19 A Fine Line to Mutiny 150
20 The Mail Run 158
21 Tymbaki — A Cruel Victory 167
22 A Costly Assault on Sicily and Leros 176

PART IV: ALL SPENT

23 Our Last Bomb Runs 187
24 Mission Behind Enemy Lines 198
25 Exit from Egypt 218
26 South Africa — Uncle Percy's Boers 223
27 Christmas Convoy 228
28 A "Screen Tour" and Tragic News 234
29 The End of My Odyssey — Going Home 244

Epilogue 253
Bibliography 257
Index 261

FOREWORD

BY GROUP CAPTAIN KENNETH MCDONALD, OBE, DFC, RAF (RET'D)

MANY BOOKS HAVE BEEN WRITTEN about the bomber war in Europe, the war that Adolf Hitler's former armaments minister, Albert Speer, called "the greatest lost battle on the German side" and which "opened up a second front long before the invasion of Europe."

Howard Hewer served in that war in Europe, but he served also in the extension of it that harried General Erwin Rommel's Afrika Korps in the campaigns of the Western Desert. These two experiences alone were enough to set him apart from fellow airmen whose operations were confined to the European theatre.

But he was not content with those experiences. In intervals between his duties as wireless operator/air gunner in Wellingtons (Wimpys), this nineteen-year-old Canadian explored England and Scotland and helped air raid wardens pull bodies from a bombed London dance hall, during which he was himself wounded by German bomb splinters. Plagued by bronchitis, he was in hospital when he learned that his crew was about to leave for the Middle East. He talked his way out of hospital, rushed to the departure airfield, and was airborne for Gibraltar at 0400 the next day. En route, their Wimpy was hit by flak off the French coast, damaging the starboard wheel, but Bill Dixon got them safely down on the airfield's short, and only, runway.

The continuation of his operational flying in the Mediterranean theatre would make a book of its own. Living conditions were bad enough at base airfields; at advanced landing grounds they were so bad, so lacking in amenities of the crudest sort, as to stand as a permanent blot on the records of successive commanding officers who failed in their first duty — to care for the men under command.

Despite those conditions — ground crews performed miracles to keep the Wimpys flying — the aircrews dropped their bombs and strafed enemy installations in the cause of holding the Afrika Korps in check.

Hewer and his crew were part of air power's long arm. Yet they share with compatriots in Burma and Italy the fate of all military units too far from the centre of authority. Northwest Europe was where the European war would be decided. Northwest Europe was where the news was written and broadcast.

Bomber crews who survived the dark nights of Europe will read with admiration and respect Hewer's matter-of-fact descriptions of low-level operations at night: laying their 4,000-pound bomb alongside a mole in Benghazi harbour; repeating that op two nights later, each op requiring an overnight stop en route at a primitive ALG and ten to eleven hours flying time; and as the lone attacking aircraft, doing a timed run to drop a 4,000-pound bomb on the German headquarters at Tymbaki, on the south coast of Crete, after they had dropped (as briefed!) leaflets on the north coast town of Candia and thus alerted the defences. All three operations were flown in the space of six days.

Howard Hewer flew 300 operational hours in Wellington Marks I and II, but it was in between the spells of official ops that he got into different kinds of trouble. Among many episodes, this one stands out. Convalescing from serious illness in Cairo, and bored by the enforced inactivity, he offered his services to the Mechanical Transport Unit. While he was there, he volunteered to drive a truck as part of a two-vehicle survey some 400 miles westward into the desert, though he had never before driven a car. A British Army captain, Sergeant Hewer, and the captain's corporal driver, set off on an expedition that took them far behind enemy lines. These and other remarkable adventures took three years of Howard's young life.

PREFACE

ADMIRAL NELSON'S signal to the British fleet at Trafalgar was obviously meant to inspire his sailors, but according to diaries of the time, reactions to what became the most famous naval signal in history were not what might have been expected.

Crusty Admiral Collingwood grumbled, "What is Nelson signalling about? We all know what we have to do." Some seamen complained, "We've always done our duty."

Those reactions reflect the fact that for centuries the soldiers and sailors of the British Isles have ever gone "once more unto the breach," often poorly led, always in discomfort and danger.

Since the air wars of 1914–1918 and of the Second World War, the airmen of Britain and the Commonwealth have earned the right to take their place alongside their sailor and soldier comrades. If I have one overriding, lasting impression of my many hours of operational flying on Royal Air Force squadrons, it is of my aircrew and groundcrew comrades shrugging off their fears and hardships, their sometimes poor leadership, and even abuse, all the while pushing themselves to the limits of duty to King and Country.

I believe that my motivation to enlist was partly influenced by my family's history of service. One of my earliest recollections is of the steel helmet, the cartridge bandoliers, and the bayonet in its worn leather sheath, all covered in a film of fine coal dust, that hung behind the furnace on the cellar wall of 198 Jones Avenue in Toronto. In one of the cartridge pouches were my father's dog tags: 342310 GNR Hewer JH CGA C of E.* He had been a gunner in the 3rd Brigade, Canadian Garrison Artillery, 11th Canadian Siege Battery, attached to the British Expeditionary Force (BEF) in Belgium in 1918, the last year of the First World War. Later I discovered that my uncle, Percy Ireland, had served in the Boer War in 1900. He had enlisted in Hamilton, Ontario, in the Lorne Rifles of Canada, which later joined the Canadian Mounted Rifles.

As soon as Canada's participation in the Second World War was confirmed by parliament, the country's scant reserve forces were called up, recruiting offices were opened, and tens of thousands of Canadians enlisted in the Canadian Army, the Royal Canadian Navy, or the Royal Canadian Air Force. All were volunteers.

For the title of my story, I finally settled for *In for a Penny, In for a Pound*, partly for the aptness — as the dictionary puts it, "things once begun must be concluded at all costs" — but also because they were the first words to greet me on arrival at our first operational squadron. An Australian flying officer, cap at a jaunty angle and a holstered revolver slung dramatically on his hip, welcomed us in August 1941, with, "Well, chaps, the glamour period is over. You got in for a penny, but now you're in for the pound!" How right he was!

ACKNOWLEDGMENTS

I am indebted to many people who encouraged me to persevere with this story when I began to flag under the stress of recalling the wartime events of over fifty years ago, and the strain, at my age, of having to unravel the complexities of a computer word processing program enough to produce a manuscript.

First of all, I wish to express my gratitude to Bill Dixon, my former pilot, and captain of our bomber crew, not only for making it possible for both of us to be here, but for correcting some of my narrative where

---

* These were the fireproof discs worn around the neck to identify soldiers killed in action. One was removed for records; the other remained with the body until burial.

it relates to piloting, for confirming the details of our operational record, and for contributing the introduction.

I owe particular thanks to Alan Brierley, who read all draft chapters and constantly urged me onwards. Alan served with the Canadian Army through the Italian campaign as one of the "D-Day Dodgers," and also in the slogging battles in northwest Europe that liberated the Netherlands. From his experiences, he was able to give me guidance on some of the land battle notes. I am indebted also to Hans Kotiesen, who brought his superior knowledge of the English language and his fine literary sense to bear on my manuscript, and helped me to avoid awkwardness.

I owe a further debt of gratitude to Group Captain Kenneth McDonald, a distinguished RAF veteran, for his professional editing of my manuscript, and for the foreword he so kindly volunteered to provide.

Finally, I'd like to thank Andrea Schneider. Without her keen eye, this edition might never have been published.

Opinions and any errors committed are, of course, my sole responsibility.

■ ■ ■

I would like to acknowledge various sources for some of the maps and photographs I have adapted for this book. The map of the European Theatre on page 76 was originally published in *The Right of the Line*, by John Terraine (Hodder and Stoughton, 1985); the map of Gibraltar on page 113 was published in *Gibraltar: The Keystone*, by John D. Stewart (Houghton Mifflin Company, 1967); the map of the Mediterranean Sea on page 118 originated in *The North African War*, by Warren Tute (Griffin Press Limited, 1976); the map of the Western Desert on page 146 was published in *A History of the SAS Regiment*, by John Strawson (Secker & Warburg).

The photo on page ii was published in *The Wellington Bomber*, by Chaz Bowyer (William Kimber); the photo of a Wellington at Gibraltar is also from Bowyer's fine book.

INTRODUCTION

BY FLIGHT LIEUTENANT WILLIAM H. DIXON, RCAF (RET'D)

I FIRST MET HOWARD HEWER IN 1941 while flying bombing operations into Western Europe during the Second World War with 218 Squadron, RAF, flying Wellington aircraft from Marham, Norfolk. After several months, I became captain of his second crew, and we served together, primarily with 148 Squadron in the Middle East.

Following training courses in Canada, a small but interesting convoy took Howard's group to Greenock, Scotland. In London, he was exposed to the horror, the suffering, and the devastation of the "blitz." His traumatic experiences during enemy air raids were his first brush with the realities of war.

With his first RAF crew from an Operational Training Unit, Howard joined 218 Squadron of Bomber Command's 3 Group at Marham. Introduced to the challenges of the bomber raids, along with his comrades Howard found strength of character and the personal discipline required to do his duty. His detailed descriptions of several operational sorties, and his crew's survival of terrifying ordeals, may not be unique, but his recording of them will give most readers an insight into experiences they may find hard to believe. He learned quickly that an

Australian officer's welcoming words, "You got in for a penny, but now you're in for a pound," truly reflected the possibility of death at the hands of the enemy.

Howard is frank in relating details of his adventures while on leave. You will not be surprised by unusual occurrences visited upon this young airman.

Few writers have so well acknowledged the efforts of the non-flying people who were essential to the success of the air war. Howard pays tribute to those ground crews operating under appalling conditions in the Western Desert, who kept our aircraft fit to fly. I share his respect for these partners in the war effort; their performance and dedication were extraordinary.

Howard tells how we came together when our commanding officer ordered me to assemble a new crew for transfer to the Middle East theatre of war. From a hospital stay, he barely made our take-off for a turbulent and life-threatening flight through Gibraltar to Malta, thence to an airport near Cairo, Egypt. The lack of navigation aids en route was a major challenge, but with perseverance and ingenuity, Howard repeatedly supplied the information our navigator needed, a remarkable accomplishment much downplayed in the narrative.

Howard's description of the aircrew's primitive living conditions at the air base of Kabrit, Egypt, where we joined 148 Squadron, will be a revelation to the reader. More shocking is the exposure of the discriminatory treatment of the few Canadian "colonial" aircrew by several pre-war RAF officers. Fortunately, this was offset by the friendly welcome and comradeship of our RAF NCO fellow squadron members.

Howard tells of how our squadron "mutinied"; it was an extraordinary affair that remains a condemnation of the failure of senior officers to care for the welfare of the fighting men under their command. It is a little-known aspect of the sometimes conflicting values and personal costs of wartime service.

Some of the operational sorties described in the narrative required exceptional courage and dedication from our crew. The reader may be particularly stirred by the peril and complications of our bombing raids on Benghazi (Libya), Tymbaki (Crete), and on Leros Island in the Aegean Sea.

When our crew finally completed the thirty-plus bombing raids required for a "tour," we reluctantly disbanded and went our separate ways, but Howard remained in Egypt to take part in some unusual and risky undertakings. This included a perilous and torturous expedition far behind enemy lines to find a landing site for fighter aircraft. In later chapters, we also read of meetings with Boers in South Africa, and of a long, adventurous sea journey back to the United Kingdom.

A short period of instructional duty in England, and his appointment to commissioned rank, precedes the welcome news that he was to be repatriated to Canada.

As the pilot and captain of the crew, I was well aware of Howard's dedication and ability. We knew that we could trust him to play his part with courage and skill; his performance was outstanding. We were fortunate to have him, not only as a fellow crew member, but as a good friend.

As someone who was there, I can attest to the accuracy of Howard's descriptions of events. I believe that Howard has written a gripping book, one that surely makes an important addition to our history of that world conflict.

Howard's book has rekindled many memories of lost friends, the exhilaration of a safe return, and the usual question, "Who's missing?" His style carries the reader along with warmth and humour, but he also describes the traumatic effects of our dangerous operations. My children have told me how interesting it is to begin to understand the experience of war through such a personal and readable story. I am pleased that Howard has been able to capture and communicate our experiences in such a balanced and engaging way.

LIST OF MAPS AND ILLUSTRATIONS

MAPS

The European Theatre of Air Operations   76
Gibraltar   113
The Mediterranean Sea   118
The Western Desert — Egypt   146
Benghazi City Centre   161
The Takoradi Route   220
The Route from Suez to Greenock   229

ILLUSTRATIONS

A Letter from the British Government   141

ONE

IN FOR A
PENNY

1
FIRST STEPS
INTO WAR

ON 18 SEPTEMBER 1939, I was strolling with a friend during lunch break from Parkdale Collegiate in Toronto's west end when we saw the bold newspaper headlines: "HMS *Courageous* sunk!" Sailing at reduced speed to recover aircraft, the carrier had been sunk about 350 miles west of Ireland by a German submarine later identified as U29. The shocking news brought the war home to me, and I was determined to seek out a recruiting office as soon as I could skip school for a day.

A few days later, without telling my parents, I found an excuse to leave the classroom, and made my way to the Royal Canadian Air Force (RCAF) recruiting office at 55 York Street. My initial inclination had been to follow in my father's footsteps and join the artillery, but a $2.00 flight over Toronto Island in a rather primitive biplane, and the sight of airmen who were beginning to appear on Toronto streets in their distinctive blue uniforms, changed my mind. I now had a burning desire to fly.

I was due for disappointment. When I was finally ushered in for my interview with the recruiting officer, he fixed a piercing eye on me and asked, "How old are you?"

I replied brightly that I was eighteen years old. "And have you gradu-ated from high school?"*

I had to admit, "Well, no." Then quickly I pleaded, "But I will next May." Not unkindly, he dismissed me. "Then you come back and see me then. Goodbye, son."

It was a long winter, but at last spring arrived along with the final examinations which, once conquered, would set me free to tackle that recruiting officer again. No scholar, I had nevertheless managed somehow to get an 80 percent average in most subjects, which exempted me from all final exams except for chemistry, in which I was some light years away from brilliance.

Major Lamb, the principal, a bemedalled veteran of the First World War, looked kindly and proudly upon students like me, among the ear-liest to enlist from Parkdale CI. With tongue in cheek, I gravely informed the good major that I would probably have to report within the next few days. After some negotiation, and another tongue-in-cheek assertion that I had been studying my chemistry and would have no difficulty with any exam "If only I had the time," I was granted my matriculation.

At the recruiting office, now nineteen years old and having com-pleted high school, I was accepted for aircrew training.** My dreams of being another Billy Bishop† now seemed possible.

At the dinner table that night I announced, as nonchalantly as I could, that I had joined the Air Force. Mother was shocked. Father was obviously concerned, and sister Marjorie looked frightened. But I got the feeling that they were proud as well.

Two weeks later, on 26 June 1940, I reported to the old coliseum building at the Royal Canadian Exhibition grounds, which had been turned into the RCAF's No. 1 Manning Depot. I was in for a penny!

Lectures on air force order and discipline and other matters were conducted in a large oval enclosure referred to as the "tanbark," which had a surface of hardened clay and sand. It was the site of international horse show and jumping competitions. There we spent a week getting kitted out and inoculated, the latter in an area of the former stables

---

* In Canada, for the first eighteen months of the war, aircrew candidates were not accepted without a Grade 12 certificate. At the outbreak no less than a university degree was expected. Later on, because of casualties and expansion, less education was demanded.
** Years later, while searching files at Air Force HQ in Ottawa, I inadvertently pulled out my own records. A quick look revealed a report on my 1940 enlistment: "This is a strong, ath-letic, and alert young man, very suitable for aircrew."
† The famous the First World War flying ace, then serving as chief of recruiting for the RCAF.

where two medical officers, one on each side, administered shots for everything from typhus and tetanus to diphtheria. Many of us had painful reactions and high fevers from the injections.

We were assigned to double bunks in stalls that only weeks before had been home to show horses and cows. They had moved the cattle out (but not the smell) and the recruits in. We were instructed in the fine art of military bed-making, and began an early morning routine of boot polishing, brass button shining, and pants pressing.

When I was all kitted out, I stood in front of the full-length mirror that was installed for us to make sure we were properly dressed, and saw myself for the first time in blue woolen tunic and trousers, wedge cap with bright brass badge, and ankle-high boots polished to a mirror-like shine. An RCAF airman, number and rank R69621 Aircraftman 2nd class (AC2). The rank might have been low (in fact the lowest) but I was proud to be in uniform, and prepared myself for the consequences.

■ ■ ■

There were hundreds of us, and we came from every province and territory in Canada. Quebecers fitted in after a round of mostly good-humoured exchanges between *maudits anglais* and frogs. Most of us were very young, between eighteen and twenty-two years of age, but there were some "really old" guys anywhere from twenty-six to thirty-two. These were the hard-rock miners from Sudbury and Timmins, lumberjacks from northern Ontario and British Columbia, and others who had been out in the world. These were the mature ones, the ones who knew the score. There were also recruits from British colonies, and from the United States.

There was one recruit from Chile whom most of us survivors remember quite vividly. He had the longest arms we had ever seen on a human being, but his use of one of them led to his early departure. Most of the sergeants and corporals who drilled and ordered us around all day were business-like, but fair. A few were overbearing and vulgar, using insulting language that shocked some of the younger chaps. One day, on the indoor parade square, we were lined up waiting for orders when one of the least-liked sergeants confronted the Chilean on some matter of dress. He thrust his jaw into the startled recruit's face and some of us heard him bark insulting descriptions of the poor fellow's mother. In a flash, one of the Chilean's long arms swung upwards like a spring released and lifted the sergeant about a foot off the ground. We heard the crack as his jaw broke, and he crumpled to the ground and lay still. There was great confusion as the service police were called and the Chilean and the sergeant were carried away. We never saw either of them again.

Most of us adjusted quickly to the routine. We had to get used to being in a large crowd of men of mixed personalities and habits. Showering naked in large groups took a little bit of getting used to for the youngest of us. City boys seemed to be less homesick than those who came from farms where a more isolated life and the daily sharing of chores made for closer family ties and dependency. Lying in my top bunk after lights out, I often heard muffled sobs.

We ran into a common problem with our uniform trousers. They were so narrow at the cuff that it was not possible to pull them on or off over our boots. We heard that this was more of a concern to some of the older guys who got into situations we only heard about from the canteen gossip.

We were given many weekend passes, and on Saturdays there was usually a line-up at a dry-cleaning and tailoring establishment called Lavines to get a "wedge" sewn into the inside of each trouser leg so as to widen the pantleg from the cuff to the knee so we could get our pants on over our boots. We also bought blue broadcloth shirts to replace the itchy flannel ones we had been issued. These alterations went unchallenged.

To get out of the gate on a weekend pass, we had to pass inspection by the Service Police (SP), which meant wearing complete uniform with cap. Caps, however, began to disappear. Capless unfortunates who arrived at the exit gate found that the SPs just happened to have one under the counter that they could let the victim have for $5.00. Often they bought back their own cap!

Wallets, moneybelts, and other valuables were also being stolen during the night hours. This went on until the RCMP put in undercover officers posing as recruits and nabbed the culprits. Several SPs we knew disappeared from the scene.

The days rolled by quickly. With the seemingly endless drill and physical training the fit became fitter; those with any excess fat soon lost it during drill sessions in the hot late June sun burdened with their old twelve-pound Ross rifles. We also sat through motivating films on Canada's role in the war, and through repeated lectures and graphic films on venereal disease, which most of us found shocking and embarrassing.

About 40 members of our group who had shown above-average proficiency in the drill sessions, and who averaged six feet in height, were winnowed out to form a crack drill team. These unfortunates were given special training until they could perform intricate drill movements at the tweet of a whistle. They went on to perform in front of audiences at the grandstands of exhibition grounds across the country, all in aid of promoting recruitment for the air force. They were a long time getting into the war.

Finally, the day came when we were judged ready to "pass out" to more serious training at an Initial Training School (ITS). We were paraded in all our new-found spit and polish and precision of step in front of the station commander, one Group Captain Denton Massey, who had found some small measure of fame in Toronto with his bible study groups. His family connections likely had more to do with his high rank.*

After the parade and a long motivational speech from the commanding officer we collected our duffle bags and suitcases and marched awkwardly to waiting buses that were to take us off to our "real" air force training.

In this we were lucky. Courses that came after us at Manning Depot were posted to guard duty and other non-aircrew jobs while the new flying stations were being built.

■ ■ ■

It was a short bus ride from Manning Depot to No. 1 Initial Training School, the old Eglinton Hunt Club at 1107 Avenue Road, Toronto. Little more than a decade before, the gentry had ridden to hounds from stables that were then surrounded by open fields. The property, now taken over by the Department of National Defence, took up a whole city block facing on Avenue Road. An old English-style manor accommodated messes for officers and trainees, as well as an indoor drill hall. Classrooms had been built on the north side of the drill hall.

The entire southwest corner was an asphalt parade square. The former stables shared the east side with the Link Trainer building and the big pressure chamber for high altitude testing. Our bunks were in the former stables, which also housed the wet canteen (beer) and the dry canteen (sundries). When we were met with the same horsey smells

---

* Denton Massey was a cousin of distinguished Canadian statesman Vincent Massey, who was high commissioner for Canada in Great Britain from 1935 to 1946, and the first native-born Canadian to hold the office of Governor General of Canada (1952–59).

that had first greeted us at the coliseum, we began to wonder if they were to be a permanent part of our air force life.

The nearly 200 trainees of our course were organized into "flights" of up to eighty students each. After this we went everywhere in flights. I was assigned to "B" flight, and discovered that we were officially ITS Course No. 4 of the fledgling British Commonwealth Air Training Plan (BCATP).*

We quickly settled into the routine. The objective of the ITS was to instruct us, analyze us, and test us to determine for which aircrew trade — pilot, observer, or wireless operator/air gunner — we were best suited. Most of us wanted and expected to be pilots, but there were a few who had other aspirations.

Our daily routine included early morning parades, and classroom instruction in mathematics, physics, elementary airmanship, and navigation, with liberal doses of air force administration and disciplinary codes. And we thought we had escaped the classroom!

We were also taken on route marches around the neighbourhood, led by Don McDonald, our redoubtable Scot, who had brought his bagpipes to war with him.

We endured the air-pressure tank, which was used to test sensitivity to the danger of oxygen starvation at high altitudes. The tank held seats for about eight trainees and an instructor/medical officer. We were given oxygen masks and taken to a simulated altitude of 20,000 feet. We were instructed to remove our oxygen masks and, after a brief interval, to write our names and addresses on a piece of paper. My writing looked perfectly normal and legible to me, and I could read it out loud.

The medical officer then said to us, "Take a look at your fingernails." We were shocked to see that they had turned purple from lack of oxygen. "Now put on your oxygen masks and breathe normally. Take a good look at what you wrote on the paper." I couldn't believe it. Just like that of the others, my writing was an unintelligible scribble! "Now that's what happens to you at high altitudes if you don't get your mask on in time. That could get you killed, gentlemen," he warned.

By now it was well into August, and we were beginning to feel like bona fide airmen. On evening or weekend pass we walked out proudly

---

* On 17 December 1939, Britain, Canada, Australia, and New Zealand had reached an agreement on what was initially called the Empire Air Training Scheme but soon became the BCATP.

  This date also marked the beginning of a long struggle by our prime minister, Mackenzie King, to bring about the "Canadianization" of Canadian forces serving, as always before, as units of British formations. We were to pay a heavy price for this nationalistic pride.

in our uniforms. I felt, as I'm sure many others did, that we were part of something really important, and that we were "serving." We had also become comfortable being part of a large group. We began to know each other as individuals and to form friendships. I was fortunate — I already knew one of our group well. Frank Cook and I had been classmates at Parkdale Collegiate.

It was remarkable how well such a diverse group of individuals got along with each other; still, there were a few dust-ups. Altogether it was a testimonial to the character and good humour of the young men of Canada, few of whom had had a comfortable or carefree adolescence in the Depression years.

We knew that selection day would soon be upon us. Who would be going off to pilot, observer, or wireless operator training? Finally, we were paraded one morning into the indoor drill square to hear an address by Group Captain Geoffrey O'Brien.

This officer was a distinguished veteran of the First World War Royal Flying Corps. He was a fine-looking figure in his bemedalled summer uniform. But he brought shocking news. After an innocent preamble, he had tongue firmly in cheek when he announced, "Gentlemen, you are about to leave for flying training, and if I were going with you and could do my time over again, I would wish that I could be a wireless operator and air gunner.

"I am here to tell you that No. 2 Wireless School has just opened in Calgary, Alberta, and needs a full complement of trainees. Regardless of what aircrew trade you might have been tentatively selected for, this entire course will be going to that school. It will be an exciting and rewarding challenge, gentlemen. Good luck and good flying."

Most of our group who had been on the pilot list, or who thought they were certain to become pilots, were crushed. My dreams of flying Spitfires or Hurricanes were shattered. I was immensely disappointed.

Not every trainee's dreams were frustrated. One of the school's instructors, a Flight Lieutenant Henchett-Taylor, was a Britisher who had managed to talk some of the trainees into forming a cricket team. Suspiciously, several members of his team left our ranks for Elementary Flying School. One or two Americans immediately called their congressmen in the States and some ensuing cross-border politics got them into the pilot ranks. A few others who were mature enough to raise hell managed to make pilot or observer training. For the rest of us there was no hope.

At the end of August, the bulk of our course, numbering 170 men, packed duffle bags and said farewell to Toronto and ITS. Although we were all glad to move on to more realistic training and actual airplanes, as we sat on the bus taking us to Union Station and the train to Calgary, we knew it was going to take some time to put our shattered dreams behind us.

2
WIRELESS SCHOOL IN THE WEST

FOR THOSE OF US FROM TORONTO there were brief goodbyes at Union Station before we boarded the Canadian National train for Calgary. It felt like the start of adventure.

I had been out west before. In 1935, with my father unemployed, my mother, sister, and I spent the summer on my grandfather's farm at Milden, Saskatchewan. We had taken Canadian Pacific Railway's scenic route, which hugs the shores of Lake Superior. Once past Winnipeg, we were treated to the vast sweeping panorama of the Canadian prairies, with boundless acres of waving golden wheat stretching out to a very distant horizon.

For troops at the bottom of the rank scale we were treated royally — bunks with white sheets made up by porters no less, and meals served to us on white tablecloths in the dining car!* We made the most of it while it lasted.

Our friends from ITS were aboard: Harry Humphries, Ike Hewitt, Gord Houston, and my high-school classmate, Frank Cook. The course

---
* This royal treatment did not survive the first few graduating classes of the BCATP.

"characters" were also with us, and would figure prominently in some of the shenanigans to come.

On arrival at Calgary's railway station two nights and three days later, we were met by scores of open-air stake trucks. To Frank and I they looked like cattle trucks. We looked at one another and wondered aloud if we were headed for the stables again.

In good order we piled our kit into the trucks bound for the city and the wireless school, which was at the top of the hill on 10th Street. It was a typical Canadian high school, surrounded by an open field. Our barracks, with the same type of double bunks we used at ITS, were in a brick building at the west end of the school itself. A flag pole carrying the Union Jack and the RCAF ensign marked a parade and drill square. The classrooms were in the main building.

As Frank and I unloaded kit at our assigned bunks, we sniffed the air with approval: "Ah. No manure!"

The next morning we assembled on the square and met the disciplinarians who were to order our every move from that day in the second week of September to graduation. For the most part they were Canadian sergeants and corporals, but the chief was a Royal Air Force regular force flight sergeant by the name of Bligh. We were to find out just how appropriate his name was, and to feel that he must certainly have been a direct descendant of that notorious *Bounty* captain.

We saw few officers, and when we did we either never knew or quickly forgot their names. The commanding officer, however, was Group Captain Russell.

Following orientation lectures, we soon settled into the routine of instruction. Every morning at 0630 hours we were routed out of our bunks, given brief moments to climb into the "Teddy Bear" fur liners of our flying suits, and herded out into the increasingly frigid air to do calisthenics — all before breakfast! Within weeks the medical officer objected to this and thereafter we were given breakfast in the mess hall before the physical exercises. The medical officer, or MO, became one of our favourite people.

This exercise was followed by hour after hour of classroom instruction in Morse code* and radio theory. For the dit-dah of the Morse code we sat at long tables, each of us with headphones on and a code-sending

---

* More correctly, "international code." Morse code was the code used between railway stations; operators read the spaces between clicks rather than the dots and dashes of the international code. Both were invented by Samuel Morse (1791–1872).

key at our right hand as our kindly instructor, Corporal Davis, sent code to us at ever-increasing speeds. We copied the messages in our notebooks, which were then checked and marked. We also learned to tap out the code as Cpl Davis listened and marked our progress. The minimum receiving and sending speed to be attained was 18 words per minute (WPM), but many of us who took more rapidly to the rhythm of the code reached speeds of 25 WPM.

We endured many hours of lectures on radio theory. We heard about beat frequency oscillators (BFOs), IF circuits, and hysteresis curves. Hours spent on thicknesses and colours of wires proved to be of little value.

In the lab we were introduced to our first radio transmitter and receiver. This was a British T1082/R1083, an ancient piece of equipment used for army liaison in armoured vehicles in the early thirties. The transmitter had two interchangeable power amplifier coils, about five inches in diameter, to set up whatever low, medium, or high frequencies were required. The receiver had an anode and a diode coil for frequency tuning. There were twelve of these inserts, each about the size of the cardboard cylinder from a toilet-paper roll. We laboured to learn how to tune these archaic contraptions. I was thankful that I had paid attention to the instructor in the lab when, some twelve months later, in much more exciting circumstances, I was suddenly confronted again with that wireless set.

More welcome was our exposure to the Aldis lamp, partly because the classes were held outdoors on a hill overlooking downtown Calgary. This device was a hand-held cylinder about the size of a half watermelon, with a glass face covering a high-power projection bulb. Red or green filters fit over the glass. There was a pistol handgrip and a trigger activating the bulb to flash dots and dashes in Morse code.* I found the lamp easy to master and, again, some nine months later, I was happy that I'd paid attention.

Our instructor was a rather dour corporal, a man of few words and a fixed expression. We named him Ned Sparks after a well-known Hollywood deadpan comedian of the thirties. "Ned" would place us over a small knoll and sit us down to send us messages with the Aldis lamp. But once we lay down over the knoll, books in hand, he couldn't see us.

---

* The navy made the greatest use of this signalling lamp, usually in a fixed mount, to send messages between ships in convoy. This was safer than wireless transmissions, which could more easily and at far greater ranges be intercepted by prowling U-boats.

During the hour-long class, small groups took turns jogging down the hill to 10th St. for a drink or ice cream. On return we copied down what we had missed. We were never caught.

We moved between classrooms in some semblance of marching order, our big boots pounding on the dark brown linoleum that covered all the floors in the building, which had been installed when the school was converted for air force use.*

We were the first airmen to arrive in Calgary, and were greeted with the heralded old-west hospitality. The army, well established in the town, was less enthusiastic. They had enjoyed the undivided attention of the many attractive young ladies, but this changed dramatically when our blue uniforms appeared, bringing images of Fighter Command battling the Nazis over Britain. It didn't hurt that the Battle of Britain pilots had just saved Britain from a German invasion.

By now we were wearing a white flash in our wedge caps, a piece of flannel inserted into the front fold of the cap to show that we were under training for aircrew. Unfortunately, the army privates somehow got the idea that we were all commissioned officers, and offered us smart salutes, which we gravely returned; they soon discovered their mistake, and relations turned for the worse. It might have been the soldiers who spread the rumour that the white flash was a warning that the wearer had VD.

In our second month of training, our drill staff decided that an inter-service boxing match would be a good public relations exercise. They began to recruit some of our group to participate against a team from the resident Seaforth Highlanders regiment, who were no doubt looking forward to getting a little revenge.

They had some tough guys to put in the ring, but we had a couple of secret weapons of our own: big Andy Miller, who had been a policeman in Kenora, Ontario, with considerable experience as a semi-pro heavyweight; and Ty Deely, an Irish welterweight from Newfoundland, who loved to fight and looked like a windmill in action.

---

* This same floor covering appeared in nearly every air force building across the country. Apparently, a senior air force officer and his civilian brother owned the Dominion Linoleum Company, the manufacturer. At all events, this product proved itself. In 1975, while in a second "mini career" with the Ontario government, I paid a nostalgic visit to the old wireless school building for a meeting with the staff of a Stationary Engineer program that now occupied many of the classrooms. Walking along the hallway with the chief instructor, I pointed at the floor and, as he confirmed, it was the same stuff, still looking like new!

The rest of the team was made up from our group; we were assured that the matches were to be strictly for amateurs. I had had great success on our high-school boxing team, and in fact was taken off the team for knocking out two opponents. I was physically fit after a summer "stooking" wheat on my grandfather's farm. Emboldened by this record, and lulled by the assurances of our corporals, I signed up.

The big night arrived. Andy knocked out his hapless opponent in the first round. Ty took almost three rounds to dispatch his victim.

When my turn came, I felt confident enough, only to feel it fade when I got to the middle of the ring. As my opponent scowled at me, I could see scar tissue around his eyes. His ears looked like cauliflower. This was an amateur?

I managed to get through the first round, but my ribs felt like they had been run over by a truck. In my corner, my buddies cheered me on. "No problem, you're doing fine." But I couldn't help thinking of that old fight joke in which the trainer says to his battered fighter, "Don't worry. He isn't laying a glove on you." And the fighter replies, "Then keep your eye on the referee, because somebody's beating hell out of me!"

Against my better judgment I ventured out for the second round, and immediately began to take another pounding to my rib cage. This angered me, and I drew back my right arm to avenge myself. But my gladiator friend had other ideas, and the lights went out before my punch landed. That was the end of my boxing career. My jaw ached for a week.

■ ■ ■

On a freezing day in November, four open stake trucks arrived with a sorry-looking group of Australians and New Zealanders, shivering and blue with the cold. They were not used to this climate. We soon got them warmed up with hot soup and coffee.

It wasn't long before they became a popular part of the larger group, although they were starting at the basic class levels we had left behind. The Aussies tended to resist the normal discipline of the school, and could often be seen doing extra drill under the tender mercies of Captain Bligh.

We had been playing some hockey, and the Aussies decided to form a team — never mind that they had never been on skates before! After crashing and slithering on the ice for a while, they gained balance and astonished everyone by winning some games in the local league. What they lacked in skill, they made up for in sheer determination and aggressiveness. They were a welcome part of the vanguard of volunteers who joined the BCATP from all parts of the Commonwealth.

During November we began our air training. We were taken by truck south of the city to Currie Airfield, which was situated on a plateau above city level. We were introduced to the Norseman aircraft, which had gained fame as a rugged northern bush plane, and to a tiny, two-seat aircraft, a Fairchild K24.

The Norseman was fitted out with four of the old radio sets. Under an instructor, usually six trainees rotated to practise sending and receiving messages with the ground station. I remember having only two flights in the Norseman, and on neither occasion did I use the wireless equipment.

I did have one scenic and enjoyable, but utterly useless, flight in the little Fairchild. We took off one bright day for the foothills of the Rocky Mountains. I sat closely behind the pilot, separated only by the wireless set, reviewing the schedule of messages I was supposed to exchange with the ground station at Currie. I struggled through the convoluted sequences of tuning dials and reading meters that, if adjusted correctly, might just get me on the right frequency.

I needn't have bothered. The pilot was on a sight-seeing trip, and was swooping happily down into the gorgeous mountain valleys. When I told him that I couldn't reach any ground station with my signals from the valley floor, he said I should relax and enjoy the scenery. I did, but I didn't learn a damn thing about operating a wireless set from the air. That turned out to be the extent of my practical radio training in Canada. At least I had made it into the air in an air force airplane.

As December neared, and we passed our frequent tests, we began to feel more like air force men. We had received our first promotion, from AC2 to Leading Aircraftman (LAC), which gave us an increase in pay from $1.30 per day to about $2.25. We were excited to receive the silver cloth propellers we were now to wear on both sleeves of our tunic, midway between elbow and shoulder. This was not a rank, but a trade classification; nevertheless we were proud of this first symbol of achievement we could wear on our uniforms. By now we had largely thrown off the hurt of not being sent to pilot training, and were quite engrossed in learning our trade as wireless operators.

On most weekends we were granted a 48-hour pass, and we made the most of our opportunities to see the surrounding countryside. On one pass, Frank and I joined up with friends Mike Daniels and Jimmy

Cline to rent horses for a cross-country ride. This was Mike's idea. He had been raised in the west and unlike the rest of us was no stranger to the saddle.

At the rental stables we were given tired-looking nags that would have looked more at home behind a plough. Mike chose a spirited young stallion more suited to his talents. Once out on the prairie, Mike and the stallion took off at a furious gallop and our steeds valiantly tried to follow. I hung on to the saddlehorn for dear life. Frank, on old Betsy, came up alongside me, looking just as frightened as I was. Suddenly, as we careered along, his horse stepped into a gopher hole and stopped dead in its tracks. Frank did not. For a brief moment, he sat there beside me, hands out in front as if still holding the reins, with no horse under him. In a split second his trajectory changed and he hit the ground at some speed. Although shaken up, miraculously neither he nor the horse was hurt. We managed to talk Mike into holding his mount in check, and made our sorry way back to the barn.

Frank and I had a much different adventure just before Christmas. On evening pass, we were walking past Eaton's on 2nd Avenue when we almost tripped over a young girl lying in the snow. Startled, we each took an arm and pulled her to her feet. She was barely conscious, and looked to be no more than sixteen years old. Somebody had fed her a great deal of liquor, and she was not warmly dressed.

Frank asked me what we should do. An older woman appeared, looked from us to the girl and, crying that she should call the police, began to beat Frank with her umbrella. Fortunately, she moved on, leaving us to carry the girl as best we could in search of shelter. We took her into a diner and helped her to sit at the counter, where she immediately threw up. We left in a hurry, carrying the girl with us.

Next, we took her into a car salesroom. The manager got some coffee for all of us, and the girl told us what had happened. She had left a party when it seemed to be getting out of hand, and realized that she had had too much to drink. She told us her address. The manager said he lived just one block away from her, that he was closing up, and, much to our relief, he would see her safely home — a typical gesture in that warm-hearted city.

There were many romances while in training, though I'd heard that saltpetre had been added to our food right from our days at Manning Depot to help suppress our raging hormones. From our observation of the "older" chaps among us it didn't seem to have any effect. (Fifty years later, this became a joke: "Remember that stuff they put in our food during training? Well, I think it's finally beginning to work!") We quite forgot that the young women's hormones were leaping about just as frantically as ours.

I even had my own romance. At a Consumers' Gas company dance, I met a lovely girl, who soon took me home to meet her mother. Her father, a major in the Canadian army, was overseas.

We had good times together. We enjoyed skating together on the outdoor ice rinks. I discovered that out west, the male partner skated on the inside, and swung his girl around the corners. Back east it was the other way around. We had long walks along the river, and I was a frequent guest at dinner, even on Christmas.

I began to realize that my girl was a few years older than I was. After we had attended the New Year's dance at the Palliser Hotel, it became painfully apparent that I was just not ready for the "more mature relationship" that my partner obviously thought was long overdue. Sadly, that was the end of our friendship.

Two weeks later, we had our passing out parade, and said goodbye to our Calgary friends and to the wireless school. We had passed our final exams and tests, and were on our way to No. 1 Bombing and Gunnery School at Jarvis, Ontario.*

Most veterans of the Calgary experience have happy memories of those days. The hospitality and friendship offered to us were outstanding; even the climate proved invigorating.

Notwithstanding, we were headed now to bombing and gunnery school back east, and we were anxious to get closer to the real air force, flying into the real war.

---

* In 1998 I discovered from copies of my records that I had placed 6th out of 167 trainees, and had been recommended for a commission. As you'll see, it was a long time coming.

3
GUNNERY SCHOOL
AND REAL WARPLANES

As OUR TRAIN CARRIED US BACK EAST to our destiny, we rattled along again over the endless prairie fields, the wheat stubble now covered with snow. We were not pampered as much as we had been on our trip out to Calgary, and we had much time for reflection. It was now January 1941, yet we had little news of the war.

We had a one-hour stop in Toronto's Union Station before changing trains for Jarvis, in southern Ontario, a dozen miles north of Lake Erie's northern shore. I had time to phone home and to call my father at the Royal York hotel, where he was then working, just steps across Front Street from the station. He must have run all the way. He arrived breathless on the platform minutes before I boarded our train. We had a joyous, but brief, reunion.

In this second week of January 1941, the bombing and gunnery school held more excitement and anticipation for us than did the other training stations. We were about to climb into battle-tested aircraft and be introduced to some deadly weapons.

After a brief welcome by a squadron leader, we were led to our quarters in one half of an "H" hut, and were allocated single beds instead of double bunks. The wash basins, toilets, and showers — the "ablutions" — were in the common central bar of the "H." On the floor, sure enough, was the brown linoleum.

Our first day began with a tour of the flight line. To us, it looked like a full-fledged operational airfield; lined up wing-tip to wing-tip were at least ten Fairey Battles. There was a great deal of activity. There were fuel bowsers buzzing about, and we could see observer trainees hanging 11-pound practice bombs on racks fixed under the bellies of several of the Battles.

One of our sergeant guides, Sgt Howell, told us a grisly story that blunted our enthusiasm. A week before our arrival, one of the observer trainees, probably confused by the roar of the engine, had placed his bombs on the racks and backed out into the fast-spinning propeller. He was cut in half. Extra safety measures were put in place after that.

No time was wasted. We were back in the classroom for lectures on flying tactics and air gunnery. Very soon we got our hands on our first machine gun, the .303-inch Browning with a firing rate of 1,150 rounds per minute, and the much slower-firing and obsolescent Vickers gas-operated gun. The Browning was belt-fed, while the Vickers was fed from a drum clamped over the breech block.

Under the patient instruction of Sgt Howell we soon learned how to dismantle and strip, not only the Browning and Vickers, but the more powerful .50 calibre Browning and the 20mm Hispano-Suiza cannon, neither of which we ever saw again.

Sgt Howell carried a powerful lesson with him: one of his thumbs was missing, lost when it got in the way of a forward-moving breech block, the steel block that carries the bullet swiftly forward into the breech of the gun.

He soon had us firing guns on the firing range. It took a while to get used to the noise, but we soon settled down. We had to clean the guns after firing, and we learned how to use the crank machine that fit links and bullets together to form the long ammunition belts. Much care had to be taken to ensure a precise fit and alignment; otherwise, the gun could jam. Of all the parts of the Browning we had to memorize, one of the most intricate is still indelibly printed on my mind — the sear spring retainer keeper and pin, which kept the powerful spring in check. When released, it propelled the breech block forward, pushing a round into the chamber for firing.

In February 1941, we were in the air, excited to be flying, firing the Vickers machine gun at targets towed by Fairey Battles at the end of long cables. The target "drogues" were recovered after the exercise and the number of hits we made were counted and assessed. On some flights we fired camera guns at pursuing Battles on our tail that simulated attacking German fighters. The photos showed how many hits we would have made on the attacker. We were in three-man crews — the pilot up front and two trainees standing in the back of the "greenhouse" in the open air taking turns firing the camera gun. Frank Cook and I teamed up for these exercises.

We flew blissfully on, firing from our Battles at towed targets or at large chunks of ice in low-level attacks over cold Lake Erie.

One exercise almost put an early end to my war. On 28 January 1941, Frank and I were scheduled for a camera gun exercise over Lake Erie. As standard practice we wore a parachute harness, but our parachutes, unlike the pilot's, were not attached to the harness. While flying, our chutes were stored in a rack on the fuselage wall. In an emergency they were clipped onto two dog clasps on the front of the harness. Where the gunner stood in the rear of the cockpit "greenhouse," a G-string wire was attached to the floor. The free end of this cable was clipped to a ring at the bottom rear of the gunner's harness to prevent the gunner from falling out of the aircraft during violent manoeuvres.

When Frank and I climbed on board, this G-string was missing. We hesitated to cause trouble, so we kept quiet about it while we went off into the blue with a Sgt Post at the controls. (He was one of the many experienced American pilots recruited to help out in the early struggling months of the BCATP.)

At 6,000 feet over the lake, I was happily firing away at a pursuing Battle when the pilot pulled the nose up sharply, and over the side I went — no G-string, no chute! With one hand I clutched the butt of the camera gun, and the heel of one flying boot stuck in the gun ring. The rest of me was hanging over the cold water of Lake Erie! I had time to look down in horror at the ice floes a mile below me before Frank reached over and grabbed the seat of my pants. I was lucky he had strong arms.

As Frank struggled to get me back into the aircraft, our pilot, oblivious to our dilemma, was happily twisting and turning the Battle about the sky. I screamed at Frank above the tearing wind, "For God's sake tell him to level out!" Fortunately for me Frank didn't try that. All we had for communication with the pilot was a Gosport tube, which led to earphones in the pilot's helmet. To reach that tube Frank would have had to let go of me. Good old Frank! Somehow he got me back in the aircraft. It took me five minutes to pry my hand off the butt of the camera gun, and my fingers ached for an hour.

We didn't mention our little drama to anyone, but we did report the absence of the G-string. This was my first, but certainly not my last, big thrill of the war.

On 17 February 1941, we graduated as full-fledged wireless operator/air gunners. We had become reasonably proficient with the machine guns and knew Morse code, but we were to find out how ill-prepared we were for operational flying. Of the three aircrew trades,* ours received the poorest training. There was a long history of pilot training in Canada, and enough qualified navigators (observers) to structure an effective training program fairly quickly. For wireless operators, however, there was little or no tradition, and only the most rudimentary equipment during the early days of the training scheme.

I don't recall that we had much of a formal "wings parade"; at least, nothing like the pilots' graduations with visiting dignitaries like Billy Bishop or relatives pinning on the coveted wings. Unceremoniously, we were issued with our single air gunner's wing, and promoted to the rank of sergeant. (We wore a patch with a "sparks" symbol stitched on it on our left arm to indicate our wireless operator trade.) We also got an increase in pay to $3.65 per day.

We were given passes for three weeks leave, and taken by bus to meet the train for Toronto. From there the new sergeants would travel across Canada to their homes for one last time with parents or wives before heading off to the war and into the unknown.

---

* The aircrew trades of bomb aimer and flight engineer were not introduced until 1942, when the four-engined bombers entered the scene.

4
ON THE HIGH SEAS
WITH HMS *RODNEY*

THE THREE WEEKS OF EMBARKATION leave passed all too quickly, especially for my family. And yet, like others about to leave home and country for the great adventure, I was anxious to get going.

At Union Station, in the lower concourse where exits led directly to the train platforms, there were many small groups of family members and friends saying their goodbyes to son, brother, or husband. For all too many, it was the last time they would meet.

My family was apprehensive. My cousin Harvey Ireland, who joined the forces after I had, and whose father had been in the Boer War, left the scene early, looking quite forlorn.*

Once on the train, there were reunions with comrades from our training courses. The trip was uneventful, and on the second day we arrived at the air base and supply depot of Debert, Nova Scotia, a holding unit until our convoy was ready at Halifax. It had rained for weeks and wooden duck-boards had been placed between barracks as the only way

---

* Harvey joined the Canadian Army in 1942 and served in the U.K. and Italy. Upon my return to England in 1943 from Egypt, we had a reunion before he left for the Sicily invasion.

to get over the deep mud. We were put into double bunks again; the living was primitive. We passed the time doing our own laundry and playing cards. I found I had a talent for ironing shirts, and when this was found out I was pressed into service for our barracks.

We were paraded for more inoculations and a patch test for TB. This turned out to be bad news for Frank Cook. His test was positive, and while this did not necessarily mean that he had TB, it was enough to disqualify him from the draft overseas.

After two weeks of misery we were assembled in one of the hangars and told that we were leaving that day for Halifax. There were cheers all around, except from Frank, who stood forlornly on the platform as the train pulled away (I was to reflect later that the TB test just might have saved his life).*

On arrival in Halifax, we were taken directly on board the MV *Georgic*, an impressive liner of some 30,000 tons, capable of 22 knots. In single file we were led deeper and deeper into the bowels of this vessel until we reached our allotted cabins, which were below the water line. Our cabins, fitted with four bunks, were at the end of a narrow passage, almost directly over the ship's propellers.

We were given our Daily Routine Orders, and the schedule for meals and lifeboat drills. Once under way, we would have daily duties such as lifeboat guards, responsible for helping to raise the alarm and getting others into the lifeboats when abandoning ship. The lifeboat guard was the last to leave the ship.

As soon as we had settled our gear in the cabin, we took off for the deck for some fresh air, and to look at all the activity in the big harbour of Bedford Basin. A great number of ships of all shapes and sizes were anchored or taking up positions in the basin as they formed up the convoys of freighters, oil tankers, and troopships. Grey shapes of destroyers and corvettes glided towards their stations, ready to shepherd their flocks through the U-boat infested waters in the continuing struggle to get food, fuel, and ammunition to beleaguered Britain.

As I stood at the railing looking out over the dramatic scene, I remembered what my father had told me about how his convoy had left just days before the great explosion that ripped apart the harbour and the city in 1917.**

---

* Frank did not get overseas, but flew operationally with Coastal Command off Canada's coasts, and became a commissioned officer.
** At 0900 hours on 6 December 1917, the Norwegian relief ship *IMO* collided with the

Two days later, our ship eased its way out of its berth. When we had passed the submarine booms, we were joined by a tiny sailboat — the pilot boat — which led us out to sea. The air was foggy, the sea smooth.

When the pilot boat left us and the fog cleared, we saw off our port side a large, two-funnelled liner, a troopship named the SS *Politia*. Apparently, our convoy was made up of only two ships. But then an enormous grey battleship swept past us majestically, and took its place in the lead, about 800 yards off our port side. It was HMS *Rodney*, 35,000 tons, turrets bristling with nine 16-inch guns. She was to be our escort.

Just before the outbreak of war, I had purchased a Kodak 620 folding camera, which had an excellent f/4.5 lens. I kept it close at my side throughout the war, and I was fortunate to get a great many photos. Many of the shots I took were borderline "legal," and I was lucky to get away with it.

I couldn't resist taking a picture of *Rodney*. In my travels around the *Georgic*, I came across a door at the base of the forward mast. Through the door lay spiral steps that led up the hollow interior. As I climbed higher the space became smaller and smaller until at last I came to a small port that opened onto a crow's nest platform. I leaned out on the platform, and looking out and downwards I saw *Rodney* just off our port side. I quickly opened the camera, set the lens opening, shutter speed, and range, and snapped my picture. Stuffing the camera into my tunic, I scrambled down the iron steps as quickly as I could. At the bottom, I eased the door open; nobody about. I had my very illegal picture of the ship that was to take part in the sinking of the *Bismarck*.

Encouraged by this success, I managed to get a photo of the troopship *Politia* when it was abeam of us, and also what I thought was a dramatic shot of the 5-inch gun mounted on the stern deck of the *Georgic*.

We assumed that *Rodney* was there because our two ships, carrying between them what must have been close to 9,000 soldiers and airmen, needed special protection. In reality, with the ability of all three vessels to maintain a speed in excess of 20 knots, the threat from submarines

---

French ammunition ship *Mont Blanc*, which, unknown to other ships in the harbour, was carrying a cargo of half a million pounds of trinitrotoluol and 300 tons of picric acid. The collision started a fire that spread too rapidly for the crew to contain, and quickly reached the highly volatile cargo of the *Mont Blanc*. The resulting blast was the most powerful accidental explosion in history. The shockwaves and fire sank ships, touched off other conflagrations, and levelled most of the lower part of Halifax and the settlements fronting on Bedford Basin. Nearly 2,000 people died, 9,000 were injured, and 400 were blinded.

was minimized, and the most serious threat came from surface attack by roaming German battlecruisers. Hence, the presence of the *Rodney*.*

Our crossing was uneventful — no U-boat scares or attacks by long-range German aircraft. Nevertheless, lying in my bunk at night, which shook constantly from the rotation of the screws, I could not help thinking that, below the water line as we were, our chances of surviving a hit by a torpedo were not very good.

Six days out from Halifax, and one day out from our Scottish port destination, we were met by two British destroyers. *Rodney* handed us over to their charge and steamed off. The next day we sighted land, and soon we were gliding under a light rain up the Clyde estuary and through the opened submarine booms to our anchorage off Greenock, Scotland. Even in the light drizzle, the deep green and patches of purple heather of the fields had an uncommon beauty. I found it hard to believe that I was about to set foot on this storied land.

Because of the limited capacity of the Greenock docks, we anchored some distance out in the estuary. We had to be taken off by lighter boats, a sort of small barge that made several trips to get everyone ashore. By this time it had become quite misty, and the light rain was still falling. We were to find that this was normal weather for that part of this country. We milled about on the docks for almost an hour, glad that we were wearing our greatcoats. We experienced for the first time that particular brand of penetrating damp cold native to Scotland, the kind felt even by men who had come recently from the Canadian West, where temperatures regularly dropped to −25 degrees Fahrenheit. We were happy to hear the order to form up for a short march to a waiting train.

Ten hours and one box lunch of mysterious content later, we came to a stop on a siding outside London due to an air raid on the centre of the city. We sat for two hours before the all-clear sounded and we reached Waterloo. Then it was into buses for a one-hour ride through the blackout of the early morning hours to the RAF station at Uxbridge, west of London, where we were sorted out and given bunks for a badly needed rest.

---

* The *Rodney* had been part of a Royal Navy battle group searching the Atlantic for the powerful German battlecruisers *Scharnhorst* and *Gneisenau*, which had spent two months scouting the high seas, sinking over 116,000 tons of Allied shipping. The battle group that *Rodney* rejoined after her escort duties with us failed to intercept the German raiders, and they reached the port of Brest, in occupied France, on 22 March. *Rodney* later joined in the hunt for the *Bismarck*, which was finally caught and sunk with nearly all hands on 27 May 1941.

No. 1 Personnel Reception Centre (PRC) Uxbridge was, in part, a holding unit for the early graduates of the BCATP arriving from Canada. Here, we were interviewed, our records were examined, and we were assigned to whatever pre-operational training we required.

Later on, all Canadian aircrew arriving in the United Kingdom were shipped to the south coast seaside resort town of Bournemouth. There they often stayed for up to two months waiting for a posting to an operational training unit, especially when the training scheme began producing aircrew faster than the RAF units could absorb them.

From all accounts, the food there was as good as the rationing permitted, and the local girls were hospitable (though competition was fierce). On the debit side, German fighters and fighter-bombers made frequent low-level attacks on the town.

We had arrived in war-torn London, but our brief stay at the holding unit was to be more exciting and risk-filled than we could have imagined.

5
LONDON AND THE BLITZ —
FIRST LOSS OF INNOCENCE

SITTING AROUND AT UXBRIDGE with nothing much to do but wait for a posting to a training unit, we were given many day or overnight passes out of camp. The immediate magnet, of course, was London, as it continued to be for most Canadians during their time in England. Uxbridge was near the western limit of the Piccadilly line of the underground system (the tube), so it was an easy thirty-five- to forty-five-minute run into the heart of the city.

Wartime London was a fascinating place. The blackout was its most striking and affecting feature. All traffic lights were hooded and dimmed, as were the headlights on cars and buses. Blue lights guided cars and pedestrians about the roads and streets. Double blackout curtains were in place at all building entrances to prevent the escape of indoor light. All windows were covered and most were taped to stop shattering glass from flying about. Traffic was much reduced due to petrol rationing but taxis continued to be plentiful. We were told that the vehicle accident rate had fallen significantly after the imposition of the blackout because of fewer vehicles and more caution.

In daytime, London revealed hundreds of sandbagged stores, and a great variety of signs warning of the dangers of loose talk. One common poster, which we thought corny, exhorted, "Be like dad, keep mum." Better known was, "Loose lips sink ships."

Looking down on "Eros," the famous statue in the centre of Piccadilly Circus, was a huge billboard on the facade of the Pavilion theatre advertising the film *Squadron Leader X*, starring Eric Portman and Ann Dvorak.

Many places became familiar to Allied aircrew, notably the Regent Palace Hotel, a favourite trysting place just off Piccadilly; also Oddenino's bar.

For the dancers there was the Hammersmith Palais, and the Royal Opera House at Covent Garden, which had been converted for ballroom dancing and usually featured two orchestras, a waltz band, and another playing the big band sound of the day. Both were on a circular stage that rotated at intervals so that only one band was visible at any one time. I was struck one night by the view from the upper balcony of the Royal Opera House, and looking down at what seemed to be a moving sea of dark-centred yellow daisies swirling about the floor. It was peroxided hair, all the rage at the time, but the centres were growing out.

Another place that became famous was the Windmill Theatre, with its chorus of beautiful girls and vaudeville acts. This theatre never closed during the war, even in the midst of the worst bombing raids; it suffered only minor damage, with no loss of life to its staff.

The Blitz, the Luftwaffe's nightly pounding of the British capital, was still raging. Every evening, as a routine, thousands of Londoners took overnight bags and blankets and headed for the deepest levels of the tube. They also brought thermos bottles of the ever-sustaining miracle tea, the standard British cure for bad nerves and for nearly everything else. I had to pick my way carefully down stairways, stepping over and around sleeping mothers and children. On the platforms of many stations, double steel bunks had been erected.

Some of the tube stations were quite deep indeed, the long escalators descending three or four levels below the street entrance, offering almost complete protection from the bombs. But even there I could hear and feel the ominous and stomach-turning crumps and concussions. There is a remarkable recording of a mother crooning to the little girl she cradled in her arms to shield the child's ears from the sound of the explosions, when the child looked up and implored, "Please mummy, would you stop singing? I can't hear the bombs!"*

---

* Dr. William Blatz, then head of the Toronto Institute of Child Psychology, told this story

One of our forays into London from Uxbridge ended in a comedy of erotic misadventure. My friend Hokie and I ended up late one evening in Piccadilly Circus outside the Pavilion movie house. This was a favourite place of business for ladies known as the "Piccadilly Commandos." As we stood surveying the scene in the dim light of the blackout, two of them came up to us, one blonde and one brunette. Blondie spoke the immortal words, "Are you lonely, dearie?"

After a little sales talk from the ladies, one of us ventured, "Well, maybe it wouldn't hurt to go along just to see what happens." With that, one of them announced, "That'll be a pound each, dearies."

I whispered to Hokie, "I haven't got a pound. You'll have to lend me one." He grumbled but agreed, and off we went, pulled along by our new girlfriends.

Nearby, on Shaftesbury Avenue, Blondie stopped and unlocked a door. We followed her through a blackout curtain and up a staircase to a second landing, where there were two doors. The brunette dragged Hokie towards one door, and Blondie pulled me through the other one.

Once inside, she motioned me to sit on a couch, which I could barely see in the dim light of a gas fireplace. She immediately stooped over the fireplace and turned up the flame, bathing the small room in a warm pink glow. Throwing off her clothes in one practised motion, she turned and faced me — stark naked! She looked to be about fourteen years old. I could feel the panic rising through my body. *What am I doing here?* I thought. Obviously, I wasn't ready for this. Panic took charge, and I leaped to my feet and lunged towards the door. Blondie had placed Hokie's pound note on a small table by the door on our way in. On the way out, I scooped it up, with Blondie in hot pursuit.

I threw open Hokie's door to see him standing with his pants in his hand. He was wearing his farmer's "union suit," but the seat flap had come undone. I grabbed his tunic from a chair and pulled him out of the room, crying, "Come on, we're getting out of here!"

We thumped down the stairs chased by our forsaken and furious ladies, one stark naked, the other in garter belt and brassiere. We outdistanced them and reached the street. Hokie was still grumbling, "Are you crazy?" as I helped him into his trousers. Fortunately, we were in the blackout.

---

to a class of the RCAF Staff College in Toronto. In l941, Dr. Blatz was in London to examine the psychological effects of the bombing on the children. He had recorded this mother–daughter discourse on tape as he sat beside them.

We had to find a place to stay for the night and still get back to the base by 0900 hours the following morning. I hurried along a still-muttering Hokie towards a Salvation Army hostel that I had noticed on a previous visit. He kept saying, "That was a fool stunt. And what about my pound that I gave that woman?" despite my having given him back the pound I had rescued. The last words I heard from him as we turned in were, "You still owe me a pound!"

The next day, safely back at Uxbridge, we were paraded and told that a British film company, at Elstree studios on the outskirts of London, was making a documentary portraying a typical bombing raid on an industrial target in Germany. Apparently, they were short of extras for the cast and our RAF masters offered most of our group of Canadians at Uxbridge to fill in. To me and my friend Ted, this didn't sound as exciting as another trip to London, and we decided to duck out, a decision I have since regretted. Not only did we give up the chance to become film stars, but as it turned out we would have been a lot safer that evening at Elstree studios.

The film was the now-classic *Target for Tonight*, featuring the Wellington bomber crew of "F" for Freddie, of Bomber Command's 33 Squadron at Millerton (fictitious number and name). The film name of the captain of "F" for Freddie was Dixon. In reality he was Flight Lieutenant Percy Charles Pickard, RAF, already an experienced and decorated veteran of Bomber Command operations.*

The film's lead-in proclaims rightly that there are no professional actors in the film, but adds that every person appearing is a serving member of the RAF. In fact, three quarters of the sergeants shown in the briefing and locker room scenes are Canadians from our RCAF group at Uxbridge. For the film's purposes several of them were given a pilot's or observer's wing to wear in place of their air gunner's wing.

I can identify most of the RCAF "actors" from our close-knit group. They include Joe Byron (O'Reilly, who goes in low!); Guy Boudreau; R.B. Martin (U.S.); Ike Hewitt; Carl Donohue; Bob Green; J.B. Gray; Robert Boby; Guy Guerin; Ken Hyde; Frank Holcombe (Hokie!); Chuck Brady; Don Calderwood; Harry Humphries; Joe Findlay; and Wilson (Willy) Poirier, friend and ill-fated front gunner of my first crew.

---

* Sadly, on 18 February 1944, as Group Captain, with DSO and two bars, DFC, Pickard lost his life leading Mosquitoes on Operation Jericho, one of the most daring operations of the war: the low-level attack on the Amiens prison. This raid, to help the escape of several hundred French resistance fighters imprisoned there, was a spectacular success; over 200 prisoners escaped and remained out of German hands.

Instead of becoming movie stars, Ted and I made our way on the underground to the city, where we toured several of the historic spots before ending up in Trafalgar Square. It was close to 2200 hours on 10 May 1941.

It was eerily quiet in the square, and Ted remarked, "It doesn't seem like much of a war going on. Where are all the bombers and bombs?" As if to answer him, a few seconds later the wail of the air-raid sirens started up. The sound of their rising and falling notes in the Blitz was unforgettable. Stomachs turned, and nerves already raw were stretched almost to breaking point, until a single steady note, held for a full minute, signalled the all-clear.

After the warning notes faded away, there was silence again. Not for long. With a sudden crashing explosion of sound, the ack-ack guns on the roof of Admiralty Arch, not 200 feet from us, opened up on high-flying bombers. Now we heard the bombers' engines; the bombs began to fall and the earth shook under our feet.

We thought it might be a good idea to look for an air raid shelter, neither of us willing to admit we were frightened. We didn't put on the steel helmets that hung over the canvas shoulder-packs that held our gas masks. We walked down Whitehall, past Westminster Abbey, then along Victoria Street, avoiding the fire engines and ambulances that were by now coursing about the city. By the time we turned down Vauxhall Bridge Road, the incendiary bombs fell like rain. The bark and rattle of anti-aircraft guns mixed with the numbing crunch of the bombs as they penetrated bricks and mortar before exploding. The whole wall of a building we had just passed crumbled and fell in a fiery curtain of rubble into the street. We could have read the proverbial newspaper in the light of the fires around us.

Shaken by all this, we agreed to put our helmets on. But that was the last I remembered until I opened my eyes to look up into Ted's shadowy face. He said, "Don't be dead and leave me here all alone!"

I was lying at the bottom of a short flight of steps that led to basement flats. I had fallen down them after being hit by a piece of shrapnel from one of the bombs. My head throbbed, and when I felt it my hand came away covered in blood. No wonder Ted thought I had been killed. But all he said was, "You must have a big hole in your head." Up on the street, we found my helmet with a four-inch gash in it.

We walked on, still wondering about a shelter. My elbows and shoulder felt bruised from the fall down the steps, and my head ached mildly; otherwise I was not in bad shape. Now we knew there was a war going on.

A few minutes later an air raid warden and a policeman came up behind us. The warden asked, "What are you two doing out here wandering about? Let's have a look at that face and head of yours." Finding nothing serious, he pulled out a first-aid kit and put a dressing on the small cut on my head. "You two look fit enough. We need your help with what we're told is a bad bombing of a dance hall. Follow us."

We followed at almost a trot for three or four blocks, and came upon a horrific scene right out of Dante's *Inferno*. Ambulances and firefighting vehicles surrounded a still-burning building. As we got closer, we saw stretchers with bodies, and parts of bodies, on them. There was a great deal of blood about. A bloody sheet covered one body lying near the curb. Above the shoulders of the corpse, the sheet lay flat where a head should have been. Stunned, and sick to our stomachs, we were pressed into service, helping to carry stretchers of the still-living to waiting ambulances and other make-shift vehicles. The badly injured but living were strangely quiet. A great many people had died.

After about two hours, we were thanked and released from the scene, badly shaken. We had been told that a big bomb had penetrated the roof of the crowded dance hall and exploded in the centre of the floor, and that the death toll was in the hundreds (my best recollection is that the dance hall was the Cafe de Paris, and that a popular band leader, "Snake Hips" Johnson, and his entire band were among the dead). Many of the dead were servicemen, including a high number of Canadians. Even at that stage of the Blitz, many people were still ignoring the call of the sirens to take shelter.

Dishevelled and frayed at the edges, Ted and I made our way back in the direction of Trafalgar Square. As we passed what looked like a police station/air raid warden post, a warden leaving the building took a look at us and probably judged from our appearance that we could stand a little refreshment, and invited us in for a cup of tea. A police sergeant and two other wardens greeted us and soon fixed each of us up with a big mug of the soothing brew.

The blackout curtain covering the doorway parted. In came a young couple with blankets thrown over their nightclothes. They looked to be in slight shock, especially the young woman, and our hosts were quick to help them in and look them over. Both had suffered minor cuts from flying glass when a bomb blast blew their bedroom windows in on them. As one of the wardens began to treat their cuts, everyone noticed that the man had cuts only to his back. The young woman's cuts were confined to her forearms. There was a short period of silence, broken when the sergeant couldn't suppress a little snicker. With a sheepish grin, the young man felt bound to confess, "Well, we had to do something to keep our minds off the air raid."

By the time we left our friends at the post, the raid was petering out. We found our way back to Trafalgar Square, and were guided by wardens to a shelter in the basement of St. Martin-in-the-Fields church. The brave ladies of the church auxiliary were still serving tea and buns, and comfort. We were shown to some wooden slatted bunks in the crypt of the historic church, and fell onto the beds in exhaustion.*

We were both shaken by the night's experience. We would never feel quite the same again.

---

* I remembered my father telling me that he had sheltered in this same crypt during a Zeppelin raid in 1918. He was within a year of the same age.

6
YATESBURY WIRELESS SCHOOL
— COLLISION OF CULTURES

SO FAR AS WE COULD SEE through a persistent light fog and drizzle, the village of Yatesbury, in Wiltshire, was a typical quaint rural English town. We were posted to RAF Yatesbury, a signals training school, for a refresher course in our wireless operator trade. But the RAF station, devoid of aircraft or hangars to lend some colour or interest to the scene, was drab.

With no formal greeting, we were taken to a barrack block to settle in for what remained of the day. Inside was a lone pot-bellied stove at the end of a long, narrow room. Along each wall, under many windows, were odd-looking half bedsteads; the bottom half telescoped into the top half. Piled on top were three square, thin mattresses about three feet in width. These "biscuits" were laid end to end on the steel slats after the bottom half of the bed had been pulled out to full length. The cold, damp spring air rose up through the cracks in these biscuits so that we needed as many blankets on the bottom as on top to keep warm. Since there weren't enough blankets, we were reduced some nights to wearing our greatcoats to bed.

The next morning we were given a brief orientation talk by one of the instructors, and a variety of tests to determine how much we knew

about operating wireless sets, which wasn't much. Then we were introduced to the radio set common to aircraft of Bomber Command, the
Marconi R1154-T1155 receiver/transmitter. This radio was much superior in every way to the antiquated 1082/1083 we had been exposed to
briefly at Calgary. We also tapped out a lot of Morse code.

What we were least prepared for was the attitude of some of the RAF
staff. For the first time we encountered the "colonial" label, usually
accompanied by some snide remark. We grew restive and increasingly
rebellious under this kind of treatment, but our reactions were mild
compared to that of the Royal Australian Air Force group that had joined
us soon after our arrival. They erupted in a near riot, and refused to
appear on parade or in class.

Things reached a climax one day in the mess hall. The food was at
best mediocre, and usually needed a liberal coating of Daddy's Sauce
("The Only Sauce You Can Give Daddy") to make it edible. This day it
was particularly unpalatable, and one Aussie grabbed his plate and flung
it against the wall just as an RAF air commodore walked through the door.
Much of the plate's contents, including the sauce, splattered over the air
officer's uniform. The accompanying sergeant major screamed for the
service police, and the Aussie with the good throwing arm was taken
away. We didn't see him again. Only later did we learn that this was not
an isolated incident. Commonwealth airmen and soldiers were not easily
amenable to the British brand of discipline, and certainly not to being
looked down upon as still rather primitive colonials.

The high-spirited Australians were most likely to give serious vent to
their frustrations, but Canadians sometimes blew the bounds of "good
order and discipline," too. For instance, a Canadian riot at Cranwell, the
RAF college, became known as the "Cranwell Revolt." It took interven-
tion by senior Canadian diplomats and officers to calm the waters.

There were two sides to this, of course. The British just could not, or
would not, appreciate that the Commonwealth airmen needed a little
time and understanding to adjust to what was, to us, a foreign environment. They showed gross insensitivity in their use of the pejorative
"colonial." On their side, the British might have argued, with justifica-
tion, that we ought to have had better briefings, and some kind of an
indoctrination program from our own masters before we integrated with
the British in the common cause.

An issue that seems to have been anticipated, and tackled, was the
matter of pay. From the time of our stay at Uxbridge, we had been

on RAF rates of pay. As sergeants, we would now be paid six shillings and ninepence a day. With the British pound trading at approximately $4.50 Canadian, this meant that we would be getting less than half our former Canadian rate of pay. But the difference between the two rates would be credited to an account set up for us at the RCAF Headquarters at Lincoln's Inn Fields in London. When in London on leave or pass we were entitled to draw on this account within certain limits — two pounds in any one leave period. This was not always convenient, but we found that there was not a great deal to spend our money on around the Bomber Command bases, so the London account was a kind of enforced savings plan for use on leave.

The reason all Canadians attached to RAF squadrons were forced into this scheme was to avoid the hard feelings and friction that would almost certainly have arisen if we were to flaunt the significant differences in our pay. Largely, therefore, we were spared the castigation reserved for the Americans who arrived later in great numbers — "overpaid, oversexed, and over here."

Soon after arrival at Yatesbury, I applied for a new uniform. My Canadian issue was the worse for wear after my Blitz experiences, and I really couldn't pass inspection on parade. I was fitted out in the supply section with an RAF uniform, and concluded that Rudyard Kipling, with his description of the "slope-shouldered Tommy," was right. The shoulders of my new tunic were not squarely cut like our Canadian tunics, but had a definite slope to them. Also, the hem of the tunic was somewhat lower in the rear than in the front, giving the tunic a sort of swallow-tail flair. Otherwise, the whole thing fit.

Soon we were issued with the blue battledress that we wore almost constantly for the remainder of our service overseas. This was a good-looking blouse, with shoulder epaulets for the rank braid of officers. General Eisenhower later popularized a similar form of this uniform as the Eisenhower jacket.

At the end of two weeks some of us were judged ready for posting to an operational training unit, the last phase of training before joining a squadron. Others were held at Yatesbury for a further five to eight weeks of training. Some were assessed as more suitable for second wireless operator, which meant that they would man the front turret of a bomber, although this wasn't usually decided until the OTU stage. Others were reclassified, often at their own request, as straight rear gunners.

One morning I was called to the orderly room and told that I was posted to No. 15 Operational Training Unit at Harwell, in Berkshire, and given a railway warrant for the next day. Dick Powell and Joe Findlay went there too, and a week or so later we were joined by my future front gunner friend, Willy Poirier.

As the course scattered across the United Kingdom to various training units or operational squadrons there was a shared sadness in the split-up of friends. We were a close-knit group, and had come a long way together.

7
OPERATIONAL TRAINING:
THE "WIMPY"

AS I STOOD ON THE STATION PLATFORM with my duffle bag and suitcase at the small village of Didcot, and feeling some excitement at the immediate prospect of finally getting to the operational training stage, I had another, different feeling: this was the first time since Manning Pool days in Toronto that I was on my own.

There was a lot of flying activity. I could see three or four aircraft circling to land at the RAF base at Harwell no more than a mile or so south of the station. My reverie was broken by a shout from the driver of a van who was there to pick me up, along with three other airmen, all RAF. We piled in with our kit and took off down the road for the OTU. As we showed our ID cards and passed through the main gate, I had my first look at camouflaged hangars, and beyond them the flight lines of operational Wellington bombers. At long last, this was beginning to look like the air force I had imagined.

I reported to the station orderly room and handed in my railway warrant and my reporting orders so that I could be taken on strength. I was soon settled in a barracks, and allocated a single bed and a large steel locker with plenty of room to hang up all my clothes. Things were definitely looking up.

Except for Dick Powell, Joe Findlay, and Willy Poirier, whom I joined in the mess and at lectures, the rest of the aircrew trainees I joined in training were RAF. They were a mixed lot, with a seemingly endless variety of accents: Scottish, Welsh, London cockneys, north-country "Geordies," and others. They were a good, friendly bunch of fellows, all eager to get the training over with and get "on ops." There wasn't the slightest hint of the "colonial" condescension we had encountered at Yatesbury.

During a week filled with classroom lectures and demonstrations on operational wireless procedures, we were introduced to that stable, docile workhorse aircraft, the Anson. This twin-engine airplane could carry at least eight passengers, including the pilot. It was fitted with a gun turret mounted just aft of amidships on top of the fuselage. One .303 Browning gun sprouted from the leading edge of the port wing. It wasn't a formidable machine, but with some incredible luck and skilful flying, the pilot of one of these obsolescent aircraft, a Flying Officer Cedric Greenhill, RAF, had downed a Junkers 88 — some reports suggest it was a Heinkel 115 or 59 float-plane — over the North Sea. He was awarded the Distinguished Flying Cross (DFC).

I had four flights in the Anson, practising wireless procedures, totalling sixteen hours flying time. All flights were uneventful and enjoyable, except for one night exercise on 7 July 1941. It was an unusually clear, moonlit night, and our flight plan took us southwest, across the coast, and a little distance out over the Channel. This seemed to me to be a little adventurous, and so it proved to be.

Finished with my exchange of messages with the Harwell ground station, I was ordered into the gun turret. Squeezing into the seat and strapping myself in, I found the old Vickers gas recoil machine gun in front of me. I was not confident that I could do much with that piece of weaponry.

I was casting my eyes about the sky as I had been cautioned to do when I saw it. Just another training flight I thought, then I changed my mind; it wasn't one of ours, and he was diving to attack us! I grabbed my microphone and shouted, as calmly as I could manage, "Captain, gunner here. There's an enemy aircraft attacking from our port beam!" No answer, no movement. I screamed, "It's a Junkers 88!" At that, the pilot threw us into a tight, diving turn to starboard as I watched a stream of tracer bullets streak past my turret at what seemed about three inches from the end of my nose. I'd had no time to fire my gun, but cocked it now and swung it about expecting the Junkers to make another attack.

I picked him up again, above us on our starboard side, and warned the pilot, but as he started to come in again another aircraft joined the party. Flashes and tracers came from our new arrival, aimed not at us but at our attacker, who must have been taken unawares as he concentrated on us. I just had time to see some fiery eruptions on wing surfaces of the Junkers before our pilot corkscrewed us out of the scene and told us we were headed home.

There was a lot of excited chit-chat on the way back to base, but nobody mentioned the alert I had given. I smugly congratulated myself, knowing that my quick signal had probably saved us from a fiery end. I have always assumed that the Junkers was destroyed. Later, I found out that our saviour was a Beaufighter night fighter.

■ ■ ■

This ended our association with the Anson. Our next introduction was to the aircraft that was to become an old friend, the ubiquitous Wellington "heavy" bomber. To us, this was a big aircraft. It was the inspired design of Barnes Wallis* of Vickers Aircraft Company.

Climbing up into this aircraft through the front hatch, using the wooden ladder always carried aboard, I was struck immediately by the unique geodetic or basket-work airframe of a duralumin alloy, combining lightness, rigidity, and great strength. There was no other aircraft like it. There was also a constant aroma of petrol fumes and oil. The nose was totally occupied with a Frazer-Nash hydraulic gun turret fitted with two Browning .303 machine guns. The tail housed the second gun turret, also with two Brownings — the "office" of the lonely rear gunner. The pilot's seat was on the port side. On the starboard side there was a swing-down seat for a co-pilot or an instructor.** Immediately behind

---

* Later to gain fame as the designer of the bomb that breached the Mohne and Eder dams in the famous 617 Sqn attack led by Wing Commander Guy Gibson on the night of 16–17 May 1943 — the Dam Busters!

** In March 1942, the Stirlings, Halifaxes, and Lancasters having arrived in Bomber Command, a one-pilot policy was introduced, along with the new aircrew trades of flight engineer and bomb aimer ("bombardier" in the U.S. Air Force). The Wellington crew of six remained unchanged.

the pilot's armoured bulkhead was the wireless operator's position, and behind him, in the aisle, was the table and bench for the navigator.

Climbing over the main spar, behind which were the valves for switching petrol tanks, a person could walk towards the rear on a "cat-walk," passing on the way the Elsan toilet, and the flare chute, on the starboard side. The chute was used to eject flares of various kinds and propaganda leaflets. Its length could be extended with a telescoping sleeve, using a short pole clipped to its side. The extension had to be employed; otherwise ejected material would not clear the side or tail of the aircraft in the slipstream.

Amidships, there were triangular windows on either side. Brownings could be fitted on a swivel mount to fire through these windows, the gunner sitting on a seat in the aisle so that he could switch from one gun to the other.

The observer (navigator), who in those days was also the bomb aimer, would lie on the padded inside panel of the entry hatch to drop his bombs, using the bomb sight mounted just in front of the hatch. A panel on the starboard side, over his right shoulder, held his bomb toggles for selecting and arming the bombs.

All my operational flying was done on Wellingtons, the Mk 1C, powered by the Bristol Pegasus XVIII engines, and later the Mk II, fitted with the superior Rolls-Royce Merlin (later marks were produced, the Mk X with a Hercules engine, and even one with an American Pratt and Whitney Twin Wasp). The designed maximum airspeed was 245 mph, but I don't recall us reaching anything over 175 mph. The maximum bomb load was 4,500 pounds, but for long flights like Berlin, with extra fuel tanks, the loads were reduced to 3,000 pounds.

The production of the Wellington exceeded that of all other British bombers, reaching a total of 11,401 aircraft. Production of its nearest rival, the Lancaster, reached 7,377 machines. The Halifax total was 6,178. For the first three years of the war, the Wellington was the backbone of the bomber offensive against the German Reich. Not until February 1942 did the mighty Lancaster begin to arrive in numbers on RAF squadrons.

The Wellington was hardly ever called by its real name, of course. It was the "Wimpy," a name coined from the popular *Popeye* comic strip character J. Wellington Wimpy, that rotund devotee of the American hamburger. The praise and affection for this aircraft were universal.

In addition to our wireless operating exercises, we had several sessions of gunnery practice on the firing range. A fully functional Frazer-Nash gun turret had been mounted on a concrete base for firing at targets placed 300 yards distant at the end of a field. This gun turret was a marvel of design. It was powered by high-pressure oil, the force of which could spin the turret on its axis fast enough to put a crick in the neck of the gunner. The gunner sat with a trigger-equipped pistol grip at each hand, at about shoulder height. Turning the grips left or right spun the turret in those directions. Twisting the grips upwards or downwards elevated or lowered the guns. The well-trained gunner could sweep the guns in full 180-degree arcs, vertically or horizontally, even in figure-eight patterns. He aimed through a lighted optical gun sight positioned between the gun mounts at his eye level. The guns were harmonized for the bullets to converge at 300 yards, the most effective range of the .303 Browning. This placed our gunners and aircraft at a dangerous disadvantage against German fighters equipped with the 20mm cannon. (U.S. Air Force bombers were better equipped with the .50 calibre Browning with its 600-yard effective range.)

One bizarre incident upset our otherwise routine firing exercises, and almost landed a fellow trainee and me in serious trouble. One of us opened fire just as a meandering cow, obviously a trespasser, wandered onto the range behind the target. The poor creature exploded into hamburger under the hail of bullets. Oddly, I cannot recall which one of us was firing the guns, but I have always wanted to believe it was my companion. Our first "kill" of the war, and it had to be an English cow! If it was a Holstein, as it appeared to be, at least it had a German name.

Which of us fired the guns didn't matter; we were both hauled up before the station commander. I tried to imagine the charge: "Conduct to the prejudice of good order and discipline, in that they did wilfully and without due regard for safety kill one of His Majesty's subjects, to wit a cow."

Apparently, what saved us was an irregularity in the firing-range procedures, which implicated the NCO in charge. Instead of forfeiting a year's pay, we were lucky to receive a severe dressing-down, and nothing would appear on our records.

Over the next week we made a few familiarization flights in the Wimpy with a random selection of crew members, but always with a screen (instructor) pilot. On one flight I was introduced to a radio procedure known as a ZZ landing approach, designed for emergency landing guidance in fog or other poor visibility conditions. On a preset frequency, I would send a Morse code signal followed by long dashes to the ground station. The ground operators would take a bearing on my signal and transmit in voice to the pilot "engines left" or "engines right" to indicate his position relative to the end of the runway. This voice communication was made using a TR9F radio set located under the wireless operator's seat, and was intended only for special, usually emergency, conditions.

On our last familiarization flight, we found ourselves in unexpected fog. The screen pilot called me up on the intercom, asking, "I say, wireless op, it would be very handy if we could do one of those ZZ approaches right now. Think you could handle that?"

I tried to sound confident as I replied, "Yes sir, I think I could do that. I'll contact ground control now to set things up if you like."

"Good show. Let's have a go, then." I had practised this drill only once, so it was with some twitching in my nether regions that I set up the two radio sets and started the procedure.

Thankfully, the whole routine went well, and we bumped in to a landing and taxied over to dispersal. I felt rather good about the whole thing, but I felt even better when we were taking off our flying gear in the locker room and the pilot came over to me and said, "Well, lad, you handled that well. You're Canadian, aren't you? What's your name?" He wrote my name down on a small pad he carried and, with a quick pat on my shoulder, left the room.

All trainees were assembled in the readiness room one morning, waiting for flight instructions, when a squadron leader came in and stepped up onto the platform in front of the schedule board. He called the room to attention and announced, "Well chaps, the time has come for you to get yourselves organized into regular crews. We've found that it's best for you to sort yourselves out, and pick whom you wish to finish the course with. What's more important, of course, is that you will probably be picking the crew members you will be starting your operational flying with. I'll leave you to it, then. Good luck." He departed, leaving us with some questions in mind. Most of us expected to be placed arbitrarily into crews by the chief instructor. Now we had to show some initiative, and figure out how to go about getting ourselves into crews.

There was a great milling about as we began to size up who we would have the most confidence in. My first thought, which I imagined was the common one, was to get a good pilot. A poor one would surely get me killed. As I pondered this, a big, good-looking observer made his way over to me and grabbed my shoulder. It was Len Mayer, with whom

I had made several flights and talked with often in the mess. Len greeted me, "Would you like to get together, Howard? I think we'd make a good team." This certainly suited me, and I told him so. I had taken an instant liking to this man from North Wigan, in northwest England, with his broad shoulders and black bushy eyebrows. He reminded me of the Canadian movie actor Walter Pidgeon. We were to develop a very close, warm friendship, based on mutual confidence in the other's abilities. Len came to epitomize, for me, the best type of an upper middle-class British gentleman.

We were interrupted by a big, burly man sporting an air gunner's wing, who announced in a cockney accent that he was George Fuller, and did we want a great rear gunner. He and Len had been talking in the locker room, and he had no doubt sized Len up as I had. We both welcomed him, and suggested that we had better look for a pilot before the good ones were signed up. Before we could move, a pilot officer wearing pilot's wings came up to us, saying, "I'm looking for some crew members," and introduced himself as Pilot Officer Langley.

Seeing that he was an officer, the thought ran through my mind, and probably that of the others, that he must be a good pilot, or the RAF would not have commissioned him. While his commissioning meant no doubt that he had passed all his tests with a very good rating, there was no evidence so far from operational flying to indicate any measurable difference between the capabilities of officer and NCO pilots. Some of the finest records on operational squadrons had been tallied by sergeant pilots. Generally speaking, however, the easiest integration into operational flying and the best leadership were evidenced by those regular force officers who had gained a great deal of flying and general service experience in the years leading up to the war.

These thoughts impelled me to join the others in replying quickly, "Why, yes, sir, I would be pleased to join your crew." P/O Langley then introduced us to the other two crew members he had already recruited. "Gentlemen, this is our second dickie, Sgt Pearson, and our front gunner, Sgt Munroe."* We traded information about home towns and family and such. I was an oddity, being the only Canadian on our new crew.

Thus, our first crew, all RAF except for me, shaped up in this way: First pilot (captain), P/O Langley; second pilot, Sgt Roy Pearson;

---

* For some reason, I have been unable to recall the first name of Munroe. Probably, that is because, as events unfolded, neither he nor Pearson was to be with us for very long.

observer, Sgt Len Mayer; wireless op, Sgt Howard Hewer; front gunner, Sgt Munroe; rear gunner, Sgt George Fuller.

We were off to a pretty good start on our operational career, and I felt fortunate to be teamed up with these men, and to be accepted so readily as one of the team members.

We began a series of flights with a screen pilot at the controls. Once we were familiar with the aircraft and the equipment, and the captain was adequately checked out on the Wimpy's stable flying characteristics, we were happily off on our own. There were simulated bombing runs, navigation exercises, and air-to-air gunnery trials. I was given a variety of wireless procedures to practise.

Of importance were air-to-ground procedures to get position fixes or bearings to assist the navigator in his continual plotting of the aircraft's course. One well-used procedure was a "QDM," or magnetic course, to steer to reach base or another given point. This was obtained by calling up a ground station, giving the specified code letters or numerals, and pressing the Morse key for a long dash on which the ground station would take a bearing. They would then transmit to me the magnetic course in compass degrees to reach our destination. A fix could be obtained when two or more direction-finding stations took simultaneous bearings on my transmission. Bearings could also be obtained by using a loop antenna in a streamlined housing on top of the fuselage to home in on a transmitting ground station.

On some sunny afternoons, we took off on navigation exercises to northern Scotland, swooping low over lochs and down beautiful valleys. Often we landed at RAF bases in Scotland, ate box lunches while lounging on the grass by our Wimpy, and could almost forget that there was a war on. These were good days.

At some stations we had lunch in the sergeants' mess before returning to Harwell. Mostly we were well received, but sometimes we noticed a certain reserve or coldness on the part of the non-flying NCOs. This was because we were never considered to be "real" sergeants, like the tradesmen who had worked their way up in rank through long service and increasing trade proficiency. We, on the other hand, had been given sergeant rank solely for the pay and status as aircrew, and there was some understandable resentment at this, particularly among the "old sweats," the pre-war types who had served many years just to get to corporal rank. It occurred to me that this was part of the reason for the troubles at the Yatesbury wireless school. It also occurred to me that they might have given us leeway because we were about to put our lives on the line, night after night, while they carried on in comparative comfort and safety.

I was surprised one day to be ordered to the control tower for night duty. At 2100 hours I presented myself at the tower, where a flight lieutenant introduced himself and briefed me on our duties for the night. We were to station ourselves near the touch-down point at the end of the live runway, and provide ancillary air traffic control for a few aircraft that would be returning from night exercises.

Once in our position, I was shown the two Aldis lamps we were to use, one with a red filter and the other with a green filter. An aircraft joining the landing circuit would flash his single letter identification, and if all was clear we would flash his letter back to him using the green filter. If the circuit was not clear we would flash the red filter. This seemed simple enough to me, and I didn't expect to have any trouble with the Aldis lamp after my instruction at Calgary wireless school.

I had just settled myself down in a canvas chair when the flight lieutenant approached. "Look, Hewer, you seem to know the drill, and there's really nothing to it. Only two aircraft will be returning anyway. Just between you and me, I have a little date with my girlfriend over yonder, so can you look after things here until I get back? I shan't be long in any case." Before I could reply, he took off towards a distant clump of trees.

I wasn't happy with this twist to our assignment, but as I had no choice I settled down to wait for something to happen. It was quiet, dark, and lonely out there, and I began to hope that the officer wouldn't take long.

Nearly an hour had passed when I heard the drone of an approaching Wimpy. It had become overcast, and a little thin fog had appeared, so I couldn't see him until he was within a quarter of a mile of the landing pattern. He flew overhead and flashed the letter "G" on his underbelly white light. I snatched up the Aldis lamp with the green filter and, aiming at the pilot's cockpit, returned his call letter. He finished his downwind leg and came in to land; no problem. I felt a small sense of relief and accomplishment.

No sooner had I settled down again when I heard another drone, and another behind it. Same procedure; I got both aircraft down and hoped the flight lieutenant would get back so that we could pack up.

No such luck. More engine noise, and soon I had three more Wimpys in the circuit! Where the hell were they coming from? I got the lead aircraft in, but right behind him were two Wimpys not waiting for an okay, one right on top of the other, both on final approach. What to do? In a mild panic, I grabbed the Aldis and flashed a green at the lower Wimpy. I then tried to aim the red flash at only the top aircraft. It worked; the top Wimpy alertly veered away and went around again. Three more Wimpys then arrived, two in poor shape, but they took their turns and I had no further problems.

I had just collapsed into my chair, feeling relieved but a little drained, when my officer friend sauntered jauntily up and asked, "Well, how's it going?" Fortunately, I was able to choke back the words that came rushing to my tongue, and instead I filled him in on what had happened. He was as mystified as I was about where all these Wimpys had come from.

As soon as we returned to the operations room we found out that all but the two of our own had been diverted to Harwell on return from a raid because of bad weather. We were one of the few stations in the south-central area still within landing limits. I was pleased that I didn't see the flight lieutenant again, and I said nothing about the incident.

■ ■ ■

From time to time we heard bits of news about members of our original group now scattered about Britain at various OTUs. One incident involved a very Irish-Canadian member of our original training gang, O'Malley. He and his crew were on a training flight from an OTU north of Harwell and strayed too far over the Irish Sea. By some mischance they had engine failure and had to make a forced landing in southern Ireland. That country being neutral, the crew was immediately interned for the duration of the war, and the Wimpy confiscated.*

It turned out that O'Malley just happened to have a wealthy aunt living in Dublin. Through some process of negotiation, and no doubt the influence of the well-positioned aunt, O'Malley was released into her custody — a most happy and fortuitous reunion. Nothing for it but that O'Malley should attend university in Dublin to while away his time, in civilian clothes. Four years later, the war ended, and the graduate O'Malley re-entered service life and was repatriated to Canada. He had been promoted on what was called the "shadow roster" from sergeant to

---

* In 1995, a neighbour told me that as a crew member of a Blenheim medium bomber of 25 Sqn, RAF, he had taken part in a raid by eight or so bombers on the Irish port of Cork, at the end of 1941 or early 1942. This was in response to reports of German U-boats being refuelled there. He remembers the raid being a show of force, with most bombs purposely landing in the bay. This may have militated against the return of our crews from internment.

flight lieutenant, and returned to Canada with veterans' ribbons. Sure and begorra, was this not the way to fight a war?*

By the end of July 1941, our crew had completed all the scheduled exercises and passed all our individual exams and tests. We were confident that we had the skills to take on the serious job of flying on an operational squadron.**

When the postings for the crews who had completed training were pinned up on the notice board, we learned for the first time that we were part of a flight automatically slated for posting to a Middle East squadron. This came as a bit of a shock to my British comrades who, understandably, would have much preferred to remain in England where their families were. I was the only unmarried member of our crew. Len's wife had just given birth to their first child, so it would be particularly wrenching for him to be sent out of the country.

A quick poll of our crew showed that all were in favour of remaining in Britain. It wasn't as important to me, but because of the close attachment I had formed with Len, and also with George, I certainly didn't want to be parted from them now.

P/O Langley and Len managed to get an interview with the station commander to present their case. Mostly on compassionate grounds, because of Len's baby, they won their point and our crew was given a posting to 218 "Wimpy" Squadron, 3 Group, Bomber Command, at Marham, Norfolk.

Just before our departure, in a little celebration party, our co-pilot, Sgt Pearson, entered into the spirit of things too well. Leaving the pub on his trusty motorbike at great speed in a cloud of gravel and mud, he left us behind. When we overtook him we found him in a ditch with a badly bent motorbike. Fortunately, he had only broken a leg, which put him out of action and, sadly, out of our crew.

This accident held us up for a few days, but we were then introduced to our new co-pilot, Sgt Ted Crosswell, who seemed like a very personable and reliable chap to us. And so we threw off our long days of training and took off for Marham, and for whatever fate had in store for us in the "real war."

---

* Shortly after the war, I ran into O'Malley. After a few beers, he confirmed the story.
** The annotation in the back of my logbook, where assessments are recorded, states that on completing OTU, I was a "steady and reliable No. 1 operator, Wellington." It adds that, having fired 1,000 rounds in air-to-air exercises, and scoring 4.5 percent hits on the drogue, I was also considered to be "slightly above average" as a gunner. Oddly enough, I cannot recall firing a single round in the air at OTU. The murdered cow, I remember!

TWO

IN FOR A
POUND

8

OPERATIONAL —
"THE GLAMOUR PERIOD IS OVER"

IT WAS 27 AUGUST 1941, our crew's reporting date to RAF Station Marham, and our designated squadron No. 218. From that date our lives were to be changed dramatically; our futures would be in the hands of others, and guided by events over which we had little or no control.

I had spent the two days leave we had been given from OTU seeing more of the sights of London. The other members of the crew had hurried home to their families. I could imagine the sobering effect upon reunions of the knowledge that loved ones were bound for an operational squadron of Bomber Command.

As I approached the station, sitting in the back of the lorry that had picked me up at the railway station in the nearby city of King's Lynn, I saw the camouflaged hangars and control tower and the circling aircraft of a busy operational station. This was it, I thought. This was what I'd been trained for. Now it was up to me.

I showed my identity card at the guard gate and was dropped off at the station orderly room. It was close to 1000 hours. Within the next hour the other members of the crew showed up at the orderly room where we had a welcome reunion, a rather boisterous one, too, until a severe-looking flight lieutenant emerged from his adjutant's office and told us to settle down. This officer then outlined to us where we were to be billeted, and arranged for a bus to take us on a quick tour of the station. Our gear was packed into the bus that would take us to our quarters after the tour.

RAF Station Marham was a permanent RAF base constructed in the thirties. It had substantial brick and steel buildings and hangars. Many of the buildings were pock-marked where low-flying JU 88s or Me 110s had raked them with 20mm cannon shells in the course of attacks made mostly during the Battle of Britain period. The station was host to two operational Wellington bomber squadrons, Nos. 115 and 218, and was part of No. 3 Group, Bomber Command. It was situated in Norfolk, sharing with Suffolk the easternmost part of England, about 100 miles northeast of London, and only a few miles from the palace of Sandringham.

The nearest city of any size was King's Lynn, an ancient and historic town tucked into the south corner of the great square bay called The Wash. This was where we frequently went on most of the nights we weren't scheduled for ops. There were so many fish and chip shops in King's Lynn that I joked that if I leaned out of the pilot's hatch as we neared The Wash on return from an op I could guide us to the airfield by smelling the fish and taking a bearing from there.

Len, George, and I found ourselves billeted together in an old, ivy-covered manor house about three miles down the road from the station. We were to share a large second-floor room, furnished rather sparsely with three iron single cots, a few chairs, and small tables, and three closets, or "armoires," for our clothes — still better than we had been used to on our training stations.

Once we had our belongings stowed away, Len and George began what would become an almost nightly ritual when we were not flying. Both were big, strong men, over 200 pounds. Trying to prove who was the stronger, they began to grapple and wrestle their way about the room. As these two leviathans careered across the room, knocking over tables and chairs, I sought refuge in a corner out of harm's way.

These thoroughly good-natured matches usually ended with both contestants sitting on the floor, completely winded, and grinning like the Cheshire cat. It seemed to me that Len was a little more fit than George and tended to get the better of the contest more often than not. Later, when we were well into our operational flights and everyone's nerves were stretched, these little bouts became good therapy for Len and George, and also helped me, as referee and spectator, to relax.

That first day we got back to the sergeants' mess in time for high tea, which consisted of buns, toast, assorted jams, and lots of strong, acidic tea. Dinner, we discovered, was at the fashionable 2000 hours. This was the standard, peacetime meal-hour routine Marham had always followed, and it remained in effect for the length of our stay. No little war was going to upset this long-established British routine. The main disadvantage was that if we waited to have a proper dinner it was then too late to catch the bus into King's Lynn to go to the "flicks" (movies), or to a dance. On most free nights, therefore, we headed for town after high tea, in time for fish and chips before the show, and often more of them afterwards. Because of rationing and shortages of almost everything, the fish and chips were deep fried in the same fat over and over again — but we were young.

The next day all the new arrivals were gathered in a small briefing room in one of the hangars. If we expected any kind of a grand welcome by the squadron commanding officer, or even by one of the flight commanders, we were to be disappointed. Seated on the edge of a table at the front of the room was a Royal Australian Air Force flying officer, cap at a jaunty angle, and a holstered revolver slung on his hip — a dramatic pose indeed, but it did get our attention. I remember his welcome to us almost word for word.

"Well, chaps," he said, "the glamour period is over. *You got in for a penny, but now you're in for the pound.*" After this had sunk in, he outlined our daily routines, and the procedures for our operational briefings. He also explained that each of the new crews would be assigned to an operationally experienced pilot (commonly called a "screen") who would take us on at least our first three or four operational bombing raids. The pilots who had been crew captains at OTU would be assigned as second pilots in other, experienced crews. (This routine saved a great many crews from disaster on their first operation.)

He concluded his welcoming address with a stark prediction: "I think it is only fair to tell you that casualties in this command have been high, and that they are on the rise as we make more and more flights further into Germany. I must tell you then that many of you will not be with us a few weeks or a month from now. Good luck to all of you." With that he got off the table and left the room, leaving us with mixed emotions.

The next member of our welcoming committee was a flight lieutenant medical officer. After the usual caution about the risks of amorous liaisons in town, he described some of the physical and mental strains and stresses that we were about to experience on our bombing raids. We found out about the sick parade routine, and were given suggestions about diet, exercises, or activities to help us cope with stress and fatigue. His last observation was a shocking conclusion to his otherwise helpful talk.

"I hope it doesn't happen to any of you, but in the event that you find yourself trapped in a burning aircraft, with no chance of escape, best to get things over with in a hurry. What I suggest you might do is lean directly over the flames, open your mouth, and inhale strongly. The fire should scorch the lungs and cause almost instant death, much preferable to burning slowly. Well, good luck chaps."

The room went silent as we digested our welcome to our first operational squadron. It was hardly the best display of leadership but, curiously, it did not significantly dampen our spirits or our enthusiasm for getting into the air war.

As we sat there exchanging opinions about what we had just heard, a number of officers and NCOs, all pilots, entered the room. One flight lieutenant, reading from a list he held in his hand, began calling out the names of the captains of the assembled crews, and the names of the operational pilots who would be taking over from the pilots who had brought their crews from OTU.

When P/O Langley's name was called out, a sergeant pilot made his way over to us. He introduced himself to Langley, and nodded to the rest of us. After a short discussion with our new captain, whom I shall refer to simply as Sgt "B," P/O Langley turned to us rather wistfully and said, "You know the drill, chaps. I have to join another crew, but I want to tell you how much I enjoyed flying with you. As far as I'm concerned, each one of you knows his stuff, and Sgt B here is getting a damn good crew. I wish you the best of luck. Hopefully we can get together again some day." Len Mayer thanked P/O Langley for all of us for the good flights at OTU.

We chorused a good luck wish to our personable and capable pilot, yet we were not to see him again. He must have been posted to another squadron. I have often wondered what became of him, and whether he survived the war.

Sgt B told us that he had already completed twenty operational flights, and that it was probable that he would finish his tour of ops with us. I was happy that we were getting such an experienced pilot. I had to wonder what he had done to deserve getting such a green crew, but that was the system, hard on the tested and "blooded" veteran, but a life-saver to inexperienced crews.

Our new captain told us to report in full flying gear to the flight planning room in our designated hangar at 0830 hours the next morning to prepare for a cross-country familiarization flight.

The next day we assembled as ordered. Sgt B appeared and outlined on a map what our route was to be for our cross-country, or shakedown, flight. Our flight time would be two hours. I had received a separate briefing in an adjacent room set up for wireless operators, with duplicates of all our aircraft radio equipment set up on benches for practice and extra instruction or training we might need.

Fully dressed and equipped, off we went on our first flight with our new captain. It was uneventful. Each one of us checked out and tested our equipment, but Sgt B didn't put us through any special drills. He seemed to take our competence for granted. Perhaps he had been given reports of our passing out levels from OTU. He handled the Wimpy with experienced hands.

After landing following that first flight as our new crew, Sgt B did not join us for a late lunch in the sergeants' mess. He was a rather short, dark-haired man, quite reserved in manner. He was slightly uptight most of the time, but I supposed that this was his make-up; or did his twenty ops account for it? He didn't socialize with us at any time in the mess, or offer to accompany us into town. I presumed he was married and that his wife lived nearby so that he could go home in his off-hours. Mostly, we saw him at briefings, during flight, of course, and at debriefings. I thought it strange that we did not get to know this man better, the pilot who was to finish his operational tour as our captain, and see us through the first part of our own tour.

During lunch we learned that we had been lucky to have arrived on the station too late to take part in the last daylight raid attempted by the squadron. On 22 July, 218 Sqn joined seventy-nine other aircraft in a raid on the German battlecruisers *Gneisenau* and *Prinz Eugen* sheltering in the French port of Brest. This was an abortive raid, causing little serious damage to the battlecruisers, but resulting in the loss of ten aircraft shot down by Messerschmitt 109s.

No sooner had we finished our lunch than the "Attention" call came over the Tannoy, the loud speaker system installed throughout the messes and in the station living quarters. All crews were to report for operations to the briefing room at 1900 hours. Ops were on!

We thought we had better get some rest in the short time left to us, so we managed to hitch a ride from the main gate to our manor house. George, Len, and I lay on our beds, fully clothed, wondering if this was going to be our baptism, our first bombing raid. George wondered "where the bleeding hell" they were going to send us, and hoped it wouldn't be the Ruhr or Berlin.

At least that's what I thought George said. I still hadn't mastered his cockney lingo. It wasn't so much the accent as the fact that he used words completely foreign to me. Often he spoke in rhyme. "What'll we do for lunch? I've got a hunch, we'll have a bunch." I learned new words. A hat wasn't a hat, it was a "titfer." It took me almost two months before I was tuned in to George's patter. Len didn't take nearly that long, but then he was English.

A station bus came to collect us for briefing, and we arrived at the briefing room at the prescribed five minutes before start time. Sgt B was already there, and we joined him to take our seats as near to the front as we could get. We didn't want to miss anything.

The briefing room was like a small theatre. Rows of seats faced a raised stage platform that had a lectern, or podium, at each side. At the rear of the platform was a large wall map of western Europe. The central portion of this map included Germany and part of France.

Wing Commander Kirkpatrick, CO 218 Sqn stood at the centre of the stage, waiting for us to take our seats and settle down. The briefing room was not full by any means. The wing commander told us that they had just finished a briefing for crews going to Mannheim, in the Ruhr valley. Ninety-four aircraft from the Command, including a number of crews from our squadron, raided Mannheim that night; two aircraft were lost.

This second briefing was for "sprog" (inexperienced) crews like ours. Our target was to be the docks of the French port of Le Havre. This was a so-called "soft" target, where anti-aircraft fire and any interference from night fighters was usually much less intense than that experienced over other targets. Also, the target was less than two hours flying time from Marham, making for a fairly straightforward navigational exercise for the green navigators' first operational sortie.

The curtain covering part of the wall map was drawn back, and we saw red tape outlining our prescribed route from Marham to a turning point near Portsmouth, thence straight across the Channel to Le Havre.

The wing commander described the taxi procedures from dispersal to our live runway, and the suggested tactics for approaching and making our bomb run-up on the dock area to the bomb release point. We were to bomb from an altitude of 8,000 feet.

The armament officer then outlined our bomb load of 250-pound high explosive bombs, totalling 4,000 pounds. This was close to the Wimpy's normal limit of 4,500 pounds. Next, the squadron navigation officer gave us more detailed instructions regarding our route and our fuel loads. To assist the navigators, the wireless ops were to be allowed the unusual liberty of getting QDR bearings on the outward leg until we reached the Channel. These were simply the reciprocals of the common QDMs, which gave a magnetic course to steer to reach base. On the homeward-bound leg, we were authorized to get QDMs to assist the navigator to find home base.

He reminded us to turn on our IFF right after take-off, and to turn it off as soon as we reached the Channel. It was to be turned on again as soon as we approached the English coast on our return flight. IFF stood for "Identification Friend or Foe." The technology involved a box, about twelve inches square, that housed a transponder sending out a pulse signal that showed up as a blip on the British radar screens, identifying a friendly aircraft.

It was important that the transponder be turned off over enemy territory because there it could allow German night fighters to home in on the signals until they were within firing range. It also was important that these sets not fall into enemy hands where they could be duplicated for use in German bombers entering British airspace. To forestall this, an explosive charge was packed into the IFF box, activated by an inertial "Graviner" switch that tripped with the shock of a crashing aircraft, blowing the box to pieces.

It was one of my jobs to set the IFF immediately after take-off, and to ensure that it was turned off before entering enemy airspace. On the return flight, it was important not only to turn the set on at the appropriate time, but to deactivate the explosive switch before touchdown at base. It was known from experience that a particularly hard landing could set off the charge, destroying the IFF box.

We were also cautioned to give a wide berth to the barrage balloons protecting London and other large cities from low-level attacks. The TR9F radio set under the wireless op's seat was supposed to activate "squeakers" to warn us of proximity to the balloons, which carried steel cables to a height of three or four thousand feet, cables that could cut the wings off an aircraft that struck them. As a partial safety measure, a cable cutter was installed in the leading edge of both port and starboard wings of the Wimpy. This was a slot, with a strong cutter activated by an explosive charge. The theory was that if one of our aircraft ran into a cable, the cable would slide along the leading edge of the wing and lodge in the slot, whereupon the cutter would explode shut, severing the cable and allowing the pilot to regain control. Unfortunately, it worked only too well when a few "erks"* working on the wing became careless and poked their fingers into the slot, quickly losing those fingers.

We were also briefed on "Darkie" procedure. This was the name given to an emergency system designed to help crippled aircraft, or those disoriented in bad weather, to reach the nearest serviceable airfield. The TR9F radio set was used to call "Darkie, Darkie" on a specified frequency. The call would be acknowledged, and a pair of searchlight beams would appear. The vertical beams would then lower to a horizontal position, pointing to the nearest station. Where other beams crossed would indicate the final location of the airfield. We would soon be grateful for this information.

The meteorological officer gave us the expected weather en route and over the target. With a final good luck wish from the wing commander we were dismissed. We had a few hours to put in before our take-off time of 2200 hours.

Before joining the others in the crew preparation room, I had a separate briefing for wireless operators in the radio room. Here we were given the colours of the day for the Very pistol cartridges, code books, and call signs for the night. We were also given a sheet of rice paper carrying codes for special messages. If in danger of falling into enemy hands, we were to eat these papers.

We were also given the three-character code that we were to transmit to base as soon as the primary target was bombed (B7J for example), and a separate code to transmit if we bombed the secondary target. Finally, we were impressed with the importance of keeping a detailed and accurate recording of all wireless traffic in our w/t logbook. Reminders were also offered on radio silence and the IFF procedures.

---

* In the RAF, all ground crew tradesmen were invariably referred to as "erks." Most probably this term, first used at Uxbridge in 1920, came from the song "One of the aircs," an abbreviation of aircraftman, and under frequent use it came to be pronounced as "erks."

When I joined the rest of the crew, I found Sgt B, Ted Crosswell, and Len huddled over the maps for England, France, and Germany, plotting our route. Len pointed out to me the approximate positions on our outgoing track where he wanted me to get some bearings from Marham for him. Like me, he was concerned with getting things right on our first op. Our gunners, having had their own separate instructions, joined us in the locker room.

The aircrews donned their "Mae West" life preservers and then strapped on their parachute harnesses. The gunners, to occupy the cold gun turrets, wore leather flying suits, some versions of which were wired for electric heating from plugs in the turret. With those suits, silk underwear was worn to guard against burning the skin. At high altitudes, the rear gunner, with no heat from the main cabin, was particularly vulnerable to freezing temperatures that often fell below –30 degrees Farenheit. The navigator and wireless operator were usually comfortably warm.

Laden with bags of maps, codes, logbooks, and bubble sextant, and walking awkwardly in clumsy flying boots, we climbed into an open lorry with three other crews for the drive to our aircraft in the dispersal area. Alongside our Wimpy with a big "N" on its side, we piled out in time to watch the final 250-pound bomb being winched with a hand crank up into the belly of the aircraft.

After Sgt B and Ted Crosswell completed their walkabout inspection in what was left of a faint evening light, we all climbed aboard through the front hatch. It was always with some difficulty that we took up our positions; British aircraft were built for utility, not comfort, thus there was the minimum room for moving about in the fuselage. One also had to be wary of all sorts of sharp projections from paraphernalia fixed haphazardly along the bulkheads and stringers of the airframe.

After an intercom check, and our own personal checks of equipment, our captain revved up the engines and taxied out to the end of the live runway. Len and I sat with our small shielded lights on our tables and equipment. The front gunner took up his place braced against the main spar. The engine noise and the vibration in the cabin increased suddenly as brakes were released and we were thrust forward, hurtling down the runway between the rows of runway lights. In half a minute we felt the lift-off. We were on our way. This was for real!

While we climbed to our assigned altitude, I opened my logbook and entered the exact time of take-off. I then turned my attention to my radio transmitter and receiver. I had a number of frequencies to set up; first of all, the one for our home base of Marham. The Marconi transmitter had six coloured knobs that were rotated until the correct frequency was registered, and tuned on the antenna meter for maximum signal strength output. The quickest way to do this was to back-tune the transmitter to the frequency preset on the receiver dial. The transmitter knobs were loosened with a small screwdriver, and then tightened to lock in the frequency selected. Each preset frequency could then be set up quickly by rotating the knobs into click stops where each frequency had been installed. Somehow, all these instruments and dials looked more challenging than ever before. I had to concentrate over the intruding noise and vibration of the engines.

As soon as we reached our altitude and levelled out, I struggled out of my seat and squeezed past Len to make my way to the rear of the aircraft to set up the IFF. Len had his head down working on his map, but looked up and gave me the thumbs-up sign and a little grin when I gave his shoulder a pat. In the semi-darkness I clambered over the main spar, grasping the criss-crossed joints of the geodetic frame of the fuselage to keep my balance. On my route I passed the pull-down bed lashed against the port side, the Elsan chemical toilet, and the flare chute on the starboard side until I finally reached the IFF box. I set the on switch and the Graviner destruct switch, and then, since I was just outside the entrance doors to the rear turret, I gave them a tap. George flipped open one of the doors, looking rather startled. I hastened to reassure him that all was okay and that I had just knocked to say hello.

The aircraft was pitching and rolling in turbulence we had run into as I made my way back to my seat. I had no sooner strapped myself in than Len was calling me on the intercom for a bearing from Marham so that he could check the heading.

I had Marham's frequency all set up, so I called the station, using the "X" signals from my code book, held down my key so their direction finders could take a bearing on our aircraft, passed the results to Len on a slip of paper, and got a relieved grin of thanks for what was my first operational exchange of signals.

I got two more bearings for Len before our captain announced we were making our turn near Portsmouth for our run to the target, the docks of Le Havre. It seemed no time at all before the captain ordered Len forward to prepare for our bomb run. I listened to the crew patter as I concentrated on bringing my logbook up to date. Both gunners asked for permission to fire test bursts from their guns to ensure they were in working order. With an affirmative from Sgt B, the crack and vibration from the .303 Brownings reverberated throughout the aircraft. Mixed with the oil and petrol fumes I could smell a faint odour of cordite familiar from the firing ranges.

Ted Crosswell spoke up, saying that he could see fires in the dock area, and some bursting flak* as the Wellingtons that had reached the target before us finished their bombing runs. Len called out the approach bearings for our own bomb run to the captain, who confirmed he had opened the bomb doors. Len would now be flipping his toggles on the bomb panel to arm the bombs, and setting wind, bearing, and airspeed into his bomb sight. On the final approach, he called out course corrections with, "Left, left . . . r-i-g-h-t. Left. Hold it. Steady. Bombs gone!"

With that exultant cry from Len, Sgt B threw the aircraft into a rather violent bank to port, aided by a severe bump that all of us felt under our seats. The interior of the aircraft was suddenly lit up in the orange flash of exploding shells as we were bracketed by flak.

As Ted Crosswell stood beside the captain, he called out where the flak seemed thickest, with suggestions for evasive action, but Sgt B needed no advice as he threw us about to get clear of the bursts on our exit from the target area.

We were soon out of it, and Len struggled back to his bench and his maps to work out a course to get us home to Marham. He soon called this out to the captain, and then leaned over to me to ask, "Howard, as soon as you can, would you get me a bearing, or, better still, an actual position point?" I had to tell him that I couldn't do that until we were nearer the English coast.

Our captain then came up on the intercom to say, "Well chaps, that's your first op in. Is everyone all right?" We all replied in turn that we were, trying to sound more matter of fact about it than we really felt. He then called up each crew member in turn to ask what we had seen over the target. Did we see where our bombs hit, and any other "gen" we might give to the debriefing officer when we got home? The rear gunner had the best view, and George said he was sure our bombs had landed in the dock area, to add to the fires already burning there. Ted confirmed this, saying he got a pretty good look as we banked away from the target. I was too busy getting my logbook up to date. My first op and I hadn't seen a damned thing!

---

* An acronym for the German Fliegerabwehrkanonen (anti-aircraft fire).

In no time at all, it seemed, Len was asking me again for a bearing, or better still a fix. The airwaves had gotten so busy and crowded that I had some difficulty picking out and identifying stations. I finally got a response from a station near Plymouth, but because of our location they couldn't give me a fix. However, I got a true bearing from them and passed it to Len. From then on I got him bearing after bearing until the final courses to steer for our home base.

At one point Ted screamed, "We're too bloody low! I can see the barrage balloons over bloody London! What the hell are we doing here anyway?" No reply from anyone but George.

"I can see the bleeding things, too!" With no comment, our captain made a swift climbing turn to get us clear of the obstacles.

As we neared Marham and decreased altitude to join the landing circuit, our captain cautioned all of us, but especially the gunners, "Keep a sharp lookout for intruders. Last week we lost two crews from a Junkers 88 that managed to join the circuit and followed them in and shot them down on final approach. They're doing that a lot now so watch out for the bastards!"

As we started our final approach, I suddenly remembered the IFF. I had switched it on as we approached our own coast, but I hadn't turned off the destruct switch. I scrambled back the whole length of the fuselage, switched it off, and just managed to make my seat before we touched down. Climbing over the main spar I fell over the startled front gunner who had taken up his position for the landing.

A lorry met us at dispersal as we climbed down through the hatch and took us to the debriefing room. As we waited our turn, we helped ourselves to some sandwiches and tea. We were soon called in and seated before a flight lieutenant who asked for all the details of the trip. Len had to answer a lot of questions from his nav log about our courses. The flight lieutenant seemed pleased enough to hear that we thought our bombs had landed in the dock area.

As soon as this was over I had a second debriefing by a flight sergeant in the W/T room. I was relieved that he approved of my log keeping. I got a ticking off, however, for not trying some other, more suitable, frequencies for bearings on our return course. I didn't admit to him that I was afraid to change too many of the frequencies I had set up in case I screwed up the dials and couldn't get tuned in again in time. I got some helpful tips from this man, however, and was a lot bolder with my equipment from then on.

Len, George, and I were taken to our billets in the old manor house. We were a little too strung out, tired though we were, to get to sleep right away, and sat discussing our first op. From their turrets, George and Munroe saw a lot more than Len or I; we were too absorbed in our work and our logs. Len thanked me for all of the help with his navigation, which made me feel that I had contributed something to the flight. We agreed that we shouldn't get the idea that all of our ops were going to be as easy as this one seemed to be. If any of us still laboured under any such delusion, we would soon be disabused of it.

Our war had begun.

9
UNTO THE BREACH —
FINAL EROSION OF INNOCENCE

On 1 SEPTEMBER 1941, THREE DAYS after our initiation raid on Le Havre, we were called to an early afternoon briefing. The Tannoy shouted out, "Ops are on for tonight."

The wing commander faced the assembled crews in the theatre and announced, "Well, chaps, it's quite a big effort tonight. Our target is Cologne, and we want to give the marshalling yards and factories there a good smashing."

The red tapes on the map of Germany showed our route into the Ruhr valley, called "Happy Valley" by the aircrews because of the casualties already suffered from raids on this heavily defended area. Cities in the Ruhr harboured the highest percentage of coal-, steel-, and chemical-producing factories in Germany, so it was defended with the heaviest concentrations of flak and night fighters in Europe. Announcements of targets in that area were usually greeted with grimaces and a few audible groans from assembled crews.

The now-familiar briefing on bomb loads, target pin points, codes, expected flak and fighter activity, and the all-important weather followed. Then off we went for rest, early dinner, and our plotting preparations.

We had a surprise waiting for us when we reached the plotting room. We were introduced to our new front gunner. I knew Wilson Poirier right away. We had trained together at OTU and I had been talking to him in the briefing theatre when neither of us knew that he would be joining our crew. Munroe was not about, and I cannot remember seeing him again. We were never given any explanation for the crew change.

Willy and I were to become good friends and frequent companions on our sorties into London on leave. He was a French Canadian from New Carlisle, Quebec, but I cannot remember him speaking anything but fluent English. Perhaps he would have spoken French if I had been able to speak it as well. I wasn't to learn until much later that, like Len, he was a "star-crossed" member of that first crew I belonged to.

Our crew plotting and preparation completed, we dressed, loaded ourselves up with all our paraphernalia, and took off in the crew lorry for dispersal.

The dispersal area where our Wimpy was parked was a beehive of activity. As with the other Wimpys nearby, the ground crew of fitters, engine and airframe mechanics, armourers, petrol bowser drivers, and other odd erks were swarming all over and around our aircraft.

The flight sergeant in charge of this particular ground crew rode about on the ubiquitous issue station bicycle, barking out orders or reproofs as he thought the occasion or the culprit demanded. Ground crew flight sergeants were called, among others things, "the Chiefie." The sergeant spent some of his time chasing erks away from their "chai and wads"* dispensed by the ever-present NAAFI wagon (the Navy, Army, and Air Force Institute snack service staffed by volunteers).

The NAAFI service was a great comfort and morale booster to the indispensable ground crews, toiling in wet, cold conditions often so miserable that we marvelled at their ability to get our aircraft repaired, tested, bombed up, and serviced in time for operations.

Sheltering under the wing of our Wimpy one wet night, I was startled by the sight of two young women of the Women's Auxiliary Air Force (WAAF) pulling a 250-pound bomb on a dolly up to the belly of our aircraft. Soaked to the skin, one WAAF cranked the winch to hoist the bomb up into the bomb bay, *while the other WAAF steadied the bomb with her back!* These young WAAFs had joined their male comrades in

---

* "Chai," (pronounced *shy*), Arabic for tea, was transported back to Britain by servicemen returning from the Middle East. "Wads" was simply British vernacular for buns.

most of the ground crew trades. Although it was probably of concern to wives and sweethearts, the companionship the WAAFs provided gave us a much-needed emotional lifeline.

I have always believed that the contributions the ground crews made to the war effort have never been adequately recognized. While they did not face the dangers the aircrew confronted, they suffered a share of casualties from the frequent bombings and strafing of the airfields. They also suffered from the considerable stress of handing over the aircraft they had laboured to prepare for the night's operation to a crew they too often never saw again.

With a thumbs up from the Chiefie, and the servicing log signed and accepted by the captain, our Wimpy lumbered out to the live runway. Cleared for take-off by the control tower, at precisely 2000 hours we roared down most of the grass runway's length and lifted off into a clear, darkening night on the second "op" of our operational tour. We learned later that we were in the company of thirty-four other Wimpys and twenty Hampdens from various squadrons in Bomber Command.

As I sat in the dim light of my small desk in front of the myriad dials and knobs of my transmitter and receiver checking frequencies and getting attuned to the steady throb of the Bristol Pegasus engines, I thought of the job Len had in front of him. He knew that on this trip I would not be able to get bearings for him on our outward legs as I had been authorized to do on our first op. At this stage our Wimpy had not been fitted with "GEE,"* but it was a clear night so far, so he should have been able to get himself some star fixes from his bubble sextant.**

Our given route to the target of Cologne was to take us over Holland, south on a diversion to the small French town of Givet, just over the

---

* "GEE" was a codename for a radio-pulse system by which the navigator could fix his position by reference to three transmitting stations in England. A more accurate radar-pulse system, codenamed "OBOE," was introduced later.

** To the layman, navigation might seem to be a fairly simple exercise. The pilot draws a line on his map from departure point A to destination point B and notes the direction in degrees. Then he flies on that heading for the time taken to cover the distance at his air speed, and voilà, he arrives at his destination. As rear gunner George would say, "Not bleeding likely." For that pure theoretical flight the conditions would have to include completely still air, a constant temperature, a totally stable aircraft, and a pilot who could keep the aircraft perfectly on the heading he had been given. I doubt that all of these conditions have ever been experienced together in the history of flight. The wind, which can vary wildly in direction and strength between a few thousand feet in altitude, is the main culprit. The winds also change constantly en route, even at the same altitude. The navigator must work constantly to compute the wind and give offsetting or compensating course headings to the pilot.

border of Belgium below Dinant, then on a heading of 045° to the target. Len had gone forward to the bomb aimer's position where he could get a clear view of the ground. Suddenly he announced to Sgt B, "The Zuider Zee is right below us. It gives us a fair pinpoint!" I left the frequencies I had been monitoring in case of a recall or other orders and clambered back to the astro dome to see the famous inland sea.

Soon we saw a "V" made up of lights pointing towards our turning point of Givet. These were goose-neck flares laid out on the ground by the Dutch resistance, at great risk, to help RAF bombers reach their targets. We wondered if they could know what our target was, or if they just knew the general direction.

Soon we were over Givet and making our turn onto course for the target. We had been told to keep our eyes peeled for night fighters, and as we neared the target I went to the astro dome. Ted Crosswell, standing beside Sgt B, cried out, "There are the fires straight ahead. Must be Cologne! There's a lot of flak bursting over the city." We could all see it, and we also saw the white searchlight beams probing the sky.

Our captain then announced, "I'm going to stooge around a bit on the outskirts just to see what's happening before we go in. Navigator, you'd better come forward now and get ready for the bomb run."

Orange mushrooms with dirty brown rings expanding rapidly from their centres began to sprout around us, and the whump of the exploding flak shells could be heard above the roar of the engines. It was accompanied by the sweet, sickly smell of cordite. Outskirts of the city or not, we were beginning to run into a great deal of heavy flak.

At 8,000 feet we began to attract the attention of the medium flak gunners. I watched with a nervous fascination as the streams of mixed yellow, green, and some red shells snaked up towards our Wimpy in an "S" curve. They appeared to leave the ground in a lazy, slow motion but accelerated rapidly as they reached our level and went past our wings at incredible speed. Most of them seemed to me to be aimed precisely at the end of my nose.

Sgt B began to jink the aircraft to avoid the increasing flak, and called to Len on the intercom that he would be making our bomb run now. Immediately, we all heard Ted's protest: "What do you mean we'll start our bomb run? We're nowhere near the railway yards, and I didn't bloody well come here to bomb bloody German cow pastures! We've got to get right into the city to get to our target, which is over there to port, about ten degrees."

This outburst must have struck a nerve with our captain, who obviously had the "wind up" (as we used to say of those whose fear or panic had taken over) and was perhaps loath to go in to the target over the fierce firestorm already consuming parts of the town centre. He told Len to stand by, and altered course as Ted had demanded.

By now the flak had intensified. We were surrounded by exploding shells whose blasts were thumping under our feet as the whole airframe shuddered. The sky was no longer clear but covered in the brown fog of the deadly fireworks display ahead.

I saw two other Wimpys over the target area. One of them was caught in a cone of three searchlights. Suddenly he exploded, and became a monstrous red and brown expanding ball. Pieces of the aircraft fell through the searchlight beams, sparkling in the white light. Later that night, that Wimpy would be marked FTR (Failed to return) on the board in the ops room for that Wimpy.

Len's voice came over the intercom with a heading of 350 to the target. "We can start our run-up now." Sgt B straightened out for the approach, and Len started his corrections with "left, left, steady . . . r-i-g-h-t, steady . . . bombs gone!"

"Let's get out of here!" cried our captain as he threw the Wimpy into violent corkscrew turns to avoid the flak that appeared as an almost impenetrable curtain of exploding shells.

I had to get back to my seat to send the "bombed primary target" coded message to Bomber Command Headquarters. With the captain's okay I immediately set up my transmitter on the designated frequency and, waiting my turn on the busy wavelength, got the message out and got the "R-Ack-R" receipt. Len than gave the captain a tentative heading for home, and we started chatting about where our bombs had hit. Ted was sure we had come very close to our target, and Len agreed.

Having gotten my important message away, I leaned out into the passageway to tell Len that I would get him some bearings as soon as we had reached the Channel. I glanced back down the fuselage at the precise moment a shell exploded halfway down to the rear turret with a sharp crack and a brilliant flash of light. The blast hit me full in the face. My eyelids closed tight, and my eyes felt as if they had been sand-blasted shut. I was blind! I felt panic rising through my body. Of all the things I had imagined might happen to me, being blinded wasn't one of them.

Len grabbed my shoulders, and I shouted that I couldn't see. Just then we were rocked again by shrapnel hitting the aircraft. Len picked up the microphone that I had dropped and called the captain to say that smoke was coming out of my wireless set.

Ted clambered back quickly to look at the equipment with Len. It had been hit by pieces of the shrapnel, but Ted announced that the smoke had cleared and there seemed to be no risk of fire. He then hurried back to the rear to check on damage from the exploding shell. He reported a few stringers and some fabric missing but no serious structural damage. George also reported that he was all right, and added a few cockney comments on the rude reception we had been given.

Len set about trying to do something about my eyes, and managed to get some water into them. This helped to relieve some of the painful burning, and I was extremely relieved that I could see something again, even if through a smoky haze.

I had trouble focusing on my dials and meters, but at least I could make them out if I really strained and concentrated. I was dismayed on a quick test of the transmitter when I got no reading on the antenna output meter — it wasn't working. At least I had gotten the bomb message away. But now I began to worry about getting bearings for Len as we left the target area. Wind up or not, our captain's experience had pulled us through it.

I concentrated now on trying to get my transmitter to work. I managed to get my hand around to the back of the set, and found some dangling wires that obviously had been broken loose. I had no idea where they had come from, but I found what felt to be connection points and twisted the loose ends into those fittings. I also found some loose plates that fixed back in positions that seemed to fit.

I had been working longer than I thought because Len was telling the captain that he believed we were nearing the Channel coast. He didn't sound very sure of himself. The clear skies that had made us better targets for flak or night fighters, but had also given Len stars for position lines, had clouded over. He was forced into straight DR, or "dead reckoning" navigation, and was having trouble finding his winds.

The captain was not pleased, and the whole crew seemed to be getting edgy, largely, no doubt, the after-effect of our rough time over the target area. Len leaned over to pull my sleeve. Rather than speak over the intercom so all would hear, he pulled my earphone aside and asked if I could get something out of my set for him. I got the distinct feeling that we were lost.

I turned all my attention to the transmitter and tried several frequencies to no avail. At least the receiver seemed to be operating. The captain kept asking Len for a new heading, sounding more and more frustrated and worried.

I worked at the transmitter for a long time. In frustration I tuned into a station at Hull, knowing it was a powerful station but that it might be too far north to hear me. On the third try I got a faint response, so I quickly sent back the code request for a fix, and held down my Morse key for a long dash. Back came the weak, barely audible code for the first four of the eight coordinates I needed, and then the signal faded out. I tried again and got up to six of the figures I needed before the signal faded again.

With Len leaning over me now, I waited a few minutes, and had a sudden brainwave. I reeled out the trailing antenna, and used the transmitter output meter to judge when I had the optimum length for the Hull frequency I was on. Then I tried again. Eureka! This time I got all the coordinates we needed for a good fix of our position. Like a man grasping at straws, Len snatched the slip of paper on which I had hurriedly written the coordinates, and soon called out a course for home base.

The captain handed over the controls to Ted and came back to look at Len's map. He was as startled as Len and I had been to find that we were over water, north of Holland, headed for the North Sea. By this time our fuel was getting dangerously low; if we had kept on our previous heading we would have had to ditch when we ran out of fuel.

We were lucky. From then on I could get nothing out of my equipment.

Our captain warned us that we weren't out of hot water yet. Our fuel was low, as he and Len had figured out, and we had to make for the nearest airfield as soon as possible. Our new course put us on track to southeast England, and as we approached land Sgt B called out that we would have to use the Darkie procedure to try to get in somewhere quickly. I had already switched on the TR9F set under my seat so we might get the "squeaker" warning of too-close barrage balloons, so I readied it to contact Darkie stations by voice.

Ted called "Darkie, Darkie, this is N Nan, do you read?" I had the IFF switched on by this time, so we were identified as friendly and back came the sweet voice of the WAAF ground operator.

"N Nan, this is Darkie. We have you all right. Follow the lights."

I hurried forward to peer over Ted's shoulder in time to see two searchlight beams switch on to project vertical shafts of light ahead of us. I could make them out through my still-hazy eyes, which burned and felt as if they were full of grit. The beams then went horizontal, pointing slightly to the northwest, and Sgt B swung us over to follow them.

Before we made our next turn, an unmistakable Aussie voice came over the radio throughout our intercom. "Darkie, Darkie, this is P Peter, do you read?" No reply. After several tries, the Aussie got frustrated and called, "Darkie, you little bastard, where are you?" This time, the sweet WAAF voice came back, but only after blowing in her microphone several times to test it, an annoying habit of some operators.

A cool Aussie shot back with, "You've blown in my ear three times, Sheila, now kiss me!" A brief pause ensued before the Aussie got his direction. This little exchange gave all of us a lift just when we needed it.

By now we had followed our last searchlight beams and were on the approach to an airfield that turned out to be West Malling, in Kent. This was primarily a night fighter station. It was some distance from our home base of Marham, but was very welcome nonetheless.

After a cursory debriefing by a grouchy intelligence officer rudely torn from his bed, we were taken to the sergeants' mess and told that we would have to make ourselves comfortable on the sofas and chairs for what remained of the night, or rather morning. We had been in the air over six hours, and it was now past 0300 hours.

Still in our flying clothes, we stretched out on sofas or the floor rug. It was hard to calm ourselves down enough to actually get to sleep, although Ted managed to doze off. Willy Poirier looked pale and strung out. He had had the front row seat overlooking all the action, of course, and it had an effect on him. I sat with him and chatted for a while until he seemed to feel a little better. I suspected that he had been airsick during our flight.

Len urged me to go to the station hospital to have my eyes treated, but I insisted that I would wait until we got back to Marham. This wasn't bravado on my part. I was afraid that if the medics got hold of me I wouldn't get back to our home base to rejoin my crew for goodness knows how long.

I turned to my logbook, in which I had neglected to make entries during all the stress of trying to get the wireless set working after we left the target. My eyes were still burning, but I could just make out the log-book pages enough to write in times of transmissions and message content. I had to rely on memory, and I hoped the debriefers wouldn't check my times too closely. Only when I finished this could I rest my back against a chair to try to get some sleep. I found it hopeless; I could not get the sight of that exploding bomber out of my mind.

In the memory of every Bomber Command survivor is the sight of other bombers exploding, and the knowledge that later the same night FTR would be entered on the ops boards at the crews' home bases. In his book *The Right of the Line*, John Terraine quotes John Pudney's poem "Security." It's about pre-take-off precautions, and for me it expresses the individual tragedies in all the losses:

Empty your pockets, Tom, Dick and Harry,
Strip your identity; leave it behind.
Lawyer, garage hand, grocer, don't tarry
With your own country, your own kind.

Leave all your letters. Suburb and township,
Green fen and grocery, slip-way and bay,
Hot-spring and prairie, smoke stack and coal tip,
Leave in our keeping while you're away.

Tom, Dick and Harry, plain names and numbers,
Pilot, observer, and gunner depart,
Their personal litter only encumbers
Somebody's head, somebody's heart.

At daylight we roused ourselves and walked stiffly into the adjoining mess hall for an early breakfast. Even the simulated eggs and the cold English toast tasted good. We were dehydrated and hungry.

Our Wimpy had been inspected, refuelled, and declared fit for flying. There were numerous holes in the wings and fuselage, and several square feet of fabric and stringers were missing, but this never seemed to upset the old Wimpy unduly. With its geodetic structure the airframe could take an enormous amount of damage before the flying stability of the aircraft was seriously impaired. We clambered aboard, and were soon on our way to Marham.

Marham operations knew all about our misadventures, and we had to undergo a long, critical debriefing. I handed in my logs to the duty wireless operator, and was told to report for a radio debriefing later in the day. I was then sent off to the duty medical officer to have my eyes examined.

The medical officer washed my eyes out with some kind of soothing potion that relieved the burning greatly; he pronounced them okay. Apparently my eyes had been filled with dirt and grit that blew off the floor of the aircraft when the shell exploded. Later I found I had a permanent tiny black spot in one eye that was annoying only when I looked into a clear sky; sometimes it made me think twice about whether it was the spot or an enemy aircraft in the distance. The medical officer ordered me to spend the rest of the day in the sick bay, and I fell gratefully into the cool white sheets of the hospital bed, by now thoroughly exhausted and emotionally spent.

When I did finally get my radio debriefing, I was told there was no possible way that my transmitter would have worked the way I had blindly wired it back together. All I could say to them, as the flight sergeants shook their heads, was that they could ask our navigator, because if I hadn't received that fix from Hull, we would be at the bottom of the North Sea.

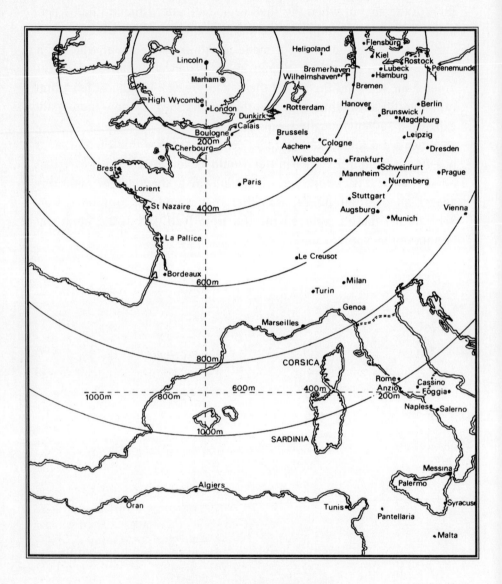

THE EUROPEAN THEATRE OF AIR OPERATIONS

10
BLOODED MEMBERS OF THE CLUB

WITHIN A MONTH, WE HAD TAKEN part in several bombing raids over Germany, and we began to settle in to the routine of squadron and station life. Now blooded in action against the enemy, we were accepted into the "club." Hardened veterans we had not yet become, but we were gaining confidence in ourselves, in spite of the new-found emotions that were beginning to gnaw just a little at our nerve ends: stress and fear.

We suffered from no moral ambiguity in what we were doing. Sometimes, when I heard the "bombs gone" call from Len, I had a troubling but fleeting thought about whom the bombs might be maiming or killing. Were they women, or children? We had no knowledge then of the unbelievable depths of depravity of the Nazis, but knowing what atrocities they had already committed in Poland, Holland, and Belgium — as well as in Great Britain, where I had seen the results with my own eyes — we had no compunction about dropping our bombs anywhere on German soil. Targets in France, of course, were different, but an unavoidable part of the war.

We learned that crew members were never "killed"; they "got the chop," "bought the farm," or simply "bought it." They were also lost when they "went for a Burton," the name of a popular dark ale.

Crews tended to stick together. They became a family that flew and socialized together. The development of close friendships outside the crew was generally avoided. We had to find our own way to deal with the loss of crews with whom we had shared lunch or early dinner just hours before.

By this time, Willy Poirier and I had been reassigned to share a room on the second floor of the sergeants' mess. I was disappointed to lose the warm companionship that Len and George and I had enjoyed in our common room in the old manor house, but Willy and I got along well together and we were happy enough with this new arrangement.

We spent a great deal of our off-time in the sergeants' mess. This pre-war mess was well organized, and comfortably furnished with leather-covered sofas and chairs. There was a large fireplace, and tables and chairs for card players. One adjoining room was fitted out with the absolutely essential dart board and a large, regulation-size billiard table.

Our meals were served in a large dining hall in the mess, with seating at several long tables. Our waitresses were WAAFs, members of the Women's Auxiliary Air Force. We were to learn that these female members of the RAF were involved in a great many roles more important to the war effort than waiting on tables, but we were grateful for their attentions, and for their presence.

The meals we were served reflected the severe rationing the entire country was enduring. There were great amounts of dried or dehydrated egg powder, and abundant slices of cold, tasteless toast that seemed to be the British preference. Brought out hot from the kitchen, the toast was placed in racks on a sideboard until it was nice and cold and ready to serve. We discovered that this wasn't solely an air force idiosyncrasy; it was common to restaurants and bed-and-breakfast homes throughout Britain.

Small Brussels sprouts were the main vegetable served at nearly every meal. Most of us enjoyed the first thousand or so, but when we began to get them for breakfast our taste buds gave up the battle. The reason for their proliferation was that the hardy devils would grow almost anywhere, even in cinder beds. Behind every air force hangar, and in nearly every civilian backyard, there was a "victory garden," heavily favouring the little green monsters. Like most Canadians who served overseas, I vowed that if I survived the war I would never eat one again.

There also seemed to be an unlimited supply of a thin, yellow custard that was ladled out over every sweet served. Even when I attempted to shield my bowl, a hand would appear from nowhere and reach over my shoulder to deposit a great glop of this custard over the contents. Someone didn't want us to know what the sweet of the day was.

The French are said to live for eating, but the British mainly eat to live. Beyond sustenance, they simply seemed to have no great interest in food, and it showed in the preparation. They did their best, however, and really performed miracles at times with the little they had to work with.

There was also the bar, serving the time-honoured ales and bitters of Britain, along with the harder spirits. I hadn't begun to drink beer or anything else at this stage, but Len, George, and Ted, while not regular drinkers, enjoyed a pint or two. Later, my painful indoctrination came in the form of a chug-a-lug contest, trying to drink a full pint of black and tan* without pause. I found, as others did, that this potent mixture of bitter and Guinness produced the most horrible of hangovers. The rules covering drinking and flying had been made quite clear to us, of course, and it was a matter of survival to keep a clear head when scheduled for flying.

Daily, at noon, the mess anteroom fell silent as the BBC radio news was broadcast, usually read by the well-known Alvar Liddell. What we found very strange was that the previous night's targets raided by Bomber Command were almost always identified. More startling was the revelation of the numbers of aircraft lost on these raids. We wondered about the accuracy of these figures, and the dangers of revealing such losses to the enemy. We found out that the numbers were indeed accurate.

These broadcasts went on for the whole of our stay at Marham. Contrary to the assertions of post-war revisionists, we were fully aware of the casualties being suffered throughout Bomber Command. Needless to say, we knew soon after our return from an operation what our own squadron losses had been, and who we would not be seeing at the breakfast table again. It was somewhat surprising that this knowledge did not cause the serious deterioration in morale that one might reasonably expect. There is no doubt, however, that this continual reminder of

---

* Because the mixture looked black (the Guinness) and tan (the bitter), the name is thought to derive from the "Black and Tans," an auxiliary group of constabulary serving in Ireland during the troubles of 1920–21, so called because of the colours of their uniform. Recruited from unemployed veterans of WWI, their tactics in a ruthless campaign against the Irish revolutionaries helped to unite the Irish population in the cause of independence, and led to the granting of dominion status to the Irish Free State in 1921.

the deadly hazards that we were facing added to the stresses that operational flying was placing upon us.

In fact, losses on operational sorties were beginning to exceed three percent, causing a great deal of concern over replacement of aircrews and aircraft. In late 1941, Bomber Command had forty-five operational squadrons in five groups, including one RCAF squadron (405 Sqn). Of these, twenty-one squadrons were equipped with the Wellington bomber. But in all, there were only 450 aircraft, with crews. All of us were aware that crews had less than a fifty percent chance of surviving a full tour of operations. Although aircrew "on ops" during 1941 were generally of the understanding that thirty operational flights constituted completion of a full operational tour, it wasn't until August 1942 that Air Marshal "Bomber" Harris, from February 1942 the air officer commanding Bomber Command, confirmed that figure. On completion of that number of sorties, aircrew members were to be transferred to non-operational duties, usually to instructing at an OTU. After four or five months, they could be returned to operations for a second tour. The chances of surviving a second tour were indeed slim.

During this period, with the lack of any sophisticated navigational aids and no organized techniques for target marking, the Command was still trying to place its bombs on small-area industrial or transportation targets. The Pathfinder squadrons of highly experienced aircrews, trained to mark targets with coloured indicators in the van of the main bomber force, were not organized until mid-1942. Consequently, the majority of these raids were not having a significant effect on the war-making capacity of Nazi Germany. This led, of course, to the controversial concept of "area bombing," with its inevitable destruction of urban areas and greater loss of civilian lives. Under the conditions of the time, however, there was simply no alternative. Bomber Command was the only Allied force capable of carrying the war to the enemy in Europe. This was the true context of operations.*

---

* Although four RCAF squadrons were flying with RAF Bomber Command by 1942, it wasn't until 1 January 1943 that a Canadian group of squadrons was formed under its own Canadian commanders. On that date, No. 6 RCAF Group was formally constituted as one of Bomber Command's groups. Initially, 6 Group comprised 8 squadrons, but expanded to 14 within the year. Crews of that group flew their first operational sortie on 3 January 1943, when six Wellingtons of 427 Squadron completed a mine-laying sortie to the Frisian Islands. But of the 93,844 RCAF airmen who served overseas between 1940–45, 60 percent served on RAF squadrons.

Our spirits were lightened considerably by a variety of radio programs. We were introduced to the soon-to-be-legendary Vera Lynn, and also to comedians Tommy Trinder and Max Miller. We were listening to the borderline vulgar sketches of Max Miller one evening when he went far beyond what the BBC and listeners of that era could or would tolerate. Mad Max was cut off in mid-sentence and replaced with military band music. We never heard from him again. Apparently, his contract with the BBC was terminated that night.

We were given many evening and weekend passes off the station. For most of us this meant a trip to King's Lynn for fish and chips and the flicks. The station provided a bus run to and from the city. On nearly every trip, some of the erks or aircrew would start up their rendition of that popular ditty "I've Got Sixpence." We came to cushion our ears against the never-changing lyrics:

I've got sixpence, jolly, jolly sixpence,
I've got sixpence to last me all my life.
I've got tuppence to spend, and tuppence to lend,
And tuppence to send home to my wife.
No cares have I to grie-eeve me,
No pretty little girls to decei-eeve me,
I'm happy as a king, belie-eeve me,
As we go rolling, rolling home.

To the tune of "Waltzing Matilda," there was also "Ops in a Wimpy":

Ops in a Wimpy, ops in a Wimpy,
Who'll come on ops in a Wimpy with me?

We might have settled in to the routine on the station, but we began to look forward to a break from this environment. We needed a change of pace and a change of surroundings to recharge ourselves. Our nerves were not quite as stable as they had been, and little things that we had shrugged off before as trivial were beginning to become major irritants. It was time for leave.

11
ADVENTURES ON
SQUADRON LEAVE

IT WAS WITH CONSIDERABLE JOY and relief that we learned of the squadron policy on leave. Aircrews flying on operations for seven weeks were given every eighth week off on leave. Up to this point, we had been given no more than daily and weekend passes. Each one of us felt the need for some renewal or restoration of body and mind. This need was particularly acute for the married members of the crew, of course, and I knew Len was yearning for some time with his wife and baby. We needed a change from the constant tension of anticipating the next briefing and from the stress of the raids themselves.

Willy had some friend he wanted to look up, and the married members of the crew took off speedily for home. I declined their kind invitations to visit with them; I knew that I would just be in the way. In any case, I had my own plans.

The grandparents of my high school girlfriend, on her father's side, lived just outside Aberdeen. I had been given the address, and since I was interested in seeing Scotland anyway I decided that I would look them up.

We were given warrants for rail travel on leave, which allowed us to save our rather meagre pay for food and lodging. We were also given a fairly liberal supply of ration coupons. These were meant to relieve parents from expending all their precious coupons on sons or daughters arriving home on leave. They were also valuable to me, of course, when I stayed with friends.

At London, I boarded one of the great trains, the "Aberdonian," at King's Cross station and was on my way to Edinburgh. For most of the four hours it took to reach that Scottish city I was glued to the window, enthralled by the unfolding scenery as we followed the east coast north.

I found a room at the YMCA and began my tour of Princes Street, with its imposing monument to Sir Walter Scott and the overpowering immensity of Edinburgh Castle. On my tour of this fabled keep, I was met by one of the security guards as I crawled along the ramparts taking pictures. I was lucky to be able to talk the guard out of confiscating my camera.

I had found one of the many canteens operated throughout Britain by the Salvation Army where so many Commonwealth servicemen far from home found tea, buns, and comfort. On my second evening I climbed to the second floor of a building just off Princes Street where the canteen was located.

There were ten or eleven British Army soldiers sitting at the tables, but I saw no other airmen. I was ordering tea from a young lady volunteer when three Royal Navy sailors came in and joined me at the counter. They had obviously been drinking, and began to speak in vulgar language. The manager came out of the kitchen and asked the sailors to tone down their language in front of the young lady volunteer. They ignored him. He then pleaded with me, "You're a sergeant, would you tell them to cut out the bad language?"

I had no naive delusions that my rank insignia would carry much weight with these inebriated fellows, but, foolishly, I decided that I should make some effort to help matters. I turned to the rough-looking sailor closest to me and said, as diplomatically as I could, "I know you're having a good time on the town, but I wonder if you'd tone down the bad language in front of the young lady here?" Big mistake! As he turned to face me he lashed out with his fist and caught me on the cheek. The force of the blow knocked me backwards on my heels, but as he stepped towards me again I instinctively struck out as hard as I could. In that split second I was sure that I felt his nose break under my fist.

His two buddies now joined him in pummeling me against the wall. A quick, hopeful glance at the soldiers in the room told me that not one of them was coming to my aid. Just as I was despairing of any hope of help, a huge soldier appeared in the entrance and immediately strode towards us. He grabbed the two largest sailors by their necks and hammered them unmercifully. I was left with the other sailor, who appeared to me to be the youngest of the trio, about my age and size. We carried on our fight, but it was no contest. By now I was thoroughly angered by the whole donnybrook, and I'm afraid I pounded him a little more than his particular actions deserved. He gave up and turned away from the fray.

In the meantime, my new friend and saviour had left his unfortunate sailor opponents lying still on the floor, and had turned towards the soldiers still sitting motionless watching the fight. The giant picked up a chair, and held it up as if it were a feather, and challenged, "All right, you yellow-bellied bastards, come on, one at a time or all together, it makes no difference to me." There was a dead silence in the room. Not one soldier made a move. I could not say that I blamed them, after what they had just witnessed.

I shook my rescuer's hand and thanked him for saving me from a brutal beating. He brushed off my thanks, and said that as he entered the room and saw the fight he recognized immediately that I was a Canadian airman getting beaten; he wasn't going to put up with that. He was a Canadian soldier in the Forestry Corps, on leave from his unit. A former lumberjack — it was no wonder that the sailors were way out of their league.

In the meantime, the manager had called for the ambulance and the police. The two sailors on the floor were obviously not in good shape. The ambulance arrived and the two victims were rushed away. Two military police also arrived and took down our story. My young adversary had disappeared. The Canadian forester, who said his name was Smith, declined my invitation to go out for a beer or two, saying he had a train to catch. With that he took off.

The next morning, not knowing where else to go, I returned to that canteen for breakfast. As I was trying to remove a tough jacket of skin from a "banger," I looked up to see the very bruised young sailor from last night's imbroglio standing beside me. He asked if he could join me. I pulled out a chair for him. He looked at me a little sheepishly, and confessed, "I say, I'm very sorry for what happened last night. I had too much to drink, and my mates shouldn't have done what they did."

This took me by surprise; I couldn't hold a grudge against him, though, and I told him to forget it. I asked him if he knew how his friends had fared at the hospital. He told me that one had been discharged with numerous bruises and a few loose teeth. The other one was in worse shape, with a broken nose and several broken ribs.

■ ■ ■

It was a short rail run to Aberdeen, that port city of granite brick buildings. I booked a room on Union Street in a hotel also called the Union. The next morning, I caught a bus for the town of White Rashes, only about five miles out of the city. I told the bus driver that the folks I wanted to visit lived near there, just outside a small village called Pitrichy.

"What's their name?" he asked.

"Dick," I replied.

"Oh, I know the old folks. I can drop you off within walking distance of the house. It's an old stone farmhouse."

The driver deposited me at the entrance to a short laneway leading up to the house. It was a quaint old place. I knocked tentatively on the door. In a few moments, the door opened, and a woman with grey hair and a shawl over her shoulders took only a brief look at me before exclaiming, "Och, you'll be the sergeant from Canada we heard about from our granddaughter. Come in, laddie." The moment I stepped into the small front room, she threw her arms around me and called for "faither." The old man came from the kitchen and welcomed me energetically.

I told them that I intended to stay for only a few hours, but they would have none of it; they insisted that I stay the night. Fortunately, I had brought a small overnight bag with me. I stayed for three days, but to say that my visit began less than auspiciously would be an understatement.

We had a good chat around the fireplace following a dinner that tasted delicious to me after eating the mess food. I handed over all the ration coupons I had, to the delight, and I'm sure the relief, of Mrs. Dick. When it came time for bed, I wondered where they were going to put me. I could see only one room off the living room that could be a bedroom in this one-storey house. I couldn't believe it when I saw Mr. Dick pull down a hinged ladder from the ceiling. I was led into the bedroom and told that there was where I was to sleep. I asked, "But where are you going to sleep?" I was told that they were going up into the loft above the living room where they would be quite comfortable. My protests fell on deaf ears. The bedroom was nicely furnished. The bed, Mrs. Dick proudly pointed out, had a thick, feather-filled mattress.

Feeling guilty about taking their comfortable bed, I lay back in this sinful luxury and fell into a deep sleep. I was more exhausted than I had realized.

I had several troubling dreams. In the last one I was floating in a pool of water. I opened my eyes to the morning light, and awoke to my horror that I was indeed lying in a pool of water — my water! What had I done? I had not wet the bed since I was four years old. I lay there in the soggy, cooling mess, wondering how I was ever going to face the dear old lady. What would I say?

A knock on the door brought me up to an uncomfortable sitting position. In came Mrs. Dick with my breakfast on a tray. I saw an egg, a small piece of bacon and some fried bread, and a cup of tea. There was also a piece of toast and a small plate with jam. With all the rationing, this was a sumptuous feast. I felt guilty again, especially in my present plight.

As the dear lady placed the tray beside my bed, telling me to relax and enjoy my breakfast, I just had to tell her what I had done. Her reaction overwhelmed me. "Och," she responded, "the wee bairns are doing that all the time. Dinna worry about it. After breakfast we will just put the tick out on the line." With that she took off, leaving me to shake my head at the way I was welcomed as if I were a long-absent son. Apparently, I was looked upon as a "wee bairn."

The next day they lent me their daughter's bicycle and I took off on a short tour of the lovely countryside. The family dog arrived and greeted me as warmly as my hosts had. He ran joyously alongside me everywhere I rode.

When I returned to the courtyard of the house, it was to meet four or five of the Dicks's neighbours, who had heard that there was a Canadian visiting. Everyone seemed to have a relative of some connection living in Canada. I was dismayed, however, to see that the mattress, with its soggy, round centre, was hanging in full view on the line. As the neighbours passed by on their way into the house, they cast curious glances at it, and I was sure that I heard more than one "tsk, tsk" as they went past. We all joined in a "wee dram," and putting my embarrassment aside I spent an enjoyable, heartwarming couple of hours with these fine, generous people.

The three days that they had insisted on keeping me came too swiftly to an end. I had used up my leave, but the stay had rested my mind and body like nothing else could have done. It was an emotional farewell. These dear old people had shared what little they had with me unsparingly, and had gathered me to them as a son. I left with the sad thought that it was not likely that I would ever see them again.

With only one train change at Edinburgh, I arrived back at Marham, and to the resumption of squadron life.

■ ■ ■

Two weeks later, there was a three-day squadron stand-down for some operational or maintenance reason. This gave us an opportunity to escape the base, even if we couldn't travel very far. I was happy to accept Ted Crosswell's invitation to accompany him home to London to meet his wife and family.

Ted's wife, Lily, was living with her parents, Mr. and Mrs. White, in the London suburb of Burnt Oak, one tube station before Edgware, the end of the northwest trunk of the Northern Line. The Whites were a retired couple. Mr. White was a Royal Navy submarine veteran of the First World War, who now took great pride in his duties as an air raid warden. Their small two-bedroom house was one of the narrow houses built in a row, called "council houses." In the backyard there was the common Anderson Shelter, built of sheets of corrugated steel above ground, which offered at least some protection from flying shrapnel and debris during the frequent air raids.

I was given a warm welcome. They insisted that I spend the night and made a bed for me in the downstairs front room. I spent two nights with the family, and we enjoyed the evenings at the local pub. Mrs. White's nerves were frayed from the bombings that had destroyed houses, and lives, within the block. She had trouble sleeping at night, and it was a great pleasure to see that, with a little gentle persuasion from me, a few "gins and orange" at the pub really relaxed her and gave her a well-needed sound sleep that night. Lily and her father seemed to credit me with lifting Mrs. White's spirits.

Lily's brother, Chris, was serving in the RAF as an aircraftman, and was then at a base in the remote, wind-swept Orkney Islands. Before I left, I also had the pleasure of meeting Ted's mother and father, who lived a few blocks away in Edgware. (Some fifteen months later, I was to become a frequent lodger at the White home, treated like one of the family.)*

---

* Mingling with the people, watching them "queuing up" in resigned good humour in long lines for whatever meagre foodstuffs might be available, I was struck by the general mood. Not only the air raids, but even the disaster that was Dunkirk seemed to exhilarate them.

It was on our next full week's leave that Willy Poirier and I began to travel together. This was when our London romantic adventure began.

We managed to find some cheap lodgings in the Sussex Court area. The first evening we took off for the popular Hammersmith Palais dance hall located, not surprisingly, at the Hammersmith station, the western mid-point of the Piccadilly underground line.

We were having a good time dancing and completely forgot that the last tube left Hammersmith for central London at 0200 hours. Finding the station entrance closed, we wandered through the nearby park, wondering where we might spend the night. We came across one of the brick air raid shelters that had been erected in most of the city's parks. With the light of a cigarette lighter, we saw wooden slat bunks on both walls of the structure. Not very comfortable, but having little choice, we each picked one and settled down for what remained of the night. It wasn't warm but in our tired state it didn't take long for us to fall asleep. Even the air-raid siren and the nearby thump of falling bombs didn't keep us awake.

When we opened our eyes to the morning light beaming into the shelter, both Willy and I looked up into the face of a nurse. Where were we, in the hospital? Had we been hit in the air raid?

Not so, we were informed, much to our relief. The nurses were walking through the park on their usual route to the London Northern Hospital when they heard snoring coming from the shelter. Curious, they looked in and found us lying there. They weren't sure what condition we were in and, being nurses, decided to investigate.

We told them our story and introduced ourselves. They were Bessie and Maureen, and they had come over from their homes in Northern Ireland to help out and work at the Northern Hospital. They were attractive, and Willy and I were bold enough to suggest that we meet them the next day, if they could get off work. We could not have looked as dishevelled as we felt because they agreed. They gave us their phone numbers at the hospital and at their residence, and we told them that we would call them the next day to arrange where to meet.

Thus began a relationship that would see the four of us keep company on every opportunity we had to visit London during the three

---

In *Glorious Summer*, Johnny Johnson and Laddie Lucas quote an observation by Air Vice Marshal David Scott-Malden-Carter, 603 Sqn (Paris 1965), on the conduct of the British people after the Battle of Britain: "For one moment in history, the nation felt like a family, un-British, often more comic in its embarrassed emotion — this was the true meaning of 'Their Finest Hour.' It is only in the aftermath of victory or defeat that greed, meanness, and self-interest flourish like weeds in a forgotten garden."

months I had left in England. Bessie and I were attracted to one another from the beginning, as were Willy and Maureen. Whatever days Willy and I could get leave or a pass from the squadron and our nurses could get time off from the hospital we spent on picnics in Hyde Park, sometimes swimming in the park lake, the Serpentine, in rented swim suits, or at dances at Covent Garden. For the picnics the girls would bring sandwiches and tea. We enjoyed each other's company and had good times together although, knowing what Willy and I were doing, Bessie and Maureen were concerned about our safety and survival.

Bessie was about five and a half feet tall, slim, with straight, almost black, hair, with bangs across her forehead. She was very much old country in her ways, but the Irishness of her laughing brown eyes and the warmth of her smile rescued her from primness. Bessie had a lyrical Irish accent, much more pronounced than Maureen's. I found her voice delightful. Bessie was several years older than I. Maureen, who was also pretty, was a few inches taller than Bessie. She had an abundance of undisciplined reddish blonde hair.

Our outings provided much-needed therapy for Willy, who was becoming disturbingly frayed. Several times I had awakened in the small hours of the morning to find him sitting on the edge of his bed across from me, smoking non-stop. The ash tray was full of butts; he had become a chain smoker, apparently unable to throw off the pressures of operational flying. We were of a different mental make-up. I had taught myself to push the images of our more stressful ops to the back of my mind.

Bessie and I became very fond of one another, but our relationship never progressed beyond the kissing and hugging stage. This was mostly because of Bessie's strict moral code; it was the way she had been brought up. I had little trouble respecting Bessie's wishes, partly I suppose because my feelings for her never became totally serious. We were soon to be parted, but I was later to find that Bessie's feelings for me were much deeper than I imagined. For Willy, however, his relationship with Maureen seemed to provide the escape valve he needed.

This was the sum and substance of my leaves during my first tour of duty in England, and I think there's little doubt that my wholesome relationship with Bessie was a blessing for both of us.

12
LONG NIGHT
TO BERLIN

Targets selected for our bombing raids varied in the degree of fear they generated among the aircrews. Heavily defended Essen, Duisburg, and Mannheim, deep in the industrial heart of "Happy Valley," were not names that crews welcomed on the ops board. But what they feared most was the briefing officer's announcement to a hushed briefing room, "Gentlemen, our target for tonight is Berlin!"

The first British aircraft to fly over Berlin were three Whitleys of No. 10 Sqn, 4 Group. On 1 October 1939, they dropped leaflets over the city on what were called "Nickel" raids. The first bombing raid on Berlin was ordered by the War Council as a reprisal for the 24 August 1940 bombing of central London. On the following night, about fifty Wellingtons and some Hampdens dropped the first bombs of the war on that city. They caused little or no damage. Six Hampdens, which had a more limited range than the Wimpys, were lost, three of them ditching in the sea, out of fuel.

From the beginning, Berlin's anti-aircraft, searchlight, and night fighter defences were steadily increased until it became the most fiercely defended target on Bomber Command's list. Heart and centre of the

Nazi regime, as well as a prominent centre of war industry, Berlin was a key target for Bomber Command.

From most Bomber Command bases, Berlin was approximately a 1,150-mile round trip. This placed it at the extreme range of available bombers. Given unexpected strong headwinds on the outward bound or return flight, some aircraft simply would not make it home. Also, the raids had to be made under cover of darkness. This restricted most of them to the longer nights of the winter months when the weather was at its worst.

Three days after our crew had been reunited, frayed edges mended from a week's leave, we were called by the Tannoy to the briefing room. *The target was Berlin!*

Some of the assembled crews had been there before, several more than once. Casualties had been severe, on occasion reaching an intolerable twelve percent of the force engaged. Now it was our turn.*

Our objective was a large chemical factory in the centre of the city. The plant sat on an island, which helped to form the river Spree into a "Y" at that juncture, a good distinguishing feature for the bomb aimer. The briefing officer stressed the importance of hitting this target, but added, "If for some reason you can't pinpoint the factory, then drop your bombs on the post office."

A voice from the back of the room asked, "Sir, which post office?" There was dead silence. We had gotten the point. If we couldn't find, or get through to, the primary target, we were to simply dump our load on the city. At this stage of our bombing tour, this didn't shock us at all.**

If we could not bomb the primary target, Berlin, then we were to bomb the railway marshalling yards of Magdeburg, approximately 100 miles west of Berlin, just twenty miles south of our intended course.

---

* In 1942, after he became AOC Bomber Command, Air Chief Marshal Arthur "Bomber" Harris sent his famous message to his squadron commanders to be read to crews about to bomb Berlin: "Tonight you go to the Big City — to Berlin. You have an opportunity to light a fire in the belly of the enemy and to burn his black heart out." (From *Wings of War*, edited by Laddie Lucas.)

** The indiscriminate dropping of bomb loads on cities had been strictly prohibited by the British War Council until late 1941. Although by this time the concept of "area bombing" had not been officially approved, the Luftwaffe's bombing of London and other cities had overcome the moral constraints against retaliation in kind. Thus began the creep towards a "total war" concept in Bomber Command's air offensive.

The morality of the Allied bombing policy between 1943 and 1945 has stirred controversy, and the subject compels attention. Most military historians are in complete agreement with Dr. Noble Frankland, who told the United Services Institution in December 1961: "The great immorality open to us in 1940 and 1941 was to lose the war against Hitler's Germany. To have abandoned the only means of direct attack which we had at our disposal would have been a long step in that direction."

We had just set up our maps in the hangar crew preparation room when the Tannoy announced that the raid had been cancelled. The next day we sat through a second briefing, updated mainly by a changed weather pattern. This time we got as far as our aircraft, standing in unexpected fog and light drizzle before the raid was again cancelled because of adverse winds on our planned track.

The effect of these cancellations was traumatic. Each man had psyched himself up for the raid in his own private way. To have the raid cancelled at the last minute, not once but twice in a row, imposed more stress on the aircrews than an actual operation. Then we were too busy; it was after the return that the stress was felt. Apart from a built-in sense of duty, it was largely the mutual dependency and support of the members of the crew "family" that strengthened each man to carry on.

On the fourth night, it was almost with a sense of relief that we finally got on our way to "The Big City."

At precisely 2035 hours Sgt B lifted our Wimpy off the Marham runway and turned us on course for Germany. Leaving the take-off position — sitting with his back against the main spar — Willy climbed the slight upward incline of our rising aircraft to get to his front turret. Passing me, he paused to give my hand a quick squeeze and offered a forced grin that I'm sure was meant to reassure both of us. By the time I had set the IFF and destruct switch and opened my log, Len was giving the captain our first heading. Ted was in the co-pilot's seat and George was getting as comfortable as he was ever going to get in his cold rear turret.

We climbed through cloud over the Channel, but by the time we were over Holland and at our planned altitude of 12,000 feet, the highest we had ever been, the sky was clearing somewhat. Without the protective cloud and the cloak of a really dark night, we felt naked and vulnerable, so none of us wished for a too-clear night sky.

With the extra fuel on board, our load of 250-pound bombs had been reduced to a total of 3,500 pounds. We would need all the fuel we could conserve to give us a decent margin for the flight home.

As I set up a few more frequencies on my transmitter, I began to think what I might do to help Len with his navigation. With the standard radio silence on the way to the target I couldn't use the transmitter, but I might find some station to take a loop bearing on. I hadn't been given any help with this at my briefing, so I thought, "Why not scan the receiver dial and see what I can find?" With a broadcast signal of any strength I could rotate the loop antenna housed in its streamlined pod over my head on the outside fuselage until I crossed two needles on a meter to give me a true bearing. I had to be careful to avoid reading a reciprocal 180° difference.

Sweeping the needle of the receiver through the six megacycle frequency range, I zeroed in on a strong signal. This German station was broadcasting the letters B-U-N-D in clear Morse code, followed by a long dash, which was perfect for a loop bearing. I took a series of bearings and handed them to Len. Luckily, he had fixed his position over the Zuider Zee through a cloud opening, so he was able to back-plot the loop bearing and locate the station's position on his map.

On my next sweep of the dial I found another station, just as strong and clear, sending the letters B-R-A-U-N and the long dash. These had to be homing aids for their night fighters. Len's backplotting gave us the location of this second station; this one was in the north, towards Denmark. The BUND station was back of us, on the Channel coast. One behind us, and one cutting our track — just right for continuing fixes for however long these stations would continue to broadcast. Len and I couldn't believe our luck. All he had to do was sit back and wait for the bearings I gave him every few minutes and confirm our position with another good fix. Len even got his ground speed from the repeated fixes.

We didn't dare hope that they would transmit for a long period, not on the same frequency at any rate. Incredibly, these two stations continued to transmit their same signal, on the same frequency. However, as we flew deeper into Germany their signal strength faded, and fell to a level too weak for bearings.

Len and I were engrossed with our work when we heard George's cry from the rear turret, "Captain, rear gunner here. I have three aircraft above us off our starboard quarter!"

Sgt B asked, "What are they doing? What are they?"

George chortled, "You won't believe this. They're old Henschel biplanes. Must be from a training station. They're looking us over now. Okay to warm up my guns?"

With a go-ahead from Sgt B, both rear turret and Willy's front turret guns opened up with a great chatter.

Ted and the captain had a quick discussion and decided that we would continue to fly straight and level until they showed signs of attacking. Len and I scrambled back to the astro dome and took turns looking for the Henschels. We were just able to make them out in the clearing night sky. In the face of the gun flashes from our turrets they obviously decided that discretion was the better part of valour. With an abrupt wing-over they plunged down out of sight.

We concluded that they were student pilots from a training school. When I joined Len for a moment to look at his map, we saw that this encounter had taken place just as we were passing about seventy-five miles to the south of Hanover.

Although the signals from the German stations had faded out, Len had a good plot and we were dead on track for Berlin.

About an hour and a half from our Henschel sighting Ted and Willy both spoke up to say that they could see searchlights and flak ahead. This was our target, and obviously many bombers ahead of us were already getting a violent reception.

Much sooner than we had anticipated, because we were barely over Potsdam, a few miles from the outer environs of Berlin, we were bumped harshly by exploding flak shells. Ahead of us was what seemed like a wall of searchlight beams. We could see other aircraft in the light of the beams.

By the time Len called Sgt B with a course to steer for our chemical factory objective, we were being pummelled by heavy bursts, and cordite fumes were finding their way through the skin of our Wimpy.

I was in the astro dome looking out for fighters when Sgt B called Len to say he was concerned about our fuel status. Len didn't see a serious problem; neither did Ted, who was so often at loggerheads with our captain. Nevertheless, Sgt B swung us over in a hard bank to starboard and announced that we might have enough fuel to get to our secondary target and home if we started now, since Magdeburg was right on our track for home anyway.

Taking no heed of Ted's and Len's protests he weaved and jinked us through angry clusters of exploding shells until we were in the clear. I returned to my table as Len was reluctantly giving our captain a new course for our secondary target, Magdeburg, which sat on the river Elbe. To a crew puzzled and not too happy about our abrupt departure from our main target, it appeared that our op-weary Sgt B had gotten the "wind up" again.

It seemed no time at all before we were on our final heading into the area of Magdeburg, where the railway yards lay. Again, we were into the flak as Len went forward to his bomb aimer's pad, and began calling out heading corrections to our captain.

For some strange reason, perhaps because he was feeling a little guilty about our abandonment of Berlin, Sgt B pressed on, taking us through a heavy pattern of bursting shells direct to our aiming point. Only when Len called out, "Bombs gone!" did he bank sharply away to escape. As on some of our other raids, I found it hard to believe that we could pass right through so many clusters of exploding shells, virtually a solid wall of searchlights and flak, without receiving crippling damage.

As we left Magdeburg behind, we saw several Wimpys over the target area, which had begun to burn fiercely. Unless this had been their primary target, we weren't the only ones to opt out of the "big one."

I confirmed to the captain that I had gotten the "bombed secondary target" coded message away, but there wasn't much chatter over the intercom as we droned on, setting course for home. In little more than an hour I was elated to pick up our BUND and BRAUN stations again, still transmitting on the same frequency. Our fixes from more loop bearings took us home across the Channel. Whatever else this op had been, Len and I would remember it as the easiest from a navigation standpoint.

Our debriefing was not pleasant. The debriefing officer gave Sgt B a hard time for not getting to the primary target, but Len did his best to give him as much support as his innate honesty would bear. Ted was glum-faced and non-committal. We did get redeeming partial marks for the successful placing of our load on Magdeburg. For all but our captain, I supposed, this op to the feared Berlin had been something of an anticlimax. We did not have a feeling of satisfaction about this one.

We learned later that a total of 197 aircraft had set out to bomb Berlin that night. Of that number, fifteen were lost: eight Wellingtons, two Hampdens, two Whitleys, two Stirlings, and one Manchester. There was damage to four war industry factories, and to transport and public utilities. Nearly a hundred aircrew had failed to return; some, we hoped, might have bailed out successfully, to survive as prisoners of war.

It was now almost 0630 hours. Neither Willy nor I found it easy to get to sleep, and we sat and talked for a while about the trip. When I finally dozed off, Willy was still sitting on the edge of his bed, smoking.

Later that night we gathered at the sergeants' mess bar for a little celebratory drink. We may not have been satisfied with our performance, but we had been over Berlin, had pasted Magdeburg, and had survived. Sgt B did not join us. We couldn't really blame him, if he was spending the day at home with his wife. We discussed what had been puzzling some of us: Why was he staying with our crew? Presumably, now that he had seen us through more than the number of ops needed to give us experience, he could have opted for a change. On the other hand, he would be better off with us than with a new, fresh crew.

I wasn't unhappy with the way he handled the Wimpy as a pilot, but I had begun to hope that very soon now, Ted would take over as captain. Len and I had a lot of confidence in him, more in fact than we had in Sgt B.

13
FEAR, COURAGE, AND LMF

Nowhere in the theatres of war did fear offer more of a challenge to the human spirit than on the squadrons of Bomber Command, and at this stage of our bombing tour, all the members of our crew were conscious of it.

Fear and stress — and courage — were not exclusive to Bomber Command, but the psychological stresses to which the aircrew were subjected would fairly be called unique. Each enemy target was different; crews took off, sometimes two and three times a week, into the unknown. We knew that the target would be heavily defended, and that the aircraft would be in danger, both from fighters pouncing unseen out of the dark sky, and from other flak belts near the route. We knew also that there would be fewer aircraft returning than the number that left base, and another group of familiar faces would be missing from the breakfast table. What stretched our already taut nerves close to breaking point was sitting through the briefing for an op only to have it cancelled, sometimes just before take-off, but still knowing that there would be more briefings, and more ops.

Mathematically, the odds of survival were probably the same on the final thirtieth op of a tour as they were on the first, but psychologically, with the cumulative effect of repeated raids, in the minds of the aircrews there seemed to be a law of diminishing returns governing survival.

We all knew, right from our second op, that our captain, Sgt B, had the "wind up." Witness the occasions when he chose not to go in to a primary target. But even to do that took a kind of courage. Moreover, by the time he joined us he had already completed twenty ops, a total we had still to reach.

Fear affected all of us in different ways. The only effect it seemed to have on Ted was that sometimes (but not often) he could become snappish and irritable. I was in a better position to observe Len's reactions. Once he had gotten over his complete preoccupation with the challenges of his navigation job on our first few sorties, he exhibited a slight ner-vousness. At other times he would cover up with a little humour or jocularity. I knew that he worried about his family and what would happen to them if he were lost. His was a completely unselfish fear.

George Fuller, on the surface, seemed irrepressible, and unmoved by the perils of the night. But here again, afterwards, when he was distracted from the group's conversation and his mind had obviously gone somewhere else, it was apparent that, like Len's, his mind was on his family.

Fear hit Willy the hardest. He had the front seat, ahead of the rest of us, thousands of feet above the dark earth, knowing that he would always be the first to see — and enter into — the searchlights and the flak.

We shared a room in the sergeants' mess. He slept fitfully, and chain smoked, sometimes into the small hours of the morning, when his restlessness would wake me up, and we would talk. On some raids, while we waited for the bombing up to be completed, he would step quickly to the far side of the aircraft where he might not be seen and throw up. Yet not once did he show any sign of unwillingness to fly.

My own reactions to the common fear were somewhat ambiguous. Like most of our comrades I coated myself in a veneer of denial, not wishing the others to see my fear. On one flight I remember standing in the astro dome, straining on tip toes to get a better look at the flak clusters, when my knees began to knock and tremble. I cast a quick, furtive glance up and down the fuselage, hoping no one had noticed. I was ashamed, and told myself that it was simply a muscular reaction to overstretching. I did not allow it to happen again.

What sustained me most of all, as I believe it did to most who served in action, was a sense of duty. Whatever the circumstances, I had joined of my own free will and had made a commitment to accept whatever fate had in store for me. I found what every one of us who carried on had to find for himself: a way to manage his fear.

Many aircrew were superstitious. They carried teddy bears with them, muttered incantations to themselves before take-off, and even wore their pajamas under their flying suits. In one way or another, the vast majority found a way to endure the strain.

But what really held us together was the bonding of our crew into a family, whose members would endure anything rather than let the others down. Leadership might come nominally from our captain, but really it came from our own self-discipline, from within.

For those few who could not find a way to manage their fear, the prospect was a certification of LMF, or Lack of Moral Fibre. This belittling label was a euphemism for cowardice in the face of the enemy, for which many soldiers in the First World War and some in the Second World War were shot by firing squad. In the Second World War Bomber Command, to be certified LMF meant demotion and disgrace, and removal from flying duties.

These men were more pitied than scorned. They had volunteered and done the best they could. We came to understand what was known as the Moran principle, that courage is not an absolute human characteristic, but expendable capital every man possesses in varying quantity. As Lord Moran put it, "They had used up their reserves of courage."* For some it was the cumulative effects of mental and physical fatigue. General George Patton knew what he was talking about when he observed, "Fatigue makes cowards of us all."

In 1941 and 1942, we heard little of LMF. We knew that some aircrew had refused to fly after so many ops and had been classified LMF, but it wasn't anything that we thought about or discussed. The odium attached to being labelled LMF may have compelled some men to carry on when they might otherwise have packed it in, but it had nothing to do with our resolve or that of anyone we knew.

With the increase in magnitude of the bomber offensive in 1943 and 1944, and the frightening increase in the toll of men and aircraft, the spectre of LMF became a more troubling issue, both within the newly

---

* From *The Anatomy of Courage*, by Lord Moran (Sir Charles Wilson).

formed Canadian 6 Group and the RAF squadrons. The cases were not well handled. In the early stages of the courts martial, there was little understanding or compassion, particularly within the RAF. We heard of entire squadrons being paraded to watch, as a warning lesson, the rank insignia and buttons torn from the tunic of a charged and convicted LMF victim.

When the American Eighth Air Force became operational in early 1943, and began to have the same problems, they developed a more humane way to deal with these casualties of war.

But despite what has been written about LMF, there was little of it. In the worst part of Bomber Command's hideously costly offensive of 1943–44, less than one half of one percent of all engaged aircrew were affected by it. Throughout the whole of the RAF, the total for all aircrew was less than 0.3 percent.

Some aircrew, whose nerve ends may have become cauterized by the repetitive exposure to danger, flew on in an almost robotic state. They could appear to be courageous. The majority called upon a great self-discipline and sense of duty; doubtless they were courageous. But the most courageous of all had to be those poor souls who were racked with fear to the point of becoming quite ill, and still forced themselves to carry on, and to go ever "once more unto the breach." Many were cursed with a vivid imagination that tortured them into constructing scenarios in their mind of the various ways in which they might meet their end.

Our front gunner, my friend Willy Poirier, epitomized this latter type. I watched his torment, relieved somewhat on our leaves together, and tried to help, but he had to bear his cross largely by himself. I remember him today as the bravest man I ever met.

14

THE END OF THE BEGINNING —
A NEW CAPTAIN AND CREW

ONE DAY WHEN WILLY AND I WERE in the billiard room in the sergeants' mess, I was just about to stroke the white ball when the Tannoy on the wall came to life. At the crackle of static, followed by the now all-too-familiar, "Ops are on for tonight. All crews to report to the briefing room at 1400 hours," I miscued and nearly tore up the felt covering of the table.

Only the day before, Willy and I had returned from a few days leave in London spent with Bessie and Maureen. It had been an enjoyable, relaxing respite. Our good nurses had made a fine picnic lunch from scarce ingredients found goodness knows where. We ate on the banks of the Serpentine, that small lake in the middle of Hyde Park frequented by Londoners for boating or swimming. The four of us had taken our swimsuits with us and had joined the others in the cool waters.

Bessie was concerned about my considerable weight loss, which was partly due to the recurrent bouts of bronchitis that had plagued me since the first week of my arrival at Marham. I frequently spent one or two days in sick bay, but fortunately always got out in time to join the crew for our ops. But it was dragging me down. In any event, we arrived back on the squadron rested, and as relaxed as was possible.

Len, George, and Ted had been home on leave for the same period, and joined us in the crowded briefing room. Sgt B came in just as we found our seats.

The forced cheeriness of the crews' chatter was silenced by the arrival on stage of the station commander, Group Captain A.C. Evans-Evans. "Well, gentlemen, your target for tonight is Karlsruhe. I don't have to tell most of you who have been there before that this target in southern Germany is one of the industrial centres vital to the Germans' war-making capacity, and that it is heavily defended. Give it a good pasting, and good luck to you."

Sgt B had been there before, but it was a new target for the rest of us. When the curtain was pulled aside to reveal the red tapes marking our prescribed route from base to the target, we could see that it was going to be a six-hour flight. After hearing the bomb load information from the station armament officer, the meteorological officer gave us the weather we might expect en route to and over the target. His forecast for decent weather and visibility on the final legs of our return to our Norfolk base was greeted with the usual skepticism. In these late winter months, finding home base and making a decent landing was the final challenge in a night of trial and tribulation.

The intelligence officer showed us slides of the target; the slides offered quite a clear outline of our aiming point, a complex of factory buildings situated less than a mile from city centre. These factories had a high output of shells and other munitions. Whether we could place our bombs anywhere close to this complex was another question; we were sent off with our individual times for take-off, ours being 1850 hours, a little earlier than we were accustomed to, but dark enough at that time of year to give us whatever real or imagined small margin of safety a black night offered.

As soon as I had picked up my codes for the night and finished with my separate wireless briefing, I joined the two pilots and Len in our squadron hangar plotting room, where I found them leaning over the maps covering our route to the target.

Len's plotted route to a turning point and then direct to Karlsruhe looked straightforward enough, but we now had something going for us that we had acquired on our last op, the new navigational aid GEE. Len had just enough experience with this new device that he had gained some confidence in it.*

The principle of GEE was simple enough. A radio pulse signal was transmitted by three stations in England placed 100 miles apart on a base line 200 miles long. The master station A controlled the pulses from the slave stations B and C. The navigator on board the bomber watched the cathode ray tube on his oscilloscope or GEE box, noting how long the pulses from stations B and C took to arrive. He then transposed the point of intersection of the time lines from the GEE box display to a special grid on his map. Soon, he had his position plotted with reasonable accuracy.

This system had drawbacks. Its range was limited to 300–400 miles, which meant it could cover the Ruhr but little past that. It could also be jammed, which forced changes in frequencies during the raid. It was certainly not accurate enough to be used as an automatic bomb release point at beam intersections over a target. It was, however, a great boon to night navigation, particularly assisting crews to reach England and home bases. On some raids more aircraft had been lost by crashing in England on the perilous return flight than over the target when tired crews lost their way in poor visibility and turbulent weather, and ran out of petrol or became disoriented. As soon as most of the bomber force was equipped with GEE, whose accuracy increased as the aircraft neared England, this wastage was dramatically reduced.

We lifted off the grass of Marham runway at 1857 hours into the blackest night I could remember. In no time at all we had crossed the Channel. We were fast reaching our prescribed altitude of 12,000 feet near the Belgian coast when we were rocked violently by multiple explosions under our belly. Ted yelled that our starboard engine was on fire. Sgt B cursed, and corkscrewed our Wimpy in an automatic reaction to get away from whatever had attacked us. There were no further explosions. What had happened remained a mystery. We believed that we had been fired on by a night fighter that had then lost us or run out of ammunition, or that we had been the victim of one of the flak ships or flak towers that were placed at numerous places on known bombing routes.

Whatever the cause of our misfortune, we had the fire to contend with. Sgt B quickly put the aircraft into a steep dive to try to blow the

---

* Three Wellingtons of our sister squadron at Marham, No. 115, had been fitted with the system for the first operational trials in July 1941.

fire out. It worked. The engine seemed to be running normally. We felt very lucky indeed.

Both Sgt B and Ted suspected that the blast to our belly had jammed our bomb doors. This was soon confirmed; the doors wouldn't budge. Nothing for us to do but to return to base. We couldn't even jettison our lethal bomb load into the Channel or the North Sea. The bombs were not armed, of course, but they still presented a great hazard if we made a bad landing.

Len gave the captain a course for Marham and we were on our way — no target bombing for us tonight. We had mixed feelings about this. There was some guilty feeling of relief at avoiding the perils over Karlsruhe, but I wasn't the only one who felt that we were somehow copping out. With a series of quick bearings I got for Len, we were soon on final approach at Marham. Sgt B made one of his few bad landings, almost ground looping the Wimpy; we ended up off the flare path near a ditch. He had warned the tower that we had our bombs aboard in a jammed bomb bay so we were met by emergency fire vehicles and armourers by the dozen. We were all glad to get clear of the aircraft. We had been airborne little more than two hours.

Debriefing was not pleasant. While our dilemma was obvious, the intelligence officers were almost accusatory in asking why we failed to go on to the target. The whole affair was a disagreeable anti-climax, not least because it also proved to be my last operational sortie from England.

■ ■ ■

Soon after our aborted mission, we flew a simple cross-country fuel consumption test that turned into a bizarre experience. At one of our briefings, a flight commander had told us that the Americans had formed one of their own fighter squadrons, called the "Eagle Squadron," that had gotten into the habit of making mock fighter attacks on our Wimpys. All very well and good, except that they had become bolder with experience and were coming far too close to our aircraft. The risk of disastrous collisions was becoming too much of a possibility. It was suggested that our gunners might fire off a warning burst near but not at our American friends to discourage them from coming too close.

About an hour into our flight, I heard George's cockney accent over the intercom: "Captain, rear gunner. I've got one of those bleeding Yank fighters buzzing about our tail. It looks like an Aircobra.* Too bloody close. Can I give him a warning burst?"

Sgt B came back with, "Okay, a short burst, but be careful."

The chatter of George's Brownings had no sooner faded than Ted yelled out, "Bloody hell, I think George has shot the bastard down. He's bailing out."

Ted got on to the frequency of the nearest airfield and reported the bailout so that a search could begin and some aid could get on its way to the pilot. In reply to Sgt B's blast at him, the only excuse George could offer was that the fighter had turned abruptly into the bullet stream just as he opened fire. He must have hit some control surfaces to force it into a spin.

When we arrived back at Marham we were informed that the American pilot had survived, but that he had a broken leg. We were also told that we were all to report immediately to the office of the station commander.

In his office, seated behind a huge mahogany desk, Group Captain Evans-Evans studied the six airmen standing rigidly in front of him in silence for a moment that seemed like ages to me. He was obviously not pleased. He suddenly erupted, "What in hell did you think you were doing? You've probably set back our relations with the Americans by a year!"

He went on at some length while we fidgeted in discomfort. For some reason he took off on another tack to tell us how scruffy we looked, and that we had better tidy up our uniforms. Finally, to our great relief, he dismissed us. Apparently, there was to be no disciplinary action.

Just as we were escaping through the door, we were surprised to hear, "One other thing. Our Yankee friends might not be such a bloody nuisance to us after this." It was this good man's way of telling us, blooded members of his team that we were, that the strip he had torn off us was really only his duty by the book. We heard no more of the incident.

At the end of a week of unusual inactivity, we were called to the crew room in the hangar. One of the flight commanders, a flight lieutenant, was there to greet us. Sgt B was not there, but another sergeant pilot was standing beside the officer. The flight lieutenant explained, "As

---

* George was sure this was an Aircobra. This was a Bell Aircraft design known in the U.S. Air Force as a P39. It was used unsuccessfully in the Pacific in 1943, but a few of them apparently found their way to England earlier. The first aircraft flown by the Eagle Squadron were mostly Spitfires.

you probably know, Sgt B has reached the end of his tour, and I'd like to introduce your new captain to you. This is Bill Dixon, who has been on the squadron for many months and is ready to take on his own crew. Well, I'll leave you to get acquainted." With that he turned and left the room.

As we overcame our surprise, Bill shook hands with each one of us, and said that he had been told that we were a good, experienced crew. He was a good-looking Canadian chap with black hair, nearly six feet tall, slim, but strong. I was somehow pleased that he was a Canadian. I immediately felt confident in his abilities. Bill had an avuncular way about him that encouraged our acceptance of him as our leader. As we discovered, he was about three or four years older than we were, and had been out in the world, from his home in Ottawa, making a living before the war. This small difference in age and experience was more significant than one might think.

I had heard about Bill before meeting him. A week or so before our meeting, I had overheard a discussion in the crew room about a Sgt Dixon whose quick reaction and skilled flying had averted a near disaster on the runway. The story went that as he gained flying speed halfway down the runway, a petrol bowser or some other vehicle appeared on the runway in his path. Apparently, in the split-second he had to react, Bill thrust down some wing flap, giving the Wimpy enough lift to leapfrog over the vehicle. The squadron CO had apparently taken note of the incident.

After some discussion with us about our operational experiences, Bill said to us, "I'd like all of you to meet me here at 08:30 tomorrow morning. I want to go over some of the bits and pieces of the Wimpy to make sure we are all on the same wavelength."

Bill and I sat down in the mess and had a good talk about Canada, and our homes and family. It had been a while since I had talked to another Canadian, other than Willy; our talk reinforced the strong feeling I had about this man. I soon found out that the rest of the crew also had a good impression of our new leader.

We did not see Sgt B again. He left as quietly as he had arrived. We were used to his not socializing with us, but I still thought it strange that he never said goodbye to us. After all, I thought we had been a good, reliable crew to him; certainly, with considerable piloting skill, if not leadership, he had seen us through some very harrowing operations. I have always wondered what happened to him. He deserved a rest.

When we gathered in the morning at a Wimpy parked at one of the dispersal bays, Bill took us around the outside of the aircraft, and then from nose to tail on the inside. He went over a thorough checklist of the flying instruments and other equipment, most of which we were familiar with, especially Ted Crosswell, but he surprised us with the odd detail that had escaped our attention. He managed to do all this without being patronizing or condescending, appreciating that we were not an inexperienced crew. Even Ted seemed to accept all this with good grace. Sgt B had never done any of this with us, and as a green crew when he inherited us, we would have benefited from this exercise.

Bill's identification and explanation of all the valves, levers, and lines of the Wimpy's fuel system was an eye-opener. He emphasized the location and sequence of use of the main and auxiliary fuel cells, and of the hand-operated pumps that fed oil periodically to each of our two Pegasus radial engines. Later on, after Bill gained confidence in me, he gave me the job of pumping the oil, and switching the petrol cocks from main to reserve fuel cells.

Two weeks later, after we had completed a cross-country fuel-consumption test, I was sitting in the mess reading when Bill sat beside me. He had some surprising news. "I've just come from the CO's office. They're looking for volunteers to go to the Middle East. I told them that I was willing to go. I think it would be a good thing for you, too, Howard. You should get to a warmer climate. What do you say?"

I had not heard of this opportunity before, so it was a surprise to me. Right away, I thought how odd it was that this should crop up. A few days earlier, while getting a check-up for my bronchitis, the medical officer had said to me, "I think that if you stay in this damp climate much longer, you have a good chance of developing chronic bronchitis for the rest of your life."

It didn't take me long to digest this and to give Bill my answer. I wanted to stick with Bill, so I was prepared to go wherever he did. I told him so, and added, "I just wonder how the rest of the crew will take it. I'm sure Len won't want to leave his family, and the others may not wish to either. But Willy has no great ties here, so he might well come with us."

Bill nodded. "Well, we'll just have to ask them, and if not, we'll have to get another crew."

That evening, Bill gathered all of our crew in a corner of the mess and put the question to them. It caused visible consternation. They were not happy with the prospect of losing this captain, but their reaction was what I had suspected it would be; after all, except for Willy, they were British, and their families were nearby. They had to tell Bill that they preferred to stay in England. Willy surprised me. After a great deal of thought, he opted to stay with Len and the others. I wondered whether this had to do with his relationship with Maureen. In any event, the die was cast. I knew right away how hard it was going to be to part company with these friends with whom I had trained and flown on the first operations of our bombing tour. Most of all I was going to miss Len.

A week later, Bill rounded up our new crew, all of whom had volunteered for the Middle East. I had not met any of them, yet they had been flying in 218 Sqn for a short time. All were English, unmarried, and except for our pilot officer navigator, who had trained in Canada, all sergeants. Our brand new crew shaped up as captain Bill Dixon, from Ottawa; second pilot Bill White, the tall, quiet son of an undertaker from Walthamstow, London (to avoid confusion with Bill Dixon, I shall refer to Bill White as "Will"); navigator P/O Trevor "Robbie" Robinson, a twenty-three-year-old from south England; wireless op Howard Hewer, now twenty years old; front gunner Tony Carroll, a meticulous, stocky man from the English midlands; rear gunner Doug Chinnery, a good-natured twenty-year-old from a farm in Surrey.

Altogether, I am sure that Bill felt as I did — that this was a good crew that would pull together.

Before we had a chance for a flight together, but after we had gotten to know one another over a few beers, Bill suggested that we should get together on leave in London. I knew that Len and the rest of my former crew were also due for leave, and that this meant that I might not see them again.

I managed to meet with Len and the others in the mess to say goodbye. It was an emotional parting; I had difficulty saying goodbye to Willy and Len especially. I had a moment aside with Willy, and urged him to give it up if the ops continued to eat away at his health, knowing full well that he would not.

Leaving Len Mayer was more than emotional, it was gut-wrenching. We looked at one another in silence for a moment, then in a mutual impulse reached out to each other. I was smothered in the arms of this bear of a man to whom I had grown so close. We muttered to each other, "Now you take care of yourself." Len turned abruptly and walked away. I knew that I would never see him again.

I don't recall who joined Bill and me in London at the Covent Garden dance hall, but we had been there only about an hour when I came to grief. It began with a sore throat, and progressed rapidly to a burning fever. I had to tell Bill that I felt terribly ill. He needed only a quick glance to tell that I was in sad shape. He swiftly got me out to a taxi and back to our hotel room, where he phoned Canadian headquarters for the duty medical officer. I was fast losing interest in what was going on when an RCAF flight lieutenant medical officer arrived. He immediately took my temperature, which proved to be astronomically high. He asked me which hospital I would prefer, the Royal Masonic in London or a Canadian Army hospital that had been established at Taplow, Lady Astor's country estate about fifteen miles west of London.* I had time to opt for the Canadian hospital before lapsing into unconsciousness.

When I awoke, I found myself lying on a bed, stark naked, with two army nurses sponging me down with cold water. I had come to enough to notice that one nurse was red-haired and the other one blonde, and both were very attractive. My expression must have given my discomfiture away because they had a good laugh at my expense. They were trying to get my soaring temperature down.

By the time they had me dried off and into hospital pajamas I had begun to feel a little better. I was put on drugs of some sort, and the medical officers told me that I had somehow picked up a form of typhoid fever, and that I was also anaemic and dehydrated.

After two weeks, when I was allowed out of bed, I enjoyed the Canadian salmon sandwiches sold in the canteen in the company of fellow Canadian soldier patients. My bed faced that of a Canadian Army despatch rider who had crashed his motorcycle on the icy winter roads and smashed both of his arms and legs. He had iron rods protruding from both knees and both elbows. Somehow, in that desperate condition, he remained quite cheerful.

I began to be concerned that Bill and the crew might leave England without me. In my third week of recovery, when I managed to reach Bill at Marham by phone, he told me that they had to leave right away for Harwell, the jumping-off airfield for the Middle East.

---

* Lord Astor had leased part of his Cliveden estate at Taplow to the Canadian Red Cross in 1940, for a nominal sum. The Red Cross constructed the hospital (as it had done on the same site in WWI) and handed it over to the Royal Canadian Army Medical Corps, 5 CGH, on 16 July 1940. As units moved to northwest Europe in 1944, Taplow changed to 7 CGH, and finally to 11 CGH.

Four days later, when I called him at Harwell, Bill reluctantly told me that they couldn't wait for me any longer and that he had to take on an Australian wireless operator in my place. I couldn't let that happen, and immediately began insisting that I be discharged to take my place with my crew. I met with great resistance from the medical officer and the head nurse, who was a bit of a battleaxe. They didn't think I was at all in good enough shape to leave. Eventually, they got so fed up with my repeated demands to leave that they gave me my discharge and a railway warrant to Harwell.

When I called Bill again at Harwell to tell him I was on my way, he told me that I was lucky — they would have been on their way without me but that the Aussie wireless op had fallen from his bicycle after too many ales and had broken his leg. Great news for me, if not for the poor Aussie. Bill said to get a move on, and that he would tell ops at Harwell that he had a replacement for the Aussie.

When I wrestled my duffle bag and half-trunk onto the dark and almost deserted platform of the familiar railway station of Didcot, it was well after 1900 hours. It took me over half an hour to get transport to the airfield. I just had time to find Bill and learn that our take-off for Gibraltar was 0430 hours the next morning. If I hadn't arrived, the flight would have had to be cancelled.

The orderly sergeant found me a bed in a room at the end of a barrack block. There were no sheets, and the blankets looked scruffy. I couldn't find my pajamas, so I fell naked into the rough blankets, which ordinarily would have driven me crazy, but I was too tired and weak to care, and dozed off immediately.

Awakened at 0200 hours, and after a quick, soggy breakfast, I joined the other crew members in the operations room for our pre-flight briefing.

Our direct route was to take us to a point just clear of Brest, then southwest to Spain's Cape Finisterre, south to Cape St. Vincent, then eastwards to Gibraltar. Flight time would be nine hours and thirty minutes, at 10,000 feet. We were warned to be alert for German fighters patrolling the Bay of Biscay for RAF anti-submarine aircraft. It was foggy, and borderline for take-off, but the fog was forecast to clear en route. Our aircraft was a Mark IC Wimpy, "D" for dog, Serial No. Z9019.

15

OFF TO A DIFFERENT WAR — GIBRALTAR, MALTA, AND EGYPT

FOG COVERED HARWELL AIRFIELD like a dirty yellow blanket as we pulled our duffle bags and suitcases from the truck that had carried us from the crew room to our Wimpy, which was waiting for us at one of the dispersal bays. As I waited my turn to shove my gear up through the front hatch of the aircraft, I caught a taste of sulphur in my mouth, which could have come only from the thick fog. It was cold and damp at 0345 hours on the morning of 1 December 1941.

My new crew members clambered awkwardly to their places for take-off as Bill taxied out to the end of the live runway. Since our route would be entirely over water, we had to wear our Mae West lifejackets under our parachute harnesses — not the most comfortable of garments.

The engines revved up to a high pitch, and the roar shook the window beside me. Bill released the brakes and my back was pressed into the seat as we surged forward down the runway. Our captain could not see the far end of the strip; he had to guide the plane by the flare pots lining either side of the airstrip. As I felt the wheels unstick from the asphalt, I entered in my logbook, "Take-off, 0430 hours." The sadness of leaving friends and memories behind was mixed with the excitement of the prospects ahead.

An hour after our departure we were barely out of the fog and passing northwest of Brest at 10,000 feet when we were suddenly rocked by flak. Bill cursed, and flung the Wimpy sharply to starboard to get clear of the bursts. "We must be too damn close to the coast, Robbie. Everybody, check to see if we suffered any damage." Will did a tour of the aircraft and couldn't see any evidence that we had been hit. "Okay, chaps, I guess we were lucky," Bill assured us.

We had just passed Spain's Cape Finisterre off our port side when we saw the sun. It was coming up from behind the Cantabrian mountain range, the western end of the Pyrenees. The black of the mountain shadows was changing rapidly to purple. The dark sky lightened to a bright royal blue, and the sun itself was a widening orb of brilliant orange. We were enthralled by the sight. We had left behind the wet, grey days and black nights of an English winter and entered an artist's palette world of blues, oranges, and yellows.

As I picked away at the box-lunch rations we had been given for the flight, I looked back at navigator Robbie's round, boyish face, and his thin, blond moustache. He was having an easy time of it with all the visible landmarks he had to fix our position. He and Bill Dixon had hit it off right away, and established a mutual confidence that was to become a constant source of reassurance for the rest of us.

By noon we had passed Cape St. Vincent and were heading direct for the Strait of Gibraltar bathed in the warm Mediterranean daylight. Robbie came up on the intercom, "Howard, could you get me a bearing of some kind from Gibraltar?" (I had been authorized to break our radio silence at about this point in our flight.) As soon as I had identified myself, I got the bearing we wanted — a great help to Robbie because we had to fly a precise course to avoid coming too close to pseudo-neutral Spain or to the coasts of North Africa.

I got periodic bearings for Robbie until we came upon the great Rock of Gibraltar, since 1704 a crucial bastion guarding Britain's lifeline to the Middle and Far East. It was a thrill for all of us to look down on this historic mountain thrusting itself up 1,400 feet from its peninsula, separated only by a thin isthmus from the Spanish mainland and the impoverished town of La Linea to the north. The entire peninsula is only three miles long, and barely one mile across at its widest point. The east side of The Rock rises almost vertically from the sea, and is coated largely in concrete to provide a catchment for precious water. On a narrow plateau on the top of the mountain we could see clusters of radio antennae, and

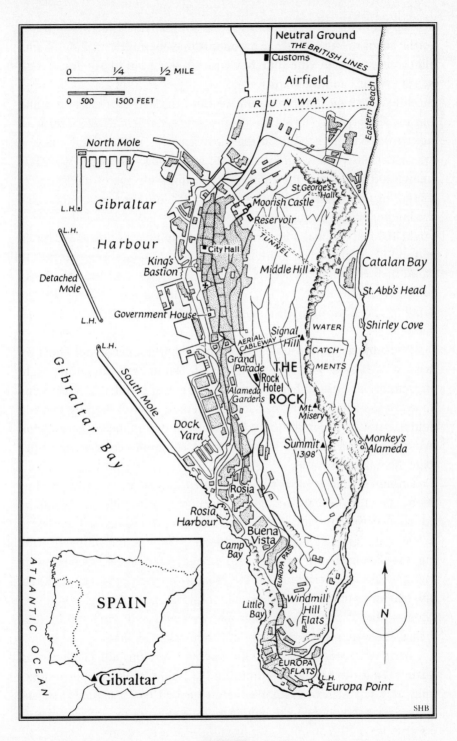

GIBRALTAR

several anti-aircraft batteries. The west side falls at a forty-five-degree angle down to the town and harbour. Concrete moles jutting out into the blue waters of Gibraltar Bay protected a large basin filled with supply vessels and warships.

Bill was given landing clearance from the RAF airfield tower and began his descent. The one and only landing strip ran east and west across the narrow isthmus at the north end of The Rock; Bill knew it was notoriously short, less than 2,000 yards long. The water was clear enough off the end of the runway to see the skeletons of the scores of aircraft that had overshot the field and crashed into the sea. The approach for landing had to be just right.

At 400 feet on final approach with our landing gear down, Will cried out to Bill, "Our starboard tire is shredded!"

At that, Bill pulled us up and announced, "I guess we weren't so lucky with that flak at Brest. We'll have to go around again." He aborted the landing and flew on a left-hand circuit of The Rock out over the west harbour.

We had just overflown a battleship at anchor in the harbour when we were shaken by at least a dozen bursts of medium anti-aircraft fire right in front of our nose. What in hell was one of our own battleships trying to do to us? I had the IFF on, and we were so near to landing that Bill told me not to shoot off the colours of the day from the Very pistol, which I had just begun to scramble to do. We were sure that we hadn't been hit again.

On our second approach, Bill swooped in at a steep angle, as slow as he dared, to take advantage of every foot of the runway. When we touched down, he had to work hard to keep the damaged starboard wheel from forcing us into a ground-loop. As it was, the starboard wing tip was damaged, and the starboard propeller and wheel assembly were ruined. The small rim holding the remains of the ripped tire had held up, keeping us from a bad loop and more damage.

As Bill shut down the engines and we clambered down through the hatch, we were met by firetrucks and emergency vehicles.

When we reported to the flight operations room, Bill made a complaint about the hostile fire from the battleship, which the ops officer told us was HMS *Malaya*.* We were allocated barrack room quarters, except for Robbie, of course, who would be going to the officers' mess.

---

* Royal Navy gunners were notoriously twitchy about overflying aircraft and often fired on our own until sure they weren't hostile.

Replacements for the damaged parts of the aircraft would have to be flown in from the U.K., so we were grounded in Gibraltar for five days.

After a late lunch in the mess, we headed for the barracks. We had been up since 0200 hours, had been flying for nine-and-a-half hours, and we needed a rest. I had been tired enough when we took off from England; now I was completely exhausted.

The next morning, Doug, Will White, and I decided to take off for a little sightseeing of The Rock. As we passed out of the station gate, we looked northwards beyond the customs gate to the town of La Linea, and saw the Spanish fortifications facing the airfield from the north end of the isthmus. Beyond rows of barbed wire there were five or six very large concrete gun emplacements and bunkers stretching between the east and west shores. Spain was no friend of Britain, still coveting ownership of The Rock as it had ever since the British took possession in 1704. It was common knowledge that a tall tower on a Spanish hill overlooking Gibraltar Bay harboured German observers who recorded all the arrivals and departures of Allied ships and the activity of the airfield.

But Gibraltar was well protected. On the mountain slopes, we could make out the tips of the barrels of the large-calibre naval-type guns that were sited tactically in their cavelike housings around the whole perimeter of The Rock. The resident garrison was in command of the strait and the waters surrounding this strategic bastion.

A short bus ride took us to the town centre, and we began to investigate the main street, which was lined with Indian shops and the flesh-pot drinking emporiums common to any port city. The garrison troops and the navy did not always see eye to eye, and we had to dodge the odd fracas as we made our way in and out of these establishments. At one point, Doug and I looked in amazement at Will White. After being starved for fresh fruit in England, he was cradling bunches of bananas and oranges in his arms, and was eating one or the other whenever we looked his way.

The next day Doug and I made our way up the hill to see the fabled apes of Gibraltar. No one knows where these creatures came from, but they have been on The Rock since the 17th century. From 1913 they have been cared for by the resident garrison of the Royal Regiment of Artillery, traditional guardians of the Upper Rock. They were allocated regimental numbers and taken on army ration strength at birth, and struck off strength upon their death, all of which was promulgated in Daily Routine Orders. There is an old legend that if the apes were to leave The Rock, the British would follow. This impressed the dramatic bent of Winston Churchill's mind. When he heard in 1943 that there were only seven apes left, he had seven more imported from Africa.

There were two ape packs on Gibraltar. They were not friendly to each other, so they were separated into two camps, one pack at Middle Hill and the other at Queen's Gate, which was more accessible to visitors.

Doug and I arrived at Queen's Gate in time to watch the 1600 hour feeding, supervised by a sergeant of artillery. This man seemed to have a slight hunch to his shoulders, and arms a little too long for his body. His walk I would have to describe as a "lope." Perhaps my imagination was working overtime, but his simian appearance prompted me to whisper in an aside to Doug, "I think he's been too long in the job!"

One morning I slipped away to make a visit to the Royal Canadian Corps of Engineers, whom I heard were engaged in tunnelling into The Rock. I found them halfway up the slope of the mountain, and enjoyed a lunch of great Canadian-tasting stew and biscuits with the soldiers. They had been posted from England to dig into the easily drilled limestone and to create a cavern for the building of an underground emergency hospital that would be secure from bombing. (Already some enterprising locals had fashioned a night club in The Rock's interior. It was imaginatively called "Le Roc.") The Mediterranean headquarters of the Admiralty and of RAF Coastal Command were to be found at the end of a long tunnel bored for a good quarter-mile towards the centre of the limestone mass. By the end of the war, almost twenty-five miles of tunnel had been drilled through The Rock. Excavations provided storehouses, magazines, power stations, and barracks. Along with its natural caves, it must have been the most honeycombed piece of real estate on earth.

There was little love lost between the Canadian and the British engineers. When the Canadians arrived, they found the British using slow, old-fashioned methods to clear away the slag rock removed by the tunnelling. This was seriously delaying the operation. The Canadians introduced and set up an hydraulic high-pressure system that greatly sped up the clearing work. This did not sit well with their British counterparts.

Our holiday was soon over, but I needed the rest, badly; the damage to our aircraft had been a blessing in disguise. On 5 December we were told to report for briefing in the operations room at 2000 hours. We would be leaving that night for Malta.

There was only one other crew in the ops room when we arrived, and they were also headed for Malta. The flight lieutenant briefing officer outlined our route, which would take us on a straight course towards Sicily, keeping at least twenty-five miles from the North African shoreline, then on a southeasterly course to Malta, skirting Sicily on our port side. An altitude of 3,000 feet was suggested, but left to the discretion of the pilot because of the variable weather conditions expected en route. The weather briefing was not encouraging. We were to expect rain and storm conditions through at least three hours of our projected nine-hour flight.

We were given several warnings. German and Italian fighter aircraft were active throughout the region, but should not be a problem until daylight and when the weather had cleared. We would be a good distance from Sicily, but we had no choice but to pass fairly close to the Italian-held island of Pantelleria in daylight. Wellingtons had been lost to fighters from this fortified island, so we were cautioned to be alert when passing it.

At my wireless briefing, I was given a special warning. German radio stations on Sicily were responding to our aircraft signals to Malta requesting bearings. Some hours out from Malta, the Sicilian signals would be stronger, and the enemy operators would promptly reply, even in our "X" codes, using Malta call signs, and give the Wellington operator a good bearing — to Sicily! We were given a challenge code, which the Germans could not possibly have, and were warned to use this challenge without fail when requesting bearings from the Malta station, whose call sign at that time was KT1.

Our briefing concluded and we were given a take-off time of 2200 hours. The other Wimpy was to leave one hour ahead of us.

We were about to leave to do our plotting preparations when a wing commander approached Bill Dixon with a British Army officer in tow. We listened as he introduced Bill to the stranger: "Sir, this is Sergeant Dixon, captain of the Wellington that will be taking you to Malta. Sergeant, this is Brigadier . . .* The brigadier is of the Royal Artillery, and he is going to Malta to take over the anti-aircraft defences of the island. He will be your passenger for the flight, and you will have to see that he is properly equipped with parachute and Mae West, etc. I will leave him in your hands." To the brigadier he offered, "Well, sir, I hope that you have an uneventful flight. Sergeant Dixon is an experienced pilot, and I am sure that you will be in good hands."

---

* I cannot remember this officer's name.

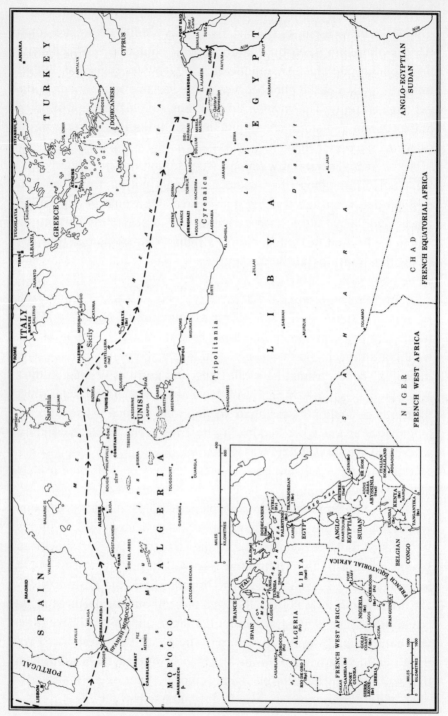

None of us was too happy with this turn of events, but there was nothing we could do about it; orders were orders. The brigadier and Bill had a chat, and Bill brought him over to us. After the introductions, Bill gave me the job of getting the brigadier outfitted for the flight. In the supply section, we managed to get everything we needed. The brigadier was a short, stocky man, and it seemed to me that he was a little cocky, and that he was inclined to throw the weight of his rank around a little bit. Perhaps that is why I somewhat mischievously recommended that he suit himself up in the full trousers and jacket of the fur-lined leather flying suit, which was more suitable for the cold flights over Europe than for these warmer climes. The poor man was going to sweat buckets in that outfit.

Armed with our codes and route maps, we boarded the bus that took us out to our Wimpy. It was a black night, and the gusty wind was not the most favourable for take-off on that short, narrow runway. I had the brigadier sit braced against the main spar alongside Tony, and took my own position as Bill called out, "Everyone ready for take-off? We're on our way, chaps."

With clearance from the control tower, Bill released the brakes and opened the throttles. The flare pots on either side of the runway raced past us as we gained speed, and I knew we were all praying that we would get airborne before the end of that short runway loomed up.

We parted company with The Rock at 2200 hours on 5 December 1941, and set course for the tiny island of Malta halfway along the length of the Mediterranean Sea.

A little over three hours into our flight, we ran into turbulence. I had fixed a fairly comfortable position for the brigadier on the canvas pull-down bed just aft of the main spar, but when things started to get a little rough, I told him that we were all going to be very busy and asked if he would mind helping out. He agreed, and I showed him how to pump oil to the engines, which was required every two hours, forty-five strokes to each engine. The pump lever was hard to push and pull when the oil was cool. I neglected to tell the brigadier that I had discovered a way to disconnect the flexible conduit that carried our cabin heat from the engine and apply the heat to the oil pump. This thinned out the oil and made pumping almost effortless.

Just as I finished, Robbie came up on the intercom, "Howard, could you take some bearings for me with the prism compass? Come and get the compass and I'll show you what I want." The compass was the size of a saucer. I sighted through a prism and lined up another sight on a target for the bearing. "If you go back to the astro dome, you'll see the city of Algiers coming up on our starboard side. I'd like you to take a series of bearings on the city lights about one minute apart and call them out to me." By this time we were pitching about violently, but I managed to brace myself and get the bearings Robbie needed. The lights of that exotic city were bright enough to see through the compass prism, and I found it a little hard to believe that I was actually looking at the coast of North Africa only seven miles away. There were no radio bearings available in this hostile area.

By now we had run into the worst of the storm, and it was frightening. The rain and hail hammered on the skin of the aircraft like machine-gun bullets, and the lightning pierced the black, purplish, roiling clouds in jagged arrows that seemed to miss us only by inches. Tony complained from the front turret that he was getting wet, and Bill called to me over the intercom, "Howard, would you get a flashlight and come forward?"

I pulled a flashlight from my bag and struggled forward to the cockpit. I don't know what Will White was doing, but our captain was having a hard time controlling the aircraft in the worst turbulence I had ever experienced. The water was pouring in over the instrument panel, and Bill instructed me, "Keep the flashlight on the airspeed and the altimeter, Howard. I'm having a hard time reading them!" This went on for some time until Will took over from me, and I went back to check on our passenger.

The aircraft was pitching so violently that it was difficult to move about. I wondered how the wings were staying on, and how Bill could possibly fly this machine. Robbie had no navigation aids whatever, so it was just dead-reckoning and hope for the best until we could get some radio bearings or some clear sky for astro shots.

I found the poor brigadier holding on to the bed supports for dear life. He did not look at all well. I reassured him, not altogether honestly, that this was not unusual for us, and that all would be well. I made sure he had bags for airsickness, and enough flight rations in the unlikely event he felt like eating. I had been keeping him informed of our progress. I didn't have the heart to let him continue with the oil pumping and took it over myself. Bill had told the gunners that they could leave their turrets if they wished for the comparative comfort of the fuselage. Tony gladly clambered out of his front office to get out of the wet, but Doug said he preferred to stay in his turret, which wasn't leaking like Tony's. There was no danger to this; no fighter could possibly find us, let alone survive, in this chaotic night sky.

We had been pounded and tossed about by the storm for over three hours when we broke out into more stable air and a lightening dawn sky. We had two tired pilots, especially Bill, who had done most of the difficult flying. I checked on Robbie and his maps. He had us well into the straits between Sicily and Pantelleria, which were only eighty miles apart.

I was seated back at my desk in front of the radio set making an entry in my log when a small bombshell went off in my head. Incredibly, caught up as I had been in all the changes of crew, the hospital, and Harwell, it did not dawn on me until now that I hadn't contacted Bessie before I left to tell her I was leaving. My stomach tightened up with guilt. How could I have been so callous? I tried to comfort myself with the fact that Bessie and I had not progressed to any deep or intimate relationship, so there probably wasn't any attachment on either side that should be cause for any great distress (how wrong I was!). I then said to myself, "Well, not to worry, Willy will tell the story when he goes to see Maureen. I just hope he tells Bessie that I was taken away in such a hurry that I didn't have time to get in touch with her. Surely that wouldn't be stretching things too much. Anyway, not much I can do now."

My mental anguish was interrupted by Robbie's voice. "Howard, I will soon need some bearings from Malta if you can manage it. We've been quite a while on DR, so I would feel better if I could fix our position so we don't come too close to Sicily or Pantelleria." I gave Robbie an affirmative, but Bill told me to wait until we got safely past Pantelleria in case somebody took a bearing on our signals.

I had just reached the astro dome to watch the brightening sky when Doug's calm voice broke the serenity of the moment, "Captain, rear gunner, we have some aircraft off our starboard quarter, about 1,000 feet above us. They're a few miles away, but they look like biplanes to me!"

"Okay, everybody," Bill shouted, "They won't be ours. I'm getting down close to the water, so they might not see us. Keep your eyes on them, and let me know, Doug, if they come closer."

As we dove down sharply to the blue waters of the "Med," Doug came up again. "Captain, rear gunner, they've seen us, and they're peeling off towards us. I count twelve of them and they look like Fiat CR 42s.* Can we warm up our guns?"

"Okay, gunners, warm up your guns and let's keep an eye on them. They'll be Italians from Pantelleria, and from what I've heard they may not be too anxious to get into a fight. If they do attack, I'll turn so they are on our beam, and both gunners can have a crack at them."

We could all see them now. They peeled off from formation and came towards us in a gaggle of line astern, but when only about 1,000 yards from us, banked abruptly and climbed away. Doug called out that they were giving up, and we all breathed a sigh of relief as they sped away and dwindled into specks in the sky. Our warning bursts may have suggested to their leader that the odds were not weighted enough in his favour.

I could get my bearings now for Robbie. The enemy knew where we were, anyway. I called up the Malta ground station and got an immediate reply. I was suspicious right away. The transmission had a metallic edge to it that I had come to identify with German radio signals over Europe. I replied, asking for a bearing to reach Malta, but added the coded challenge for the day. No reply! I was right, this was a German station trying to lure us to Sicily. The bearings would have looked plausible enough, since the southeastern tip of Sicily is only fifty-five miles from Gozo, the northernmost island of the Malta group.

I waited a few minutes and tried Malta again. This time I got back the correct answer to the challenge and accepted the bearing, which I handed to Robbie. From then on, I obtained periodic bearings, each one authenticated by challenge. I was smugly satisfied with myself.

Robbie had given Bill an ETA of 0700 hours and sure enough, with a few minutes to go, Tony called out, "There's Malta ahead just off our port bow." After nine hours of flying and the roughest storm we had ever encountered, it was with relief that we all had a good look at this tiny island, and the sheer cliffs that made up nearly all of its coastline. It was damn good navigating on Robbie's part, helped of course by a pilot who could keep to a heading in spite of the almost impossible flying conditions.

There were columns of smoke rising from many points on the island. As we got closer, we could see that most of them were coming from the

---

* The CR42 was the top biplane fighter of the Italian Air Force, quite on a par with its frequent British adversary and counterpart, the Gloster Gladiator. Both were soon made obsolete by the single wing fighters like the Hurricane.

capital, Valletta, and its Grand Harbour. When Bill contacted the tower at Luqa airfield, our destination just outside Valletta, we were told that one of the daily air raids had just finished. Bill took us down through the brown smoke patches to a good landing on an airstrip that was barely long enough for Wimpys. Just beyond the end of the runway, there was a ravine filled with a great deal of aircraft wreckage, testifying to the many aircraft that had overshot and come to grief.

Taken by jeep to the operations room, we were informed that the Wimpy that had taken off from Gibraltar an hour ahead of us had failed to arrive. Either it had been shot down, perished in the storm, or, as the ops staff believed was more likely, and was later confirmed, they had been lured to a landing on the Sicily airfield of Comiso. I was saddened to hear this, along with the rest of the crew, but I was also tremendously relieved that I had challenged the Sicily radio operator. We were given a take-off time of midnight the next day for our flight to Egypt. We would not have much time for sightseeing. For the moment, we just wanted some sleep. Our brigadier passenger simply took off and disappeared. I don't know whether he mumbled a brief word of thanks to Bill, but he didn't say anything to me.

After a breakfast in the airfield mess we were taken to our quarters in Valletta, in an ancient stone building that had been converted to service living quarters from its former use as a leper hospital. In spite of being bone weary, I had trouble getting to sleep. Two of the wireless operator staff at the operations room had told me that Wimpy Z835 had left Malta on 22 September for Egypt but had not been heard from since. The wireless op was Dick Powell, who had been one of our group at Uxbridge and with whom I had trained at Harwell OTU. Dick was a fine fellow, and I had liked him very much. This was an all-too-common story; we had to learn to shake it off and get on with our job. It wasn't easy.

We spent part of that night in an air raid shelter. It was a short run from the Sicilian airfields to Malta, so the German and Italian aircraft were able to pound the island night and day. The next day, all of our crew ventured into Valletta, but again part of our time was spent in the air raid shelters. Before we made it into one shelter, Doug and I narrowly escaped being washed away in a torrent of water bursting from a reservoir blown up in a direct hit from a Stuka dive bomber. Although the casualties from the bombings numbered well into the thousands, the toll was minimized by the deep cellars and air raid shelter tunnels that were excavated from the easily worked Maltese rock.

From the air force staff at Luqa we gained a better appreciation of the strategic importance of Malta, and Doug and I got a short history lesson on this ancient island from the curators of the ancient Church of the Knights of Saint John of Jerusalem.*

At 0200 hours we assembled in the operations room for briefing for our flight to Cairo. We took on some passengers who had lost their aircraft to the bombings. We were introduced to Jimmy Chalmers, an American in the RCAF, and to three Canadians: Alec Balinson, Art Charron, and Joe Findlay, all of whom I already knew from training days. All were wireless ops or air gunners. Our take-off time was to be midnight, and our flight time would be approximately nine hours. We found time to get some sleep.

At 0001 hours we lifted off the Luqa runway and turned on course for Egypt. We got clear of the island just as one of the night raids on Valletta was beginning.

Our long flight proved to be uneventful, except for some ineffectual fire from an Italian destroyer we overflew. Traversing the catwalk to take some rations to Doug in his rear turret, I had to step over the sleeping bodies of our passengers.

By the time the sun came up, bathing us in the bright Mediterranean light, Robbie asked me if I could get him some bearings from Egypt. The station in the best position to give us some navigational help seemed to be Mersa Matruh, on the coast just west of Alexandria. That station replied promptly, and I was able to get periodic bearings until we were into the Nile delta area. I had made sure the IFF was switched on before we reached the coast. I looked down upon the ancient land of the pharaohs almost in disbelief as the green delta area, the Cairo metropolis, and the Nile River and Suez Canal unfolded beneath us.

We were directed to land at El Faiyum, just south of Cairo, and we touched down there at 0910 hours on 7 December 1941. The next phase of our war, very different from our European experiences, had begun.

---

* Malta had been a thorn in Germany's side ever since the outbreak of war, particularly after Italy entered into the conflict. British aircraft and ships were in a position to play havoc with Axis ships trying to supply the Italian and German armies through the port of Tripoli in North Africa. Malta was described as being "like an unsinkable aircraft carrier anchored in the Sicilian Channel astride the Axis lines of communication to Libya." (From *The Right of the Line*.)

THREE

THE REMAINING FIFTEEN SHILLINGS

16
THE LAND OF
THE PHARAOHS

AT THE RAF BASE AT EL FAIYUM, we were told that we would be parting with the Wimpy that had brought us safely from England. We would not see this particular old friend again.

We managed to get some breakfast before we piled into a truck with all our gear, bound for Cairo. Even in the middle of winter the temperature was a balmy seventy degrees. On reaching the city about an hour later, we stared wide-eyed at the mosques and other strange architecture, and at streets teeming with people, most of whom were dressed in what looked to us like white nightgowns. We were dropped off at the headquarters of the Middle East Air Force, and Will, Doug, Tony, and I waited in a hallway while Bill and Robbie were taken to see some group captain about our new destination. Our passengers were taken off to some other office.

Bill and Robbie did not reappear for about half an hour. When they did, they had some startling news — the Japanese had bombed Pearl Harbor!

When we had settled down from that news, Bill told us that we were posted to 148 Bomber Squadron, based at the pre-war RAF station of

Kabrit situated due east of Cairo, on the shore of the Bitter Lakes through which the Suez Canal ran. This was a Wellington squadron, now part of 205 Group of RAF Middle East Bomber Command. The Canadians we had brought from Malta as passengers were also posted to 148 Squadron. But first we were to have a few days leave in Cairo, followed by a week or so at another RAF base at Shallufa to get kitted out for the Middle East. This base was about seventy miles southeast of Cairo, halfway between Kabrit and Suez.

We were all billeted in a small, nondescript hotel called the Gloria, on a narrow street not far from the Cairo city centre. Doug and I shared a room located on the roof of an adjacent building. To reach the room we had to cross over from our building to the other on a narrow plank. Oh well, we thought, we were in another world. We might as well start adjusting.

We didn't know where our other crew members had gone, so, after an afternoon of much-needed rest and dinner of mysterious content, Doug and I decided to investigate what looked like a cabaret or night club right across the narrow street from our hotel.

We entered through a beaded curtain into the smoky atmosphere of a scene right out of a Hollywood Foreign Legion movie. I half-expected to see George Raft or Gary Cooper sitting at one of the tables that covered most of the floor space. To the right of the entrance was a long bar, and just beyond that, a small dance floor and a raised platform holding a fifteen-piece orchestra. The place was crowded with colourful locals and a mixture of uniforms, some of which we had never seen before. The noise of the multi-language babble and of the blare from the Egyptian band was overpowering at first. We decided to chance a beer at the bar.

Before we could elbow our way close enough to order our beer, we were greeted by a big Australian soldier wearing the distinctive Aussie hat with one side of the large brim turned up. He was in shorts and a short-sleeved shirt carrying corporal's stripes. He knew from our white, untanned skin that we were new to the country. He shouted out to me, "Welcome to Egypt, cobber! These are my mates, Jack and John, and I'm Ian." Jack was the youngest of the trio, and John, obviously the more mature one, turned out to be the steadying influence on the others. They, too, were corporals.

Over the beers that they insisted on buying they told us that they had just come out of Tobruk. They had to be taken out by sea because Tobruk was surrounded and under siege at that time. They had been part of Major-General MacKay's 6th Australian Division, which had taken Tobruk from the Italians on 21 January 1941 in General Archibald Wavell's brilliant sweep west to Cyrenaica, Libya. But after German General Erwin Rommel's arrival in Libya with his Afrika Korps in February, most of Wavell's gains were erased, and Tobruk, resisting capture, had been under siege almost without respite since April. Our Aussie friends were part of several battalions relieved at Tobruk and taken out by sea, probably earmarked for return to Australia because of the new Japanese threat.

While we exchanged stories with our new friends, Doug became fascinated by a slender, dusky woman in an almost transparent silk dress who paraded past the bar every few minutes. No doubt employed by the club, she carried a small monkey on her shoulder and seemed unaware or uncaring that the creature was piddling quite frequently down the back of her dress.

As the woman approached the bar on one of her circuits, big Ian whispered mischievously to Doug, "That dress she's wearing has a zipper that runs all the way down the back. When she gets here, pull the zipper down, Dougie, and let's see what happens." This kind of stunt was completely out of character for staid and naive Doug, but under the unfamiliar influence of several beers, it didn't seem like such a bad idea to him.

As the woman came abreast of Doug, our hero reached out, as challenged, and pulled her zipper down as far as it would go. The woman let out a shriek that almost shut out the band music and all other noise, and as she turned abruptly towards us her dress fell to the floor. Doug's mouth fell open and his eyes bulged like saucers as he looked at the completely naked figure in front of us. All the woman was wearing was the monkey! "You really scored this time, mate," Ian chortled.

Suddenly I was pushed roughly to one side by a bulky, gorilla-like man — the club bouncer. He grabbed Doug by the tie and drew back his other arm to pound our stunned friend in the face. Before he could uncoil his arm, Ian's ham-like fist came over Doug's shoulder and connected with the bruiser's jaw with such force that he was propelled backwards into one of the crowded tables ringing the dance floor. Pandemonium erupted. We looked on in astonishment as everyone started fighting with his neighbour. What had we started? Was this standard practice in these places?

Sensible John enticed a gleeful Ian from a melee at the end of the bar, and urged the rest of us, "Let's get out of this. Follow me." With that we formed line astern behind him as he led us, all in a half-crouch, through the wrestling bodies to the front door. From our escape we crossed the road to the Gloria Hotel, where our Aussie friends suggested we order another beer and sit in the big front window of the lounge so we could watch the progress of the mix-up that big Ian and Doug had started.

It wasn't long before police vans arrived. Out poured Cairo's finest with rifles in their hands. We sat as if watching a movie as the police roughly threw scores of people into the vans and roared away. For Doug and me, our first evening in Egypt was quite an introduction to the nation's night life!

Near 0200 hours, our Aussies finally decided to leave, and it was just as well, as Doug and I had about reached the end of our endurance. The Aussies would return and pick us up later in the morning to take us on a little tour of the city.

We had taken in far more beer than we were used to, and Doug and I had some difficulty climbing not only the three flights of stairs to the roof, but the even more precarious passage across the plank to the other roof and our room.

Lucky for us, our three corporals didn't arrive until noon to take us on a tour, which turned out to be a sampling of haunts familiar to them but utterly shocking to Doug and me. We entered the infamous "Birka" area, and the *muski*, the native bazaar that was clearly marked "Out of Bounds," signs that were just a welcome mat to Ian. To say that we had entered the seedier part of Cairo would be an understatement. It was the centre of prostitution and the home of the "Exibish," the troops' jargon for the depraved shows put on in some of the "cribs" that lined the inner streets.* Doug and I soon had enough of this and persuaded our hosts to take us out of the area to a more civilized part of the city.

The sights, sounds, and smells of this exotic city, so foreign to our experience, were almost overwhelming. Masses of people crammed the sidewalks, and the natives seemed to conduct normal conversations as if they were involved in shouting matches. Five times a day, from the towers of numerous minarets, the haunting call "Allahu Akbar" (God is greatest) of a *muezzin* summoned the devout to prayer. Pungent odours of stale incense mixed with fetid smells of the sewer. Exhaust fumes

---

* In the First World War, the "Birka" was almost demolished by some rampaging groups of Australian soldiers, so the "Out of Bounds" signs in this war were probably partly an attempt to prevent a recurrence of the riots.

emanated from the military and civilian vehicles whose drivers leaned on horns to help clear a passage through the teeming streets of a city swollen by troops to over three million people.

The main streets of Cairo were impressive. There were numerous small parks and squares featuring imposing monuments. The main sidewalks were inlaid with coloured mosaic tiles in blues, greens, and browns, and ivory. We were told that the city owed its splendid layout to the influence of Parisian architect and engineer Pierre-Charles l'Enfant, who had designed Washington, D.C., in 1791.

There were many good restaurants, the most outstanding being Groppi's and Salt's, but the "unwashed," the non-commissioned troops, were discouraged from patronizing some of these establishments. At the posh and celebrated Shepheard's Hotel, which had become a haven for underemployed or defaulting senior officers until they were rooted out by General Montgomery, other ranks were strictly barred. There were also many cinemas, one with a novel sliding roof that opened to provide a ceiling of sparkling stars during the movie. Performances ended with the playing of the Egyptian national anthem, which some soldiers and airmen sang to their own bawdy concocted words that, thankfully, were not understood by the Egyptian patrons. One popular version began with, "Up your pipe, King Farouk, up your pipe!"* and deteriorated from there.

If one had the time, of course, there were magnificent things to see, like the pyramids at nearby Giza, and the fabulous Cairo museum.

We met up with Bill Dixon, Tony Carroll, and Jimmy Chalmers, who had rented a *gharry*, or *arabeya*, a horse-drawn carriage driven by an Egyptian. We all piled in to some protest from the driver that his carriage was overloaded, but who drove off anyway under threats and cajoling from our Aussie friend Ian.

At the insistence of our new friends, we ended our afternoon tour by getting our group picture taken at one of the several photo studios off the main street of Sharia Soliman Pasha. We were each given a copy of this great picture. We took our leave of the companionable Aussies, and were never to see them again.

---

* King Farouk had succeeded to the Egyptian throne in 1936. In an alliance treaty that year Great Britain assumed responsibility for the defence of Egyptian frontiers, and virtually dictated the affairs of the country. Farouk was a tragic figure who meant well, but was overcome by events. On 26 July 1952, he was deposed by General Nasser and his revolutionary Constituent Council, and sent sailing into exile on the royal yacht.

A day later our crew was picked up by an RAF truck, and we left our Cairo adventures behind as we took off southwards on the highway to RAF Shallufa. We were not to see the other Canadians we had brought from Malta until we reached Kabrit later on in the month.

It took almost two hours of driving behind army convoys and various donkey carts on a narrow highway bordered by seemingly limitless acres of grey-brown sand hills before we reached Shallufa. This was another large pre-war RAF base, hosting the old the First World War–experienced Nos. 37 and 38, and later No. 70, Wimpy squadrons, and there was a lot of flying activity when we arrived.

We were assigned to our first tents, and paraded to the supply section to be kitted out with summer shirts and shorts, and summer uniforms of drill.

There wasn't a great deal to do while we acclimatized ourselves to the dry, mild climate, but what proved to be of great interest was the large prisoner-of-war compound. The high wire fences, topped with barbed wire, ran close to our tent site. This compound held all non-commissioned ranks of the entire royal regiment of King Victor Emmanuel III of Italy, a hapless puppet of Mussolini. Neither the king nor his loyal troops were anti-British, however, and had no stomach for the entry of Italy into the war on Germany's side. On the outbreak of hostilities in 1940 in Africa, this regiment was part of the Italian force facing the thin outpost of the British garrison on the Libyan–Egyptian frontier. They immediately defected and crossed the lines to surrender themselves to the British commander. They were transported, with all their household equipment, to the hastily prepared compound at Shallufa.

The gates of the compound were locked only during the night hours; these prisoners had no wish to leave the comparative luxury of their new home. They had brought with them their stoves, cooking utensils, cots and bedding, and all their personal effects, including a great array of musical instruments. These men were the cream of the crop of the Italian forces. Their ranks included talented singers, musicians, boxers, and wrestlers, who held instructional classes in all these skills for interested personnel on the station. All this in the midst of a war.

The prisoners had their own night reserved to attend the station cinema. One night, an RAF orderly sergeant had unwittingly locked the gate to the prisoners' compound. On their return from the movie, the POWs could not get back into their home. Great consternation! The duty officer was summoned, and had to get the gate opened for the Italians, who were quite put out by this upset of their routine. They had no wish to exchange the comfortable beds they had constructed for themselves in their compound for the kind of rude canvas cots we had been given in our Spartan tents.

Our stay at Shallufa came to an end when we were ordered to pack up our kit and board a truck for the trip to Kabrit. We were on our way to our new squadron home.

17
KABRIT —
INTO THE DESERT WAR

IT TOOK ABOUT FORTY MINUTES driving north to reach the guardhouse gate of the RAF station at Kabrit. The guard, armed with rifle and bayonet, passed us through after examining our identity cards, and we started down the road to the headquarters building. It was 21 December 1941.

On our right were four or five large hangars. The main airfield and runways were just beyond them, and we could see many Wimpys parked on the tarmac. The main buildings of the station, officers' and airmen's quarters and messes, the supply section, the briefing theatre, and the base headquarters were on the left side of the road. None of the structures was painted; they had weathered to blend with the beige of the sandy terrain. The roofs of the hangars had been camouflaged in an effort to make them blend into the ground when seen from the air. There were Wimpys in the circuit above the field, and men and vehicles scurrying about the side roads. It was a busy station.

Our driver stopped first at the headquarters building, where Robbie was taken to the adjutant's office, and we were joined by the orderly sergeant. Our next stop was the supply section, where we were issued with blankets and, much to our surprise, with army winter battledress. The idea was that the brown khaki uniform would not show up against the sand like our blue battledress that we were still wearing would, and we would thus be a little safer from strafing by enemy aircraft. We always suspected that it was just a supply problem.

Our next stop was a big surprise. On the narrow asphalt road we left the main camp behind. About four hundred yards east of the camp we came upon a small village of tents scattered in a hodge-podge pattern over several acres of sand. Our truck left the main road and we rumbled through the rocks and sand to stop in front of one of the tents. The orderly sergeant called out, "Right, this is your home, chaps. This tent and the other one over there have been allocated to your crew. I'll leave you to sort yourselves out then." With that he waited until we had removed our gear from the truck and then he took off for the main camp.

There were many aircrew sergeants going to and fro among the tents, and several came over to greet us and to offer help in getting us settled into our tents. Peter Mayhew, an RAF pilot, and his navigator, Norm Wakeham, were among the first to make us welcome and to initiate introductions all around. Peter was tall and slim, with a shock of blond hair that seemed a little too long for service standards. Norm was more reserved, but we were to find that he was one of the best-liked fellows on the squadron.

Peter informed us that this was home to 148 Sqn NCO aircrews. The officers were billeted in more comfortable quarters in the wooden buildings next to the officers' mess. Even the airmen were quartered in buildings on the main station site. No doubt this was much more convenient for the tradesmen, who had to work on the aircraft daily. We never did discover what the rationale was in placing the NCO aircrew in the primitive tent quarters outside the main camp.

Each tent site had been prepared by digging out an area some nine feet by twelve to a depth of four feet. Walls of sandbags had been put in place, leaving a corridor for the sloping entrance. The main tent canvas covered the living space. A fly-sheet covered the main canvas to provide an air space that helped keep heat out in the summer and some warmth in during the winter. The tents were camouflaged by creosote that had been sprinkled over the fly-sheet with sand over the entire top. The sand stuck to the wet creosote. The tents, seen from the air, would blend into the ground to minimize our vulnerability to attack from German bombers.

Inside the tent we found one small table holding a coal oil lamp. On the sand floor there were three straw mattresses. There were also three small orange-crate boxes with one shelf in the centre. With a grand sweep of his arm, Peter announced, "Gentlemen, welcome to the Ritz. This is your living room *and* your bedroom. I hope you have some blankets. It gets bloody cold here during the night."

Peter pointed out the tents that housed the sergeants' mess and the dining hall. With exaggerated flourish he also pointed out the communal shower. This was a single pipe, about six feet high, curved at the top to create a downspout. There was no fancy showerhead. There was a concrete square to stand on, and a drain that led off into the sand. The water was heated simply by the sun's warming of the pipe! The shower was out in the open — no need for privacy since there were no women around.

The northern limit of our village was the beach, part of the southern shore of the Great Bitter Lake. Not far from the beach, two long slit trenches had been dug in a zigzag pattern some ten feet deep and lined with sandbags as a shelter from bombing raids. The road from the main camp extended past our site and ended at the promontory dividing the Great Bitter Lake from the Little Bitter Lake to the south, leaving room for the passage of ships traversing the Suez Canal, which entered the northern lake and exited the southern lake on its way to its terminus at Suez.* At the end of that road on the promontory was the residence of the station commander. This sumptuous two-storey permanent home looked out of place in its bare surroundings.

Bill and Tony and I opted to take the first tent. Will and Doug settled in an identical tent just fifteen feet away.

No sooner had we unloaded our gear into our tents when a truck arrived to take us back to the main camp. The driver informed us that we were to meet one of the flight commanders.

We hadn't been used to any great welcomes, or any praise for what we had done, so we were not expecting a ceremony, but we were not prepared for the kind of reception we got. The sign on the flight commander's door read "Squadron Leader Baird." When we entered his office and lined up in front of his desk, he ignored us for some time while perusing some documents in front of him. Finally, Baird looked up and spoke to us without the slightest warmth in his voice: "I see from these records that you have some experience. Well, you might find operations here a different kettle of fish." He paused, and his disdainful gaze settled on Bill and me. "I see that two of you are Canadians. Well, I'll tell you right now that if we have any trouble with you it's the high jump for both of you.* You'll be attending the squadron briefing in the briefing room at 0800 hours tomorrow morning. That's 0800 sharp! That's all."

We were dismissed. Bill and I looked at one another in disbelief. This was our welcome to our new squadron? I wondered if Bill was thinking, as I was, that we two probably had a great deal more operational experience than this bastard. And what kind of trouble had Canadians on this squadron been into? Fortunately, we were not to have any further direct contact with this officer.

We filed out of the office and boarded the truck to return to our tents. Our first day on our new squadron — not an auspicious beginning.

■ ■ ■

The next morning, after our first night sleeping on straw mattresses in our tent home, we joined the other aircrew members of the squadron in the long walk up to the main camp and to the briefing room. There were folding chairs for the crews, facing a raised stage that had a large map on the back wall and easels for smaller maps. It wasn't quite as elaborate as the theatre back at Marham, but it was adequate for the purpose.

Operations had been cancelled for the week, so this briefing was simply to bring everyone up to date on the operational situation in the Western Desert, where the British Eighth Army had been engaged in a series of see-saw battles during the summer and fall with General Rommel's Afrika Korps and his Italian allies. We had our first look at the station commander, one Group Captain Fall,** not knowing that he was to become our nemesis. He spoke briefly before handing things over to our squadron CO, Wing Commander Rainsford.

Neither the station commander nor the squadron CO mentioned that our crew had arrived to join the squadron. We were never introduced to them, nor to any other officers for that matter. Robbie, an officer, may have been introduced to the squadron CO and even to the station commander in the officers' mess.

---

* The "high jump" was RAF slang for the stockade or disciplinary camp.
** Group Captain J.S.T. Fall, DSC, AFC, was first commissioned in the RNAS in January 1917. He was promoted to temporary Group Captain 1 September 1940, and retired before the end of the war (11 March 1945) in that rank.

■ ■ ■

Because of the frequency of attacks on Benghazi, the raids came to be called "The Mail Run" (sometimes called "The Milk Run"), and were the subject of a famous squadron song with a mournful chorus, sung to the tune of "Clementine." Although the wording of the original eleven verses varied slightly depending upon the singers, this version was among the most popular:

> *Take off for the Western Desert,*
> *Fuka, 60 or 09.*
> *Same old Wimpy, same old target,*
> *Same old aircrew, same old time.*

Chorus: *Seventy Squadron, Seventy Squadron,*
> *Though we say it with a sigh,*
> *Must we do this bloody mail run*
> *Every night till we die?*

> *Navigator, have you lost us?*
> *Come up here and have a look.*
> *Somebody's shot our starboard wing off.*
> *That's all right then, that's Tobruk.*

Chorus: *Seventy Squadron, Seventy Squadron,* etc.

> *Oh, to be in Piccadilly,*
> *Selling matches by the score,*
> *Though we'd feel a bit chilly,*
> *There'd be no blessed Mail Run anymore!*

Chorus: *Seventy Squadron, Seventy Squadron,* etc.

■ ■ ■

We left the briefing room with a better idea of just what was going on in the desert war on the day of our arrival. We learned that 70 Sqn would be leaving Kabrit for Shallufa right after Christmas, to be replaced with 104 Sqn coming from Malta.

It was only three days until Christmas. We filled our time getting settled in our tent and getting to know some other members of the squadron. I was interested in talking to the wireless operators, of course, and had good discussions with Len "Wiz" Evans, Alan "Bris" Brisbane, "Marsh" Scarborough, and Jack Butterfield. I already knew the Canadians, Joe Findlay, Alec Balinson, and Art Charron, and our American, Jimmy Chalmers.

Naturally, Bill Dixon was more interested in the other pilots, like Peter Mayhew and Sid Payne, but he and Howard Douglas, a Canadian observer, became good friends. Howard was a lawyer in civilian life and, like Bill, was a little older than most of us.

Despite some minor personal eccentricities, Peter Mayhew was recognized as one of the most skilful of the squadron's pilots, and his antics and those of his crew members had gained them some celebrity, however colourful.

Allegedly, on one raid, en route to Benghazi, they had come under attack from one or two Junkers 88s. The rear gunner, "Mad Joe" Keenan, ran out of ammunition, but had a brainwave. He took a roll of tough, government-issue toilet paper, which was always carried, and let it unravel from his turret. The paper snaked out in long undulating waves in the slipstream and was illuminated by the moonlight. It must have looked frightening to the German fighters, for they banked away suddenly and disappeared. This story was given credence by an intercepted German instruction to their Middle East fighter groups, warning that the British were suspected of using some new air weapon.

On another night, during a bad storm over the Mediterranean, Peter lost one of his engines. He knew he would have to ditch into the sea. He and his crew gradually lost altitude until they broke out of cloud over water. They had enough light by this time to make a landing on the water, with the Wimpy floating on the surface. On impact, as designed, the six-man rubber dinghy ejected itself from an engine nacelle and inflated as it hit the water. It was tethered to the fuselage by a long rope. Following the prescribed crew drill, John Fisher, the second pilot, clambered out of the pilot's hatch and grabbed the dinghy rope. The rest of the crew came out of the astro dome and slid down the wing into the dinghy. Peter had yelled at them to hurry because the Wimpy was known to float for no more than a few minutes. Everyone was thinking, "Here we are in the middle of the Mediterranean. God knows if we will be found and picked up!"

Dawn was breaking as the irrepressible John unhooked the dinghy lanyard from the wing and jumped into the water. He was stunned when his feet hit bottom and he found he was standing in water no deeper than his armpits! Their navigation had been a bit off. Instead of ditching in the Mediterranean Sea, they had come down on one of the salt lakes that dotted the northern plain of the Western Desert. Usually dry, this one had filled with a few feet of water from the recent storms.

Quickly regaining his imperturbability, John announced gravely, "We've boobed, chaps! But no use all of us getting wet." With that he took the lanyard over his shoulder and began to pull his crew-laden dinghy towards the shore, which all could now see was only some 300 yards away. They were well within the British lines, and were picked up by an Eighth Army patrol within the hour. It's no wonder they were known as the "eccentrics."

There were a few things we had not been issued with at Shallufa. At the Kabrit supply section our crew was "paraded" and we each signed for the following items: one silk escape map of the Egyptian Western Desert and Libyan Cyrenaica; one .38 calibre Enfield revolver with canvas holster and belt, and a pouch of bullets (I seldom used the holster, but stuck the loaded revolver into the top of my right flying boot); one cloth-mounted certificate or letter bearing the British Government coat of arms and featuring these words, in Arabic and in English:

> To all Arab peoples — Greetings and Peace be upon you. The bearer of this letter is an Officer of the British Government and a friend of all Arabs. Treat him well, guard him from harm, give him food and drink, help him to the nearest British soldiers, and you will be rewarded. Peace and the Mercy of God upon you. The British High Command in the East.

The letter included some points on conduct when meeting Arabs in the desert, such as removing footwear when entering their tents, and ignoring their women. The letter also included a few useful words in Arabic. The day before Christmas, I was standing near our tent talking to Tony when we heard sounds of a great commotion coming from the cook's tent. The bottom of the tent wall parted and a pig came racing out across the sand, squealing in anguish. Hard on its heels came the cook in his stained white smock. With a butcher's knife in his hand, he

BRITISH GOVERNMENT

الحكومة البريطانية

الى كل عربي كريم

السلام عليكم ورحمة الله وبركاته وبعد ، فحامل هذا الكتاب ضابط بالجيش البريطاني وهو صديق
وفي لكافة الشعوب العربية فنرجو أن تعاملوه بالعطف والاكرام . وأن تحافظوا على حياته من كل
طارىء ، ونأمل عند الاضطرار أن تقدموا له مايحتاج اليه من طعام وشراب . وأن ترشدوه الى
أقرب معسكر بريطاني . وسنكافئكم مالياً بسخاء على ماتسدونه اليه من خدمات .
والسلام عليكم ورحمة الله وبركاته؟

القيادة البريطانية العامة في الشرق الاوسط

To All Arab Peoples — Greetings and peace be upon you. The bearer of this letter is an
Officer of the British Government and a friend of all Arabs. Treat him well, guard him from
harm, give him food and drink, help him to return to the nearest British soldiers and you will
be rewarded. Peace and the Mercy of God upon you. *The British High Command in the East.*

SOME POINTS ON CONDUCT WHEN MEETING THE ARABS IN THE DESERT.

Remove footwear on entering their tent. Completely ignore their women. If thirsty drink
the water they offer, but DO NOT fill your waterbottle from their personal supply. Go to their
well and fetch what you want. Never neglect any puddle or other water supply for topping up
your bottle. Use the Halazone included in your Aid Box. Do not expect breakfast if you
sleep the night. Arabs will give you a mid-day or evening meal.

REMEMBER, NEVER TRY AND HURRY IN THE DESERT, SLOW AND SURE DOES IT.

A few useful words

English	Arabic		English	Arabic
English	Ingleezi		Day	Nahaar or Yom
Friend	Sa-hib, Sa-deek.		Night	Layl
Water	Moya		Half	Nuss
Food	Akl		Half a day	Nuss il Nahaar
Village	Balaad		Near	Gareeb
Tired	Ta-eban		Far	Baeed

Take me to the English and you will be rewarded.	{ Hud nee eind el Ingleez wa tahud { Mu-ka-fa.
English Flying Officer	Za-bit Ingleezi Tye-yara
How far (how many kilos?)	Kam kilo ?
Enemy	Germani, Taliani, Siziliani

Distance and time: Remember, Slow & Sure does it

The older Arabs cannot read, write or tell the time. They measure distance by the number
of days journey. "Near" may mean 10 minutes or 10 hours. Far probably means over a days
journey. A days journey is probably about 30 miles. The younger Arabs are more accurate.

GOOD LUCK

A LETTER FROM THE BRITISH GOVERNMENT

shouted out to us and to the other airmen standing about their tents, "Catch that bloody pig. He's your Christmas dinner!"

The aircrew sergeants formed a circle to trap the elusive pig. He wasn't greased, but he was still hard to catch. It was obvious from the doomed creature's wild eyes and terrified squeal that he knew very well what was up. I couldn't believe the speed he attained in the soft sand. He plunged between our legs and bowled over one pursuer who fell flat on his face but managed to hold onto a leg. The triumphant cook pounced on the poor beast. Grabbing him by the snout, he plunged the long blade of his knife into the pig's throat and down into its chest. Its piercing death shriek haunted me for some time afterwards. What price Christmas dinner!

That Christmas Eve, I sat down on my straw mattress in our tent, and by the light of the coal oil lamp tried to write a letter home. We had been given aerograms, which had a postcard size space for address and text. With the censorship it was difficult to know what to say, except that I was all right, and hoped that they were as well. Any mention of squadron or location or operations would be deleted. Some parents received letters with so many cut-outs that the paper looked like lace.

I lay back on my straw bed, with my head on a pillow made from my folded bomber jacket, and mused silently about the sequence of events that had brought me to this, my second Christmas away from home. I thought that the other members of my crew, and indeed most of the other crews in the other tents, were likely thinking the same thoughts, and wondering too if they would see another Christmas.

■ ■ ■

Christmas Day started with a line-up at the communal shower pipe and progressed to drinks at the bar of our mess tent. Our enterprising Aussie mess committee president had bribed an Egyptian in Suez to truck ice to us for our drinks. Packed in straw, the ice had not begun to melt when it arrived at the mess. It was a real luxury.

Christmas dinner was served in the dining tent. I looked at my plate — roast pork! The last cry of the poor pig who gave his life for our dinner rang again in my ears. I couldn't eat one bite of that meat. I contented myself with potatoes and beans and a white bun that appeared to have caraway seeds in it. I remarked that the bun was quite gritty but had a nutty taste to it. The older hands grinned and informed me with sadistic pleasure that those little seeds were flour weevils. I tried to pick them out but this reduced the bun to sawdust. Eventually I gave up like the rest and ate them along with the sand that got into most of our food. In any event, the weevils were reputed to be a good source of protein.

Our Christmas ended in tragedy. After too many beers in the mess, one of our Canadians, a Sgt W, stole a truck from the transport compound. He talked an inebriated Jimmy Chalmers into going with him on a wild ride down one of the perimeter roads of the airfield. Sgt W lost control and the truck rolled over in a ditch. He received minor injuries. Jimmy was killed.

This tragic incident cast a pall over our little village. Jimmy had been well liked. It put an end to any further Christmas celebration. Sgt W was charged and placed under close arrest awaiting courtmartial. He was eventually convicted, sent back to England, dismissed dishonourably from the service, and sentenced to several years in the penitentiary.

My second Christmas away from home had given little cause for celebration. This whole affair seemed like an end to a chapter for us in the Middle East, and so it turned out to be. Five days later we took off on our first operational flight with our new squadron.

It was a totally different war we entered — Britain's Eighth Army needed all the help we could give them in its desperate defensive battle to keep Rommel from taking all of Egypt. Our crew was ready.

18
IN SUPPORT OF EIGHTH ARMY

ON 30 DECEMBER, AT 0900 HOURS, our squadron was called to the briefing room. Robbie joined us in the crowded room, and we sat near the front row casting our eyes over the large map of the Mediterranean Sea that formed the backdrop for the stage.

Bill leaned over to whisper to Robbie and me, "I've been told that we're getting a screen pilot for this op, a Flight Sergeant Burr. It means leaving Will behind. I'm not happy about this, but there isn't anything I can do." We were not happy about it either. We didn't think Bill needed any help or guidance, new theatre of ops or not.

Wing Commander Rainsford, our squadron CO, was there, and said a few words about getting back to our tasks after Christmas, and the need to give some support to the navy and, indirectly, to Eighth Army. The briefing officer then gave us our target. We were to bomb the dock area of the small town of Salamis, which was part of the harbour facilities of Athens, Greece. German vessels would be loading there to resupply Rommel's Afrika Korps.

The weather briefing was not encouraging. We were in the midst of the Mediterranean winter storm period. We were warned to monitor our radios closely in case we were sent a recall message. In my separate wireless briefing I had been given the frequencies and codes for the night.

The Wimpy did not have the range with a full load of bombs to reach any of our current targets in the Med or further west to the Benghazi area. For this reason, forward airfields, or Advanced Landing Grounds (ALGs) as they were called, had been established in the Western Desert at distances varying from 250 to 450 miles westward from Kabrit. We were to become familiar with ALGs 09, 060, 075, 104, and 106.

Most of these ALGs were situated on dried-up salt lakes, the flat, hard surfaces of which provided smooth runways stretching in some cases over a mile or two. Large petrol drums, filled with a combustible mixture of sand, oil, and petrol, were used for runway lighting. These were lit by hand, and could be smothered in a hurry to avoid detection. Landings at night were usually no problem, but daylight sun turned the shiny surface into a shimmering mirror that distorted the depth perception of the pilots and caused some bumpy landings.

There was no bombing-up here. We carried our bomb load from base, and had to land fully and lethally loaded. Even if the bombs were not armed for dropping, it was an unwelcome procedure. When we carried the extremely sensitive 4,000-pound "cookie," we could feel the tension on the landing approach. Shortly before our arrival, another bomber had come in for a rough landing, and its cookie had detonated, blowing the crew to bits.

There was a maintenance crew of erks on detachment at each site to refuel the bombers and to provide whatever light repairs were required. There were no creature comforts. The erks lived in tents, and since there was not even a mess tent, they prepared their own basic meals of tinned sausage, beans, or bully beef. These men were truly unsung heroes of the desert campaign. How they managed to make the repairs to engines and airframes that kept us flying we could never fathom. The constantly blowing sand covered tools, got into every crack and crevice on the human body, and penetrated instruments, engines, and hydraulic systems, aggravating the primitive and harsh conditions under which they laboured. It made maintenance a nightmarish task. One of the erks, who probably worked on airframes, is credited with this verse:

THE FITTER'S LAMENT
We the willing, led by the unknowing, have done
the impossible, for so long with so little, we are
now qualified to do anything with nothing.

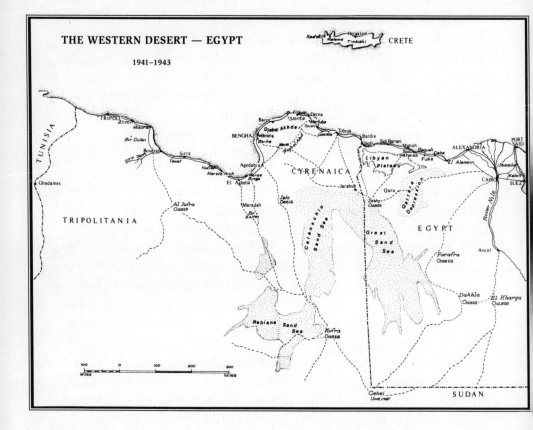

The morning flight to the ALG was followed on the same day by the night bombing of the target, but on the long return flight the crews needed rest before the flight back to base. We slept where we could, either on the floor of the aircraft in winter, and under the wings during the summer months. The winter nights were perishingly cold, and even in summer the nights were cold enough to require our fur-lined bomber jackets. The sand did not hold the daytime heat. We were not issued with sleeping bags. I couldn't understand why there was no provision for meals or for sleeping accommodation for the aircrews. Altogether, it was a punishing regime.

■ ■ ■

As it happened, after two hours on our first operational flight in the Middle East, we had to turn back because of storms before reaching our ALG.

It wasn't until 2 January 1942 that we were briefed again for the same target. This time we stayed overnight at ALG 060 and took off from there for Salamis. An hour and a half into that flight we ran into turbulent, stormy weather that cut visibility to zero, and made it quite unlikely that we would ever see the target even if we reached it. Fortunately, I picked up the coded broadcast ordering all aircraft to return to base, in this case back to ALG 060, for another cold night on bare flight rations. Some operators failed to pick up the recall message, and wasted their time and fuel for another few hours before giving up.

Ops were on again for 25 January, and again we were given a screen pilot, this time a Pilot Officer Crossley. Crews were given separate targets. Ours was Agedabia, in Libya, some twenty-five miles inland from the Gulf of Sidra, due south of Benghazi. This was one of Rommel's major tank and transport parks, and our job was to destroy as much of it as we could with low-level attacks, in what was hoped would be bright moonlight. Our 250-pound bombs were "rodded" — fitted with foot-long rods inserted into the nose. The rods would strike the ground first, detonating the bombs above ground, giving the greatest spread to the blast and shrapnel fragments. This caused the maximum damage to vehicles and to personnel.

Agedabia was over eleven hours flying time from Kabrit, so we had to refuel at the farthest western ALG, No. 075, to give us the range to reach our target. It was 2200 hours in a clear night sky when we roared down the flare path at 075 and lifted off with our captain, Bill Dixon, again in the unfamiliar right seat.

We had no electronic navigation aids like GEE, but navigation over the desert was usually uncomplicated. Unlike in European skies, nights were most often clear. There were no desert landmarks for visual pin-points unless over the coast, but stars were available for astro shots; the abundance of stars in that latitude made it difficult to identify the stars listed in the log. For course corrections because of varying winds, Robbie simply had me throw out a four-pound incendiary, day or night. Doug, in his rear turret, would then take a sighting on the smoke puff or fire flash and call out the degrees of starboard or port drift. The flat edge of the rotating ring of his gun turret was marked off in degrees starboard (green) and port (red) for this purpose.

My wireless work was also different from what I had experienced in Europe. I didn't have to fight to get a turn with a ground station on crowded airwaves. There simply weren't as many bombers in the stream to and from the targets. But there were fewer stations available for bearings to assist with the navigation, and seldom any broadcast signal useful for passive loop bearings. Our return flights to base were nearly always made in daylight, however, and map reading over the Nile delta region was simple. But target-bombing messages to base and monitoring frequencies for reports remained a critical exercise.

Three hours from the ALG Robbie announced that we were only a few miles from our target, and P/O Crossley started our descent to 1,000 feet. I scrambled back to the mid-fuselage position where we now had a single .303 Browning fitted on mounts in each of the port and starboard windows. The gunner sat on a swivel seat in the middle of the catwalk so that he could swing from one gun to the other as the aircraft swung about over low-level targets. This position was now my responsibility.

The night wasn't quite as clear as expected, but Robbie called out from his bomb-aiming position that he could see the transport park ahead. Our pilot announced that he was making the bomb run, and Robbie started giving his heading corrections. Crossley told the gunners that we were not to open fire on the ground vehicles until the bombs were released. We were suddenly greeted by a poorly directed barrage of medium and light flak. This park was well defended by 88s and many lighter calibre anti-aircraft guns. With Robbie's "Bombs gone!" I joined Tony and Doug to spray the ground with armour-piercing and incendiary bullets. We were much too high to see what we were aiming at, and I had no expectation that I was doing any damage to anything. But it all added to the fireworks.

As we pulled up and banked sharply away from the area, our stick of twelve 250-pound bombs exploded above ground and sent successive expanding shockwaves out over the desert ground, momentarily bathing the whole area in a brilliant yellow light. We were followed by the last of the flak, which had come close to our aircraft but failed to put a hole in us. Robbie and I got back to our seats, and after a few minutes Robbie gave our captain a course for home. I prepared to send my "target bombed" message. Here again, unlike our European ops, we were hardly ever given a secondary target. We were usually stretching our fuel capacity to reach our primary target, so there were seldom any worthwhile secondary targets within our range.

We landed at ALG 075 at 0300 hours the following morning and rested there until 0900 hours when we hopped to ALGs 09 and 104 before returning to base. None of us ever figured out the reason for these short visits. Our debriefing was routine, with P/O Crossley and Robbie claiming to have placed the bombs within the bounds of the extensive transport park. Our screen pilot had not been much of a communicator with us at any stage of the flight, and we were not to fly with him again. Bill was particularly happy with this; he had not been impressed with Crossley's flying. Neither did he think that Crossley had placed our bombs anywhere near the centre of the tank park as planned.

A few hours flying and three days later, we came upon a DRO notice on one of the tent poles of the sergeants' mess that was to lead to a shocking affair, and would shake up not only the whole squadron, but the whole station and Command Headquarters.

19
A FINE LINE
TO MUTINY

THE POOR ENVIRONMENT IN WHICH WE LIVED and flew at Kabrit created a growing tension, which would soon throw us into a most unsettling predicament.

When flying operations from bases in the United Kingdom, aircrews returned to comparatively comfortable living quarters, and their frayed spirits were mended by visits to the nearby pubs and by the companionship of WAAFs. Living quarters for crews in the Middle East, however, were Spartan to an extreme, and there was no female companionship. Nor was there any entertainment other than the station cinema, the bar in our sergeants' mess tent, and whatever we could find to do on our infrequent leaves in Cairo.

On our Middle East operations we suffered much less from German night-fighter attacks en route to and returning from targets than we did when bombing Europe. But our flights were much longer, and the hostile reception we received over targets such as Benghazi equalled the intensity of targets in Germany.

We also suffered from lack of leadership. While much has been written about RAF leadership inspiring squadrons and individuals to reach great heights of endeavour, less can be found about quality of leadership of bomber squadrons. Many squadron commanders, especially those of fighter squadrons personally leading their flock in daylight against the enemy, provided great inspiration. But commanders of bomber squadrons had less opportunity to impose their personality on their aircrews. They did participate in target briefings, and they could be a positive and strengthening influence if they offered themselves as examples or role models by flying frequently on the more dangerous operations. But once the bombers left the ground the crews were on their own in the darkness of the night, and the only leadership that counted or existed was that of their captain.

From my perspective as an aircrew sergeant, the exercise of leadership was confined largely to officers. In the officers' mess there was frequent opportunity for senior officers to impose their personality and character upon the junior aircrew officers, whereas in the sergeants' mess there was no such opportunity. In Britain, in fact, the senior warrant officers and NCOs in our mess were non-flying airmen, usually permanent force, some of whom looked with disdain upon the aircrew who wore only token sergeant stripes. At Kabrit, NCOs in that category were not members of our mess; they had their own mess in a more comfortable and better-equipped wooden building at the main camp.

At Kabrit, I cannot remember that any officer ever visited our tent village to inquire about our welfare. The only senior airman to visit us was Warrant Officer Streeter, a regular force RAF airman, not aircrew, whom we felt had earned the nickname we had pinned on him — "Louie the Rat." He usually visited our tents only to censure us for some infraction or other or to interfere with whatever actions we had taken on our own initiative to try to better our living conditions.

One example in particular illustrates the mean spirit of Louie the Rat. Knowing that we were sleeping on the sand, two enterprising erks of the maintenance section scavenged enough wood from the station dump to make up eight or ten beds, which they offered to us for sale. They covered the bed frame with a stout burlap, and strengthened the covering with strong fibre cross-straps. Our crew was quick to take advantage of this opportunity to get off the ground, and we found that, with our straw mattresses, the beds were quite comfortable. Our euphoria was short-lived. Louie discovered the enterprise and placed the two entrepreneurs on charge for taking material unlawfully from the dump. He also ordered our beds returned to the dump.

Somehow, our resourceful and persuasive captain managed to strike a deal with the Rat for the return of our beds. I believe the deal involved some captured German weapons that had fallen into his possession.

Our tribulations were not quite over. We awakened from our first night in our new beds covered with bites — the wood was infested with bed bugs! Fortunately, one day's soaking in the heavily salted Bitter Lake purged our new bunks of these vermin and we had no further problems.

The station commander, Group Captain Fall, a veteran of the First World War, was an anachronistic leader in the operational environment of this modern war. His occasional actions helped to create the climate in which conduct to the prejudice of good order and discipline was likely to occur.

On one occasion as I walked up the road from our tent camp to the main base, properly dressed in tunic and cap, our station commander drove by and stopped his staff car. He approached me with a stern look in his eye. I saluted, of course, and he responded by upbraiding me for sporting an unpolished brass button. I tried to explain, truthfully, that this particular button was pitted and would not take a shine. This irritated him even more, and he placed me on charge for being improperly dressed. He ordered me to report to the station warrant officer for punishment.

For my offence, I was ordered to spend two nights in a six-foot-tall square box on top of the station water tower, ostensibly as an air raid observer to sound the alarm in case of a German bombing attack, an utterly useless exercise. The bombs would fall a few seconds after I could raise an alarm. These were cold, eight-hour vigils with no company other than huge rats that arrived periodically to sniff me.

Three days later I was appointed the "Prisoner of War Sergeant of the day" and given instructions to pick up two truckloads of Italian prisoners from the huge POW compound near Ismailia, at the north end of the Great Bitter Lake. The Italians were brought to the base frequently to work on runway repair and construction. German prisoners were never so employed; they were too unruly and rebellious.

I was given the drivers of two stake trucks and two erks armed with rifles and bayonets. I wore my Enfield revolver in its holster.

At Ismailia, after showing my identity card to the Ghurkas who were guarding the main gate of the compound, I left the trucks to be loaded with prisoners, to be selected by other Ghurkas inside the camp walls.

I wandered over to the high wire fence where some German prisoners were lounging. I had studied German for a couple of years and decided to try some basic conversation with one. Before I could open my mouth, the German facing me spit at me through the wire, hitting me. In an angry, split-second reaction I grabbed my revolver from its holster and put pressure on the trigger before some rational thought intervened to stop me from raising the gun higher. I don't know what stopped me; in my then stressful state of mind I very nearly shot the German prisoner. The consequences would have been calamitous.

I had recovered my sanity, but I still had to do something in return. I worked up as much saliva as I could, and spit back through the wire at my offender. What luck — I hit him right in the face! I believe he would have been less furious if I had shot him. Feeling rather satisfied with this small victory over the enemy, I walked back to take charge of the two trucks, now filled with Italian soldiers, and began the drive back to Kabrit.

On arrival at the base, I formed the prisoners up into two sections, each with one of the erks guarding them, and marched at the head of my little army down the main road to the runways where they would be put to work. Halfway to the workplace, I turned to look over my charges and found one of the Italians holding a rifle with the bayonet about two feet from my posterior. The erk had tired of carrying his rifle and had given it to one of the prisoners! I couldn't believe it. If that had been a German prisoner, instead of an Italian, I might well have been run through with the bayonet. Because of what we had been going through, I didn't have the will or inclination to charge this erk as he well deserved, but contented myself with dressing him down with the most caustic words I could bring to mind.

■ ■ ■

The morning of 29 January 1942 was unseasonably hot. Bill Dixon and I decided to make our way to the sergeants' mess. Inside the tent we found a group of sergeants clustered around one of the main tent poles in a state of great agitation. No wonder. We read the notice pinned to the pole: "All aircrew are to report, properly dressed, to the Station Warrant Officer's office at 1300 hours." Most of us had been flying on ops during the preceding week, and some had just returned that morning. We were supposed to have at least one day of rest after an op, and most of us were highly suspicious of this unusual order. Nevertheless, the squadron NCOs reported on time as ordered.

Nearly fifty of us assembled in loose order outside the SWO's office. A flight sergeant "discip" paraded us to the station armoury and told us to draw rifles for rifle drill. He was told firmly that we were sergeants, and sergeants carried revolvers, not rifles. The impasse was broken when Warrant Officer Streeter — Louie the Rat — arrived. Once Louie had our muttering and unruly group lined up in some semblance of order on the parade square, he announced that the station commander had said that we, the squadron NCO aircrews, needed smartening up, and gave orders that we were to do rifle drill. He added that he, Warrant Officer Streeter, was going to see that we did just that.

As I stood there in the heat among my squadron comrades, I reflected that, yes, we probably were a motley-looking group most of the time. But the conditions under which we were living in our tents made it well nigh impossible to live up to the spit and polish image the station commander dreamed about. We were not there to parade, we were there to fly on ops, and to die, and we were doing both. I thought that, discipline and authority notwithstanding, the warrant officer was indulging in some marked wishful thinking if he thought he was going to get this group to do rifle drill, especially in front of the numerous erks sitting about off-duty in front of the hangars.

At Louie's command, "Order arms," one of the Australians in our group rudely told the warrant officer where he could shove his rifle, and threw his weapon with a great clatter onto the asphalt. "That man," screamed Louie, "report to the guard room, under close arrest!"

That order ignited our volatile group like a match thrown into a barrel of gun powder. Nearly fifty rifles hit the ground with a resounding crash that echoed off the hangar walls. Quite apart from our rebellion against the preposterous rifle drill, the majority must have thought as I did that if we let our Aussie friend go it alone he was going to be crucified. Surely there was some safety in numbers.

We ignored Louie's orders to remain on the parade square and, except for a few individuals weren't sure quite that to do, we marched en masse behind the Aussie to the guard room and demanded that *all* of us be placed under close arrest.

The station adjutant, who had been summoned to deal with the crisis, quickly realized that placing our whole group under arrest was impossible. King's Regulations for Air prescribed that a person under close arrest must always be escorted by two persons of equal or superior rank, and as we made up the bulk of the squadron there were nowhere near enough senior NCOs to perform this duty. He had to settle for placing us under open arrest, a condition requiring no escorts. We would be in this state until our disciplinary cases could be dealt with by the proper authority.

Not one of us was proud of our lapse in discipline on the parade square. We were part of the military system, and we believed in it. Our actions were an aberration. They were not brought on by the strain of flying operations or the casualties we suffered. Nor were they directly the result of the desert environment, which made our living conditions so harsh. Without exception, we accepted all of this as part of the "contract" we had entered into of our own free will. Our morale was sustained because we believed fervently in what we were doing. The cause was right. We also drew strength from our pride in our individual skill and the skill and comradeship of the members of our crew. No, the only explanation for our intransigence was that a long period of minor abuse and a lack of caring, a condition of "negative leadership," culminated in an order to do rifle drill which, in the midst of our operational flying against the enemy, would have been considered by most squadron commanders of the day to be outrageous.

When we arrived back at our sergeants' mess tent, we found a very distraught squadron commander, Wing Commander Rainsford, waiting for us. When he calmed down, we told him with one voice that we wanted to keep on flying, whether or not we were under open arrest. He told us that this would be possible. I believe he was impressed with our spirit, if not with our conduct.*

King's Regulations also prescribed that a formal charge and description of the offence had to be made within forty-eight hours of the infraction. This effectively put us into a state of limbo, and added to the palpable tension that this fiasco had created.

Early the next morning, a rumour circulated that any squadron VRs who had participated in the previous day's misconduct were to be charged with mutiny. These men were members of the peacetime Volunteer Reserve, an auxiliary arm of the RAF, who were automatically

---

* In May 1993, at a 148 Sqn reunion held at RAF Station Marham, Air Cdr F.F. "Turkey" Rainsford, CBE DFC, joined our group of surviving "mutineers," and told us that he had always blamed us for costing him the Distinguished Service Order usually awarded to squadron commanders at the end of their tour. He died 13 February 1999, at age 89.

called up at the outbreak of war. Apparently, because they had some experience in the service and therefore ought to have known the rules better than the civilian volunteers, an example was to be made of them.

If true, this was a shocking development, and the threat heightened the tension in our little tent village to near-electric levels. The charge of "mutiny while on active service" could bring the death penalty! Our own crew was in the forefront of the general anxiety because one of the four VRs in the squadron was our own rear gunner, Doug Chinnery.

We held several meetings to discuss our plight. We reached the consensus that we could not let our VR comrades be singled out for extraordinary punishment. We could not accept the idea that these men, who had been flying against the enemy with disregard for their own lives, would be subjected to court martial and possibly sentenced to death.

The tension pushed some thoughts to illogical extremes. Our group had collected a veritable arsenal of various types of weapons. There were Luger automatic pistols by the dozen (I had one myself), German Mauser rifles, and even an Italian light machine gun on a tripod mount. We had considerable ammunition for each gun. More than a few of us vowed that these weapons might be used if there was an attempt to take our VRs away for trial separate from the main group.

For the most part, these weapons had been given to us by the NCOs of the New Zealand Maori 28th Battalion,* whose rest camp was situated just five miles down the road from our airfield. On frequent occasions, we had hosted NCO members of that very battle-tested battalion in our sergeants' mess. These were welcomed parties, often featuring a so-called Maori war dance known as the "Haka." The Maori shared with us their renowned voices at some great singing performances. Their leader was a Warrant Officer Waitiri Lloyd, who told me that he often sang on the radio in New Zealand.

Because of this camaraderie, our friends were upset when they heard of our predicament and there was talk that they might even join in our resistance to any extreme punishment of our VRs — such were the lengths to which the affair was driving our thoughts while we sat out the two days waiting for judgment.

On the second day of our suspense, we were surprised by the arrival at our tent site of an Australian air vice-marshal who was on the staff of Air Force Headquarters in Cairo. He had heard of the incident, and

---

* In the second and main battle of El Alamein, in October, the 28th Maori Battalion was almost wiped out.

because a countryman had been placed in custody awaiting court martial as the leading actor in the "revolt," decided to investigate for himself.

The A/V/M sat among us with the lack of pretension typical of Aussie senior officers, and listened to our stories of the event. Apparently satisfied, he advised us to keep our emotions under control, and suggested that we ought not to fear the worst. Altogether, this was an unusual but comforting visit from an understanding and compassionate senior officer.

On the third day following "the incident," the suspense was broken when we were officially informed that each one of us who had participated in the breach of discipline was charged with "conduct to the prejudice of good order and discipline." This was a serious enough charge, especially on active service, but it was nowhere near the fateful charge of "mutiny." There was a collective, almost audible, sigh of relief when it was confirmed that our VRs were included in the group charge.

Having been officially charged, we would have to wait until 4 March before facing the station commander to hear our punishment.

By 4 March we had a new squadron commander, Wing Commander Rawlinson. Louie the Rat had disappeared; we heard that he had been demoted to permanent corporal. Group Captain Fall soon returned to England; it was rumoured that he had retired. The Aussie who had touched off the "revolt" had been dealt with expeditiously. He was reduced to the ranks by court martial and sentenced to thirty days in the "glasshouse," a military prison. He served his sentence on his immediate return to Australia. In the interim, we put the affair behind us and got on with our jobs. Before our sentencing, our crew carried out six bombing raids. In the history of air warfare, our unit had the unenviable distinction of being the only squadron the bulk of whose members were flying on operations against the enemy while under open arrest.

20
THE MAIL RUN

WITHIN A FEW DAYS OF our small-scale rebellion, we were out again pounding the tank and transport parks of the Afrika Korps. Rommel had reopened his offensive, and on 23 January had retaken Agedabia, which became once again a major assembly point for supplies, trucks, and armour.

On 2 and 5 February, our crew bombed the Agedabia area. These were both low-level attacks. Again, we had "rodded" bombs, which did satisfyingly widespread damage to equipment in the assembly area. On the latter raid, where we concentrated on a particularly heavy assembly of German armour on the Agedabia–El Agheila road, we were roughly shaken up by a heavy barrage of medium and light flak. While Tony, Doug, and I sprayed the ground with our Brownings, not only to damage vehicles but in an attempt to suppress some of the anti-aircraft fire, Bill threw our Wimpy about in bone-shaking turns to escape from the ground fire.

Bill's skill took us out of the flames and dense smoke we had ignited, and kept us at low level until we were clear of the area and could more safely climb to altitude for our long flight home. As usual, these flights required us to spend at least one night at one of our ALGs; in this case ALG 09. This meant a total of nine to ten hours in the air.

Once I had returned to my radios from the mid-gun position and had sent off the "bombed target" message to base operations, I had time to reflect on the raid. When we had dropped our lethal load on our targets in Europe in the dark of night from great altitudes, we could well imagine, of course, the damage our bombs were doing, but our minds shrank away from the pictures of shattered bodies that tried to invade our thoughts. It seemed an impersonal act; the enemy was faceless. But out here, on this very low-level raid in the startling brightness of the desert moonlight, I was able to follow the path of my bullets as they struck vehicles and the German troops trying to take cover from the deadly spray of metal. My God, I could see the faces of the soldiers! I was disturbed by this intimate contact with the enemy and what I had inflicted upon them, even though they were doing their best to shoot us down. I had not experienced this before. My war had become much more personal, and I would have to harden myself to it even more from here onwards.

With two days rest, Bill took us off for ALG 09 and the beginning of what were to seem like endless raids on the Libyan port of Benghazi. We were joining earlier squadrons such as 37, 38, and 70, whose members originated the mail run to Benghazi, immortalized in the 70 Sqn song. We asked ourselves the same rhetorical question posed in the song's chorus:

Must we do this bloody mail run
Every night till we die?

Three hours flying from the ALG, in a clear, star-filled, and moonlit night, took us near the Agedabia area, which we overflew into the Gulf of Sidra before turning north towards our target.

Cloud was starting to build up over the Gulf, and I watched fascinated and speechless from the astro dome as we entered a seemingly endless corridor buttressed by towering walls of cloud turned varying shades of purple and dark green by the moon's rays. Tall, greenish-white spires rose from the tops of the purple masses and turned these sculptured clouds on either side of us into celestial cathedrals. The ethereal beauty of this scene was awesome. It struck me that there was something acutely incongruous, and somehow godless, about flying down this heavenly hallway loaded with 500-pound bombs ready to blow to bits the people and ships in the harbour of Benghazi.

I had barely shaken off the impact of this scene when we left the clouds behind and reached the turning point for our run to the target. Bill called out to all the crew, "All right everybody, we're turning for our run to the target. Robbie, you had better go forward, now. I want everyone to keep a sharp eye out for fighters. We're probably going to get a lot of flak when we get closer."

I scrambled back to take my place in the astro dome. There was little or no cloud to offer us any cover from the bright moonlight, which offered almost daylight visibility. The port of Benghazi was dead-ahead and the details were coming into focus as we roared in from seawards at 5,000 feet. The large map we had been shown at briefing was clear in my mind, and we could all see the two long moles (massive piers or breakwaters formed of masonry and large stones, layered with concrete) that snaked out from the shore to form a harbour and anchorage for the ships. They were named the Juliana and Cathedral moles. The ships alongside them and the warehouses on the docks were our targets. The features of this port were to become very familiar to us.

Fires were already burning in the dock area from attacks by other Wimpys, two of which we could see getting away from the scene.

Two miles from the docks, Robbie started his bombing patter. We were suddenly greeted by the familiar dirty brown puffs of flak. By the time Robbie shouted, "Bombs gone!" we were enveloped in the thunder of the exploding shells and rocked by the shockwaves the bursts created. It seemed to take forever to reach the outer limits of this fierce barrage. Smoke and the usual smell of cordite filled the cabin.

As we cleared the target area on a course inland, Robbie called Bill to say that it had been a good run. Our bombs had landed on the Juliana mole and had run across the dock area. There were explosions and fire! With an affirmative from the crew that everyone was okay, Bill remarked that it was our first run at storied Benghazi, and that the flak was what we had been told to expect. He added that, for our low-level attack, it was heavy stuff. In his opinion, the Germans or Italians had short-fused their heavy shells.*

---

* Shells were set by a timed fuse to explode at certain altitudes. Inserting a shorter-timed fuse would cause the shells to explode at a lower altitude.

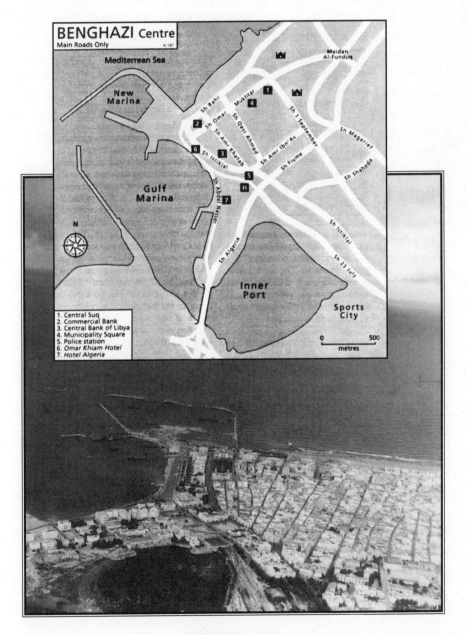

BENGHAZI CITY CENTRE

"Home" for what remained of the night was ALG 09. Three hours later, we landed there and tried to get some rest on the floor of the aircraft. Despite our fur-lined leather flying jackets, the bone-chilling desert cold denied us sleep. In any case, two and a half hours later, we were refuelled and off again for the two-hour flight to base. Debriefing was quick; the intelligence officer was pleased with the report Bill and Robbie gave him.

Two weeks later we repeated the raid with almost identical results with bombs on the harbour, but before we took off yet again on the mail run, the station personnel were surprised by a most unusual visitor. Little did we know that our crew was to figure prominently in the purpose of this visit.

During the last week of February all station personnel were ordered to parade on the main station square, properly dressed, at 1300 hours. When we were all assembled in a large U-shape formation, we faced a raised dais covered in a red carpet. There was a formal-looking table and chairs arrangement, the whole platform being sheltered from the sun by a canvas screen.

We were brought to attention as a large party of officers and guests ascended the dais. The station band played a national anthem unfamiliar to us — it certainly wasn't the Egyptian anthem — followed by the British anthem. An air vice-marshal held his salute while standing beside his guest, a tall, bearded man with a commanding presence, resplendent in colourful, regal-looking Arab robes. The station commander, squadron commanders, and at least ten members of the visiting Arab group stood behind them.

The A/V/M gave a speech welcoming our distinguished guest, whom he identified as King Abdul-Aziz ibn Sa'ud of Saudi Arabia. What a surprise this was! He then announced that His Majesty was here to formally purchase a 4,000-pound bomb to be dropped on our common enemy.* The king then gave a short speech in creditable English praising the British war effort and the men of our station. As the band played suitable ceremonial music, three Wellingtons flew past overhead, followed by a low-level sweep by a Beaufighter.

---

* Our royal visitor was not all that he seemed. The British were not fully aware of the strong pro-Axis sentiment among members of the Sa'udi family. Indeed, months before the outbreak of the war, the king had entered into arms agreements with both Germany and Italy. But the buying of the bomb was one of many modest overtures the skilful monarch made to prove his loyalty to Great Britain and her allies, whom he predicted would be the eventual victors. As one historian was later to remark, "Abdul Aziz ibn Sa'ud was clearly adept at being all things to all men."

Then something went drastically wrong. As the Beaufighter approached the parade square at less than 200 feet altitude, its 20mm guns opened up with a staccato burst so loud that it overpowered the band's efforts. The royal party flung themselves to the floor of the dais in a reflex action as the shells ricocheted with a terrible clatter off the corrugated tin roof of a nearby shed. The fighter kept on its course and disappeared.

This put a heavy damper on the afternoon's ceremony, but the senior officers did their best to reassure and placate the royal party. This probably speeded up the closing remarks and our dismissal from the parade square. A few weeks later, a story circulated that the wing commander who had been flying the Beaufighter had accidentally pressed the firing button, and that he had since disappeared from his squadron. No doubt he had been returned to Britain.

On 1 March, most of the crews of 148 Sqn were assembled for briefing. The target was again Benghazi. Our route was little different than that given to the other crews, but our bomb load wasn't the same. Instead of the usual load of 250-lb or 500-lb bombs, we were to carry a 4,000-pound bomb, the "cookie." Bill was told that this was the bomb bought in the symbolic gesture by King Ibn Sa'ud. Why were we selected? I suppose we ought to have considered it some kind of honour. It didn't impress us that way, but we had to think that it did reflect the squadron commander's confidence in our crew, mainly in our captain, of course.

We were given a special briefing by the armament officer. The bomb was a delayed-action bomb, which had to be dropped into the water. Instead of being fitted with an instantaneous fuse, the bomb was fitted with an acid bottle and a fuse cut to a specific length. On impact with the water, the acid bottle was designed to break, allowing the acid to eat away at the fuse. The length of the fuse determined the interval between impact and the explosion. On this particular raid, the length of the fuse was fixed so that the explosion would take place shortly after the arrival of a major convoy from Italy. It was therefore critical that our ETA (estimated time of arrival) over the Benghazi harbour was precisely that specified in our briefing.

What was also critical, and a potential for disaster, was the necessity to place the bomb close to the Juliana mole, but in the water. To do this we would have to go in at low level, and if the bomb was to hit the concrete mole it would explode from the impact and likely blow our aircraft (and us) to pieces. Low-level attacks at Benghazi were hazardous enough without this added peril.

Because of the danger of landing at the ALG with the 4,000-pound bomb in our Wimpy's belly, the acid bottle and fuse were installed by armourers at the advanced desert base.

On 1 March at 1600 hours, we joined several other Wimpys of our squadron at ALG 09. As we were refuelled and the armourers worked on our bomb, we were informed that our attack schedule had been changed, no doubt by intelligence reports on the convoy, and that our raid was to take place the following night. This meant that we would have to spend a cold night at the advanced base along with the other aircrews.

For the first time, we did not have Robbie with us. He was ill, and for this flight we had been given navigator John Mahood, who had trained with Robbie at Winnipeg.

The next night we took off at the unusually late hour of 23:10, glad to get into the warmth of our cabin. We had more unpleasant surprises ahead of us than we had bargained for.

Four hours later, as we made our turn from seawards towards the Benghazi harbour, we were silhouetted nakedly against a moonlit sky. We could see fires burning in the dock area, and smoke from flak thrown at the Wimpys that had bombed ahead of us hung over the area.

As John went forward to his bomb sight, Bill called out to us, "Okay, chaps, here we go. This is going to be tricky. Keep your eyes peeled." We dived steeply as we got down to our bomb-run altitude of a mere 4,000 feet. John had to have a steady run-up if he was to place our cookie where it had to go, so we were more vulnerable than usual to the dense, angry curtain of flak that now greeted us. We knew from the heavy bursts at this low altitude that they were short-fusing their heavy shells again, but the medium stuff, which came up in a swarm like thousands of ferocious gnats, seemed even more lethal.

As John gave heading corrections on our bomb run, Bill suddenly shouted, "We're overshooting! Drop the bloody bomb now or I'll have to jettison!"*

It was a blessed relief to all of us when John instantly called out, "Bombs gone!" but at that moment we went into an unexpected violent dive.

Bill yelled out, "Something's jammed the controls! Will, get back there and find it!" But Bill quickly gave up on Will and ordered him

---

* The pilot had a toggle switch on his instrument panel with which he could override the navigator's control of the bomb drop and jettison the entire bomb load.

back to take over the controls. Bill then caught up with me as I was searching frantically for the cause, and we found a four-pound incendiary bomb jamming the assembly for the starboard wing aileron. It had obviously slipped from its stowage near the pull-down bed. Bill yanked it out with all his strength, and immediately Will was able to level the Wimpy out. But as Bill took over the controls we had fallen to barely 900 feet over the harbour, and the medium flak and the searchlights had us bracketed. Bill cried out to us to grab our parachutes because it looked as if we might have to bail out. At that I had the strangest thought — not "will my chute open?" but, "My God, that black water in the bay is going to be cold when we hit it!"

As Bill struggled to get us out of what seemed to all of us a fatal predicament, one of the departing Wimpys obviously saw the trouble we were in and turned back over the harbour. I watched as he turned on all his navigation and landing lights in an attempt to draw fire away from us. This was an incredible act of cold courage! He had escaped from the target area, but deliberately turned back into a sky filled with exploding shells to help us. He did draw fire from us, and Bill pulled us out of our plight to skim low over the town and into the black desert. I had time to see that our rescuer had also escaped from the target area, and thanked God that he was safe. How our minds would have been plagued if he had not survived his brave act.*

As we cleared the area and gained altitude for the three-hour flight back to ALG 09, John said he was certain that our bomb had landed right where it was supposed to be planted. He and Bill had a right to be proud of themselves.

After another frigid night in the desert, we arrived back at base to a lengthy debriefing by the intelligence officers. They were pleased with our results, but had a very strange story to tell us. The armourers at the ALG had discovered that they did not have the correct length of fuse for our bomb. To solve (really, to hide) their dilemma they inserted a shorter fuse. This meant that our bomb would explode some six hours before the expected arrival of the convoy.

A week later we were told that by some quirk of weather and sea conditions the enemy convoy had arrived earlier than our intelligence had predicted, and that our "improperly fused" bomb had exploded

---

* Bill reported this courageous act to the intelligence officer. That captain, who we discovered was a New Zealander, was awarded the DFM or DFC. He certainly deserved that at least.

under the laden ships, causing sinkings and a great deal of damage. We didn't know if the erks who had shortened the fuse should be sent to the glass-house or given medals.

Our feelings of satisfaction about this raid were soon squashed. We had lost two crews on this mail run. We had known all of the crew members. Both captains were only ninteen years old. Reports filtered back from pro-British Arabs that the bodies of one crew had been found in their smashed Wimpy at the bottom of a small mountain. The captain had been impaled on the control column. The other crew was listed as missing.

Ten days later, as I walked from my tent towards the sergeants' mess, I came face to face with four members of the missing crew! They had just arrived back at camp from a gruelling trek across the desert. Over Benghazi, their starboard engine had been shot out, and they lost altitude gradually until crashing in a shallow gully called a wadi, whose rocky sides had torn off both wings. Miraculously they survived, suffering only numerous cuts and bruises, and set out eastwards in the dark. Luckily, they met a friendly Senussi Arab, who gave them water and led them eventually to a patrol of the British Long Range Desert Group (LRDG). They were then transported through Siwa Oasis, on the Libyan–Egyptian border, back to Cairo.

I pulled out my ever-present camera, and the "missing" crew posed for me. Standing there, with an assortment of broken ribs and other injuries, they even managed to give me big smiles. They were Jimmy Wild (captain), Tony Farrant (rear gunner), Dudley "Pop" Egles (navigator),* and Jeff Barton (front gunner).

The night we dropped King Ibn Sa'ud's bomb was a memorable one.

A few days later, Jimmy Wild confided to me that it was largely "Pop" Egles' leadership and navigating skill that had seen them through their gruelling trek. Luck had been with them even more than it had been with us.

---

* The whole crew was "Mentioned in Despatches" for their escapade. Dudley Egles went on to survive a ditching in the Mediterranean Sea, and escape by parachute over Romania during a second tour with a Pathfinder squadron. He also escaped from a POW camp in Romania and reached Allied lines. He describes his ops and charmed life in his book *Just One of the Many*, to which I was privileged to write the foreword.

21
TYMBAKI —
A CRUEL VICTORY

Our RELEASE FROM THE CONDITION of open arrest, under which we had been flying for a month, came on 4 March, one day after our return from dropping King Ibn Sa'ud's bomb on Benghazi.

The order came down to us in the morning to assemble outside the station commander's office. It was a long line. There were fifty of us, dressed similarly in tunic, shirt, and tie, but in the widest variety of footwear imaginable. We knew we were there to receive, finally, our "severe reprimand" award for our micro-mutiny of 29 January.

One by one we were paraded by two service police sergeants into Group Captain Fall's office, to stand at attention while he reprimanded us for our transgression. When my turn came, he looked up at me from his desk in obvious disgust, and proceeded to upbraid me in such a caustic manner that my blood pressure rose until I could scarcely restrain myself from making an outburst that would surely have gotten me into even greater trouble. I fully expected to be criticized severely for my actions, but this insensitive man brought up the old colonial label and went to great lengths in his denigration of Canadians. I was fortunate to escape from that office before I exploded in anger. Bill and the other Canadians received the same treatment.

We had to put this behind us now and soldier on. At least the air had been cleared, and we could get on with our job.

■ ■ ■

On the following day, another attempt to attack Benghazi was frustrated by bad weather and an enemy air raid in progress at the ALG. Our next briefing held a surprise for us. Our new squadron commander, Wing Commander Rawlinson, announced that he was taking our crew to Benghazi! He would replace Bill as captain. We weren't happy to go without Bill, but I consoled myself with the assumption that as our commander, and with that rank, he must know what he was doing.

Fortunately, everything went well, and Robbie managed to place our bombs in the midst of the harbour installations. An hour into our return flight, the wing commander came back for a little conference with Robbie on the state of our fuel. He then instructed me to inform our base operations that we would be returning direct to Kabrit and to give them our ETA. This was unusual; we nearly always stayed over at the ALG to refuel. Kabrit would have to keep the airfield open for our arrival. Unusually strong tailwinds had greatly reduced our usual fuel expenditure, enabling us to make the long flight direct home from the target. I coded up the message and was able to give a quick confirmation of its transmission and receipt to our captain.

We discovered that our commander was taking several of our squadron crews on raids to Benghazi or other targets. The reason for this became apparent before the end of the month.

In the meantime, between ops, our group was making the best of living conditions in our tent village. The lake was our salvation. Now that the air and water temperatures were rising, we spent most of our time naked, either swimming or sun-bathing on the sandy beach. With Louie the Rat gone, we were given permission to take surplus wood and other materials from the station dump. Several enterprising sergeants, including our own Will White, began constructing boats of their own design. Some professional-looking craft soon appeared.

With some help from Doug and Tony and me, Will put together a two-man boat of intriguing design. The square shell had pointed ends but seemed to me to have a coffinlike look to it. I reflected that Will might have been influenced subconsciously by his childhood environment — his father was in the undertaking business. To fasten a keel to the boat was beyond his skill, so Will cleverly fashioned a south sea–type outrigger with a pontoon held out from the starboard side by two long wooden poles. This held the boat stable in the water. He made a mast and a boom from some discarded hollow magnesium pipes that had once carried the control cables for the rudder and rear stabilizers the length of the Wimpy fuselage. He scrounged up enough factory cotton for a sail. It was an impressive achievement. Will and Doug made a triumphant maiden voyage in this odd but impressive craft to the cheers of the other crews.

After another trial, Doug and I set sail for a lengthy, more adventurous voyage out into Great Bitter Lake. A nice breeze propelled us along at a good speed, but the water soon became much rougher, and we decided that we were already much too far out from shore. As we started to come about, the two spars holding the pontoon snapped with a loud crack. Almost instantly, the boat tipped over, throwing us into the water.

As Doug and I held on to the hull, a black triangular fin glided past us. My God, I thought, a shark! Thankfully, it soon became apparent that this was one of a small school of dolphins, some of which playfully came up under us to give us a gentle nudge. They were probably trying to help us, as dolphins are known to do.

We were assessing our perilous predicament when a large Arab dhow, which we hadn't noticed, came up alongside. The Egyptian captain hailed us, and with the help of one of his three crew members, pulled us up onto his deck. With my little Arabic, his few words of English, and many gestures, we were able to identify ourselves. He then surprised us by ordering his crew to gather in and pull aboard our boat, including the sail and the pontoon. What a marvellous gesture this was.

The captain was a tall, wiry man, wearing nothing but a loin cloth. He had been blackened from the sun, like his crew members. With a big smile, he invited us to have chai, which we gladly accepted. He then astounded us. With a small hatchet, he began chopping up a small circle of the thick deck planking. The deck was empty — they had probably off-loaded their cargo of stones or wood at Ismailia or some other Bitter Lake port. He then placed a wire cage over the shallow hole and set fire to the kindling he had made. On this "stove" he placed a tin of hot water for our chai. It was only then that I noticed that the deck was covered with black, burnt spots where they had been making their chai. I supposed that, with the thickness of that deck, they could keep this up for a long time.

As we sat sipping the welcome brew, the captain eyed the onyx and gold signet ring I wore. He finally got around to asking me for the ring. I would gladly have given it to him for saving us from the waters, but, as I explained, it had been given to me by my mother before I left for overseas and I was loath to part with it. At that, this fine fellow (or *fellah*) waved his hands and exclaimed, "La, la, [no, no]," and that he could not take it from me in that case.

Our saviours not only put us ashore in a port south of Ismailia, but off-loaded our boat onto the dock before waving us goodbye. In spite of our mishap, Doug and I had enjoyed a unique encounter that few, if any, of our comrades would ever experience. Along with several other incidents, it served to strengthen my growing respect and affection for the Egyptian peasants, who seemed ever-willing to share what little they had with others, even with strangers to their land.

Eventually, we managed to flag down an army truck on its way to Suez and talk the driver into delivering us, boat pieces and all, to Kabrit. Our crew members and our tent neighbours welcomed us back with relief. They wondered whether we had drowned. Will seemed as happy with the return of his beloved boat as he was with our rescue.

Soon after, we had our first experience with the dreaded desert sand storm, the *Khamseen*, which appears most often in the spring, when the wind direction changes from north to southwest, bringing with it an immediate high rise in temperatures. The wind velocity rose to fifty or sixty miles per hour, whipping up the sand and dust, reducing visibility to zero and making breathing very difficult. A deep breath would produce an agonizing scorching sensation in the lungs. At the storm's peak, a hand thrust outside the tent could be reduced to bare, bloody bones in an instant by the blasting of the hard sand silicates driven by the wind. The fabric covering of the aircraft also suffered from the sand-blasting, and the fine dust penetrated engine cylinders and pumps, and fouled the oil lines. Flying was out of the question, of course, and all we could do was hunker down in our tents and wait out this violent assault of nature. For most of a week we were reduced to infrequent ventures from our tent to obtain water and food, most contaminated with the fine dust.

As soon as the storm settled down, and the aircraft could be made serviceable, we were off again on our bombing runs to Benghazi, the

LEFT: The author in his first uniform, at 1 Manning Depot, June 1940.

BELOW: The barracks at 1 Manning Depot, Coliseum, Toronto, June 1940.

BOTTOM: Vic Grant in front of a Fairey Battle at 1 Bombing and Gunnery School in Jarvis, Ontario, January 1941.

Top: HMS *Rodney*, taken from MV *Georgic* in the Atlantic Ocean, March 1941.

Bottom: MV *Georgic* off Greenock, Scotland, March 1941.

LEFT: Author on the *Georgic*, off Greenock, Scotland, March 1941.

BELOW: The first crew of our Wellington I, 218 Sqn., at Marham, September 1941: Len Mayer (L), Jim Munroe, George Fuller, author, Ted Crosswell.

TOP: Piccadilly Circus, London, May 1941.

RIGHT: Marconi radios R1155 (top) and T1154 (bottom) used on Wellingtons, 1941–42. When installed on the aircraft, the receiver was positioned at the bottom of the desk.

LEFT: At a former leper hospital at Valetta on arrival in Malta from Gibraltar, December 1941: Bill Dixon (L), Doug Chinnery, Will White, and Tony Carroll.

BELOW: A Wellington at Gibraltar, December 1941.

TOP: During our adventures in Cairo, December 1941: Jimmy Chalmers (L),
Aussie John, author, Aussie Ian, Bill Dixon, Aussie Jack, Tony Carroll.

BOTTOM: At the Bardia Club in Cairo, 1942: Will White (L), Robbie Robinson,
Bill Dixon.

TOP: The Sphinx and Cheops pyramid, Giza, just outside Cairo, 1942.

BOTTOM: Arab dhows on the Nile River, 1942.

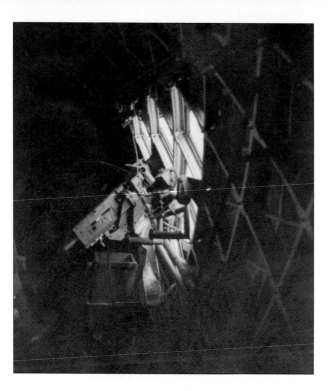

Top: Mid-gun position aboard a Wellington II, 1942.

Right: Doug Chinnery in the rear gun turret of a Wellington I at Kabrit, February 1942.

TOP: The "home" of 148 Sqn at Kabrit, on the shores of the Great Bitter Lake, 1942.

BOTTOM: The return to Kabrit after the crash in the desert, March 1942: our pilot, Jimmy Wild (L), Tony Farrant (rear gunner), Dudley "Pop" Egles (navigator), Jeff Barton (front gunner).

Top: At Kabrit, May 1942: Tony Carroll (L), unidentified airman, WO Walker, Will White, Peter Mayhew, Sid Payne, Norm Wakeham.

Bottom: Radios 1082 and 1083 aboard a Wellington II. This photo was taken during the flight to bomb Leros, May 1942.

TOP: Over the desert battlefield, en route to bomb German tank parks, February 1942.

LEFT: Author at Kabrit on return from raid on Tymbaki, Crete, March 1942.

RIGHT: Bill Dixon at Kabrit, May 1942.

RIGHT: Author convalescing
at El Ballah, July 1942.

BELOW: My companion
convalescents — Eighth
Army Cpl and WO at
El Ballah, July 1942.

TOP: The first day out from Cairo on the desert drive to Siwa Oasis, August 1942.

MIDDLE: Following Captain S's station wagon, Western Desert.

BELOW: Captain S washing up on the Western Desert drive, August 1942.
You can just make out the bullet hole in the back window of the truck.

Top left: The author, bandaged, after the fight with Italian troops near the Siwa Oasis, August 1942.

Top right: Jack Kelly outside his tent at Durban, South Africa, November 1942.

Bottom: The welcome committee at the Siwa Oasis, August 1942.

TOP: Table Mountain at Cape Town, South Africa, 20 December 1942, as we left Africa.

BOTTOM: Christmas convoy in the South Atlantic aboard the *Almanzora,* en route from Capetown, South Africa, to Scotland, December 1942.

Top: Bill Dixon and the author at the 148 Sqn. reunion at RAF Marham, May 1993.

Bottom: Together again: "Turkey" Rainsford (L), Marsh Scarborough, Alan Brisbane, author, Stan Thorogood, Len Evans, Bill Dixon, Dudley "Pop" Egles. Seven of the original "mutineers," after 51 years.

mail run. We did this until 23 March when our morning briefing for operations gave us a dramatic change in target.

Wing Commander Rawlinson spoke to the assembled crews from the centre of the small stage. "Gentlemen, most of you will be going to Benghazi, but two crews will be going to Tymbaki, a town on the south coast of Crete. This will be a very important strike on an unusual target. The small town of Tymbaki houses the complex for a large German headquarters controlling their operations in the Mediterranean. We have fresh intelligence from British army sources on the island that a successful strike on this complex would be a serious set-back to their current operations. Sergeant Dixon, you and your crew will carry out the primary attack on this installation. A second crew will provide a diversionary attack elsewhere on the island and be available for back-up.* I'll let the briefing crew take over from here." Bill looked over at us, and I knew he was thinking as we were. This is why the CO had tested several crews on the mail run. And we had "won"!

We soon had the details. We were to drop a 4,000-pound bomb on the centre of the headquarters complex. We needed to take a good photo to assess damage, so a long steady run-up was essential — not a recommended practice for those who wished to survive their tour of ops! We would have to come in from the sea in what was forecast to be a clear, bright night. First of all, however, we were to overfly the larger city of Candia on the north coast to make a drop of propaganda leaflets. This would have to be at an even lower altitude than the 5,000 feet prescribed for our bomb run on Tymbaki. We found the Candia assignment puzzling — we might lose much of the element of surprise that would help us on our south coast attack, and it was to be expected that this enemy headquarters would be heavily protected by anti-aircraft batteries. Night fighters could be an additional threat — German squadrons were based at Heraklion airfield, adjacent to Candia.

This was going to be a sticky operation. Indeed, the other crews not involved treated the situation with black humour, suggesting that Doug Chinnery leave behind his excellent black leather flying boots because it would be a shame to have them lost. No doubt calculated to lighten things up a little, it didn't do much for our morale at that moment.

---

* Bill Dixon recalls that the captain of this "back-up" crew was a Sqn Ldr Pritchard, one of our flight commanders. A sergeant leading the strike supported by a senior officer? It was one of the war's strange anomalies.

For the first time, the distance to target enabled us to fly direct from Kabrit without our usual refuelling stop at an ALG in the desert. After a little conference with our captain about the flight, Bill took us off at 1720 hours in Wimpy Z8369 with the 4,000-pound cookie in our belly.

Halfway to Crete, droning along in the clear, starlit night, I picked up a coded transmission on the frequency I was monitoring. It was being sent from our back-up aircraft. I decoded the message. It informed Kabrit that they were returning to base because of engine malfunction. I passed the message to Bill, who wasn't at all happy with the news. We were on our own.

Three hours from take-off, we were approaching the outskirts of Candia, and I informed Bill that I was going to the rear to prepare to drop the leaflets. There were about twenty large bundles of leaflets, each held together by a thick rubber band. I had to push out the extension on the chute to ensure that the bundles would clear the tail assembly after I'd thrown them out.

Bill announced that we were going in over the city and that I was to get rid of our leaflets. Suddenly we were shaken by bursts of flak that came perilously close. Bill threw the Wimpy around to evade the bursts as I struggled to brace myself and get the packages down the chute. I decided I would leave the rubber bands on; the wind stream would break the bundles open.

Just as I threw the first bundles down the chute, the intercom blasted in my ears: "Howard, Howard, this is Will!"

I thought we must have been hit by the flak! I grabbed my microphone, which was swinging wildly from a projection above my head, and shouted, "What's going on?"

Back came Will, "Howard, you know those rubber bands that hold the leaflet bundles together?"

Mystified, I could only reply, "What about the bloody things? I'm throwing them out as fast as I can."

I couldn't believe what he said next. "Well, it just came to me that those rubber bands are just what I need to fix the sail to the boom on my boat, so save them for me."

For a moment I was speechless. Here we were, with Bill trying every stunt he knew to get us out of a wicked barrage of flak, and me trying to hang on while I got rid of our paper cargo, and he's thinking about the damn boat! I had to wonder if he was hallucinating because of the fireworks. When I recovered my breath, all I could think of to say was,

"You stupid bastard, is that all you have to think about?" Nevertheless, I decided to try.

The only way I could recover the rubber bands was to thrust the bundles down the flare chute as far as I could reach and yank the band off, letting the leaflets exit and scatter as the wind hit them. I did this with the rest of the bundles, pushing the bands into my battledress pockets as I pulled them free. Each time I did this, however, I jammed the aluminum rim of the flare chute into my right armpit. In the stress of the moment I didn't feel the impact or realize the damage I was doing to myself. I would later. In any event, I had the rubber bands for the bloody boat! Bill was too busy at the time to take much notice of this farcical exchange, and later on could only shake his head in disbelief.

With the leaflets gone, we got away from the smoke and thunder, and Robbie gave Bill a southward course to steer for the sea so we could make our approach on Tymbaki.

It seemed no time at all before we were out over the sea, turning to make our approach to the target. Robbie went forward to his bomb sight and release toggles as Bill cautioned all of us to keep our eyes open for enemy fighters and for the flak patterns.

The target was clearly visible ahead of us, nestled on the coast between small mountains that must have been 1,000 feet in height. With the bomb doors now open, Robbie started his timing for our long run-up. His bomb-bay camera was set; he would be dropping the photo-flood flare just seconds before the bomb release. This magnesium flare would float down on its parachute, illuminating the target with something like five million candle-power. The rolling film in the camera would take successive pictures showing the impact area seconds before, during, and after the explosion of the bomb.

As Robbie began his heading correction calls to Bill, the expected flak arrived, giving us several rude bumps, but Bill couldn't take evasive action as it would destroy the accuracy so critical to our strike. Some of the medium flak was coming from the mountains on our left and right in streams that seemed to be almost on a horizontal line with us.

Our mouths were dry and our breathing was shallow from the tension, waiting for the release of our bomb. We listened to Robbie's fearfully slow, "Steady . . . steady . . ." then the blessed, "Bombs gone!" Bill could not alter course immediately because of the camera run, but in a couple of seconds relieved our tension with his cry, "Let's get out of here!" As we banked sharply away from our brightly illuminated target, the huge explosion of our bomb sent out shockwaves that we could feel before we got clear of the area. Robbie sounded elated as he reported that we had made a direct hit on the centre of our objective.

As I coded and transmitted the message to base operations that confirmed our successful strike on the target, I shared the crew's feeling of satisfaction with what we had accomplished. Robbie and Bill were also confident that they had gotten a good photo of the hit on the headquarters complex.

After five more hours of flying and an overnight stop at ALG 106, we arrived back at Kabrit. The debriefing officers were immensely pleased with the detailed reports from Bill and Robbie, especially when our photographs were developed and showed in clear detail how accurate and devastating our strike had been. I then took off to see the medical officer. Dried blood had fused my shirt to my body. The skin covering my armpit and my ribs looked like raw meat. I was to fly in great discomfort for the following two weeks.

But the drama of this operation was far from over. Two weeks after the raid, our crew was called to the briefing room. There we were introduced to a British army major who had an amazing story to tell.

The major, part of the secret service network, had been on the island of Crete, disguised as a native, to gather intelligence. One of his accomplices was a woman, a native Cretan patriot. Tragically, she was captured by a German Gestapo unit, and he had to watch from hiding while she was tortured to make her reveal the whereabouts of the British agents. She was then shot. The major, his cover blown, had to make arrangements to get off the island as quickly as possible. The clandestine radio net set up his escape by submarine.

Purely by chance, this officer was on a hillside overlooking Tymbaki waiting for his submarine contact when we approached the target. He watched our run-up and the release of our bomb. He said he was shaken by the noise and the violence of the explosion. He had never seen a 4,000-pound bomb detonate before. Not long after the smoke had cleared, he watched as hundreds of bodies were carried out of the rubble that had been the headquarters building complex. It was total destruction. Having watched, helpless, as his patriot comrade had been tortured by the Gestapo, he confessed to us that he felt little remorse at the wholesale slaughter for which our solitary Wimpy was responsible.

The major was generous in his praise of Bill for what he termed a brave attack on the German position. In response, Bill was quick to identify all the members of his crew. He made it clear, as he always did, that this raid, like all our other ops, was a team effort.

Although this personal account from a critical observer of our raid confirmed its complete success, the major's description of the human destruction we had wrought dampened the satisfaction we had felt with our performance. Though the flak had not been as intense as expected — the barrage over Candia had been worse, and the absence of fighters remained a mystery — this strike equalled the emotional drama of any raid in our bombing tour.

Rumour filtered down to us that Bill was to be awarded the DFM, the Distinguished Flying Medal, for this raid, which the rest of our crew felt he richly deserved, and that Robbie and I were to receive an MID for the Mention in Despatches that had been part of the final report to group headquarters. In the event, none of the awards was made, apparently because of the severe reprimand on Bill's record, and mine. Robbie had not been involved in that, of course, but must have been judged guilty by association.

But despite the flattering comments by the British officer and the devastating results of our raid, to us, in more ways than one, our raid on Tymbaki seemed a cruel victory.

22
A COSTLY ASSAULT ON SICILY AND LEROS

IN THE SIX DAYS FROM OUR ATTACK on Tymbaki, we had carried out two more raids on Benghazi. On the second raid we had dropped another 4,000-pound bomb, this one a delayed action beside the Cathedral mole that curved out from the northern part of the harbour in a half-circle to meet the tip of the Juliana mole. For some reason, our crew was picked far more often than the others to carry this monstrous weapon. Bill thought part of the reason for this was that he was one of the few pilots on the squadron with previous experience on the Mark II Wimpy. This improved mark was powered by two Rolls-Royce Merlin engines, favoured because of its increased power for carrying the big bomb.

The second raid started out badly from the beginning. On take-off, Bill was not getting the power he needed to lift our heavily laden aircraft off the runway. He quickly discovered that the supercharger levers had been pushed back to the "off" position. Just in time, he thrust the levers forward and we got the surge we needed to clear the ground. But as we began our climb over the lake, we saw the tail section of the Wimpy that had taken off just seconds before us sticking up out of the water. We had no choice but to carry on. We had to wait until our return to find out that all the crew of the other Wimpy, with the exception of the tail gunner, had perished in an engine-failure stall off the end of the runway.

Over the target, we managed to get the bomb in the water without hitting the concrete mole, always a tongue-biting exercise. The flak was even heavier than usual, especially at the low-level approach we had to make for the thin-skinned cookie we dropped. We were lucky to get away with that one.

There had been air raids on several of our ALGs and when we dropped down in a dark landing at ALG 106 and taxied off the end of the makeshift runway, we stopped near a still-smouldering Wimpy. We got out of our aircraft quickly and headed for a small sand dune for shelter against what we expected would be strafing runs from the enemy attackers. On our way we passed two or three bodies lying in and out of the skeleton framework of the burned Wimpy. We were happy to get refuelled and on our way back to base.

On our return we were greatly relieved to hear that we had been granted a week's leave. Our youthful resilience, at that point, had been wearing thin. We were feeling the strain of a long period of operational flying, and the burden of watching the thinning of our squadron ranks from casualties, although we did rejoice rather guiltily over the fact that, so far, the crews with whom we had forged the closest friendships had survived.

The strain was not just a mental one. Each of our ops averaged a little over ten hours in an aircraft shaking from air turbulence and vibrating from the noise of the engines. The pilots had the additional physical effort of constant manipulation of the flight controls (we did not have automatic pilot).

We all carried our chest-type parachutes to and from the aircraft, and Robbie and I also carried a heavy bag full of navigation tools, maps, Very pistol cartridges, logs, and other gear. After each flight, the gunners had to remove their heavy guns from the turrets and take them to the station armoury where they would strip them down, clean and oil all parts, and reassemble them. The two waist Brownings were my responsibility, but quite often Tony would generously take these guns and work on them and his. The sleep-robbing Spartan conditions at the ALGs also contributed to the physical strain. We were simply mentally and physically drained.

In Cairo, we found a small, cheap, but comfortable hotel called the Tin Hat, whose Greek proprietor, Aristides Etickulous, gave us a warm welcome. From there we toured the city's highlights, sometimes splitting up as our interests diverged.

Our crew had dinner together at Salt's, one of the best eating places in the city, and even managed an evening at Groppi's, which was a haven of elegance and luxury in the midst of a metropolis whose general tone was one of poverty and misery. Non-commissioned ranks were not encouraged to frequent places like Groppi's. The finer places were reserved for the commissioned ranks. The British Army, for example, had established a high-class brothel at the Gezira Sporting Club on Gezira Island, not far from city centre; it had become the site of an officers' mess. Apparently, it was well controlled and inspected by army medical officers, so much safer than the "shops" in the native quarter. Common soldiery were strictly banned from this knock-shop, of course, but we knew of some NCOs on the squadron who had put up flying officer's rank braid on their uniforms and visited this house, risking court martial if discovered.

The anti-British feelings of the middle- and upper-class Egyptians became obvious to us from their attitude and from signs in some shop windows praising the Afrika Korps. Even an English-language Cairo newspaper delighted in printing anything that would show the Germans in a favourable light. I cut out one amusing piece from that paper that reflected the known contempt of the Germans for their Italian allies. This purported to be an intercepted communiqué put out by the German Middle East Command, and it illustrated humorous but biting sarcasm on the part of the German writer. It read:

COMMUNIQUÉ FROM GERMAN MIDDLE EAST COMMAND

0745 HRS 2 MARCH '42 A strong motorized patrol of the 31st Ariete Division of our gallant Italian allies reports encountering a lone British cyclist at Kilo 142.0 on the Derna-Gazala coastal road. Fierce fighting immediately broke out.

1000 HRS 2 MARCH '42 The local action developing on the Derna-Gazala road has been the scene of heavy fighting. Despite withering fire from the British cyclist, a spirited attack by the Italians has forced the cyclist to dismount. Fighting continues.

1500 HRS 2 MARCH '42 A radio report from the scene of what is being referred to as the "Battle of Kilo 142.0" describes a further attack by our intrepid allies which gained them possession of the handlebars, front headlamp, and tyre pump of the enemy bicycle. The Italian force has suffered many casualties.

1800 HRS 2 MARCH '42 The last report received from Kilo 142.0 describes a final assault by the Ariete force, which has succeeded in gaining possession of the remainder of the bicycle, along with two empty despatch cases, two billy cans, one folding dart board, and thirty bags of Lipton's tea. Unfortunately, under cover of a sudden sand squall and a withering volley of rifle fire, the British soldier made good his escape.

Our change of environment, good food, and much rest in clean, comfortable beds really had knitted up the ravelled sleeve of care, and we arrived back at our squadron tent village greatly refreshed in mind and body. It was timely, because I have to wonder how well we would have coped, otherwise, with what lay ahead of us.

■ ■ ■

Except for a few air tests, we had a week's respite from flying until called to the briefing room on 19 April. A detachment of six aircraft from our squadron was to proceed to Malta to carry out bombing attacks on the German and Italian airfields on Sicily. It was imperative that something be done to reduce the enemy air attacks on Malta.

March and April 1942 were the worst months of the air assault on that small island. In April alone, enemy aircraft from Sicily flew some 4,900 sorties against Malta, dropping over 6,000 tons of bombs. Damage was enormous, but because of the deep shelters civilian casualties were limited to 300 dead and 330 seriously injured. The most critical damage was to supply ships in and approaching the harbour of Valletta, and to the ability of the island to interfere with the supply convoys from Italy to Benghazi to support Rommel's Afrika Korps. The mail run attacks by our Wellingtons on Benghazi had so disrupted these supplies that Rommel had to postpone his major offensive, which ultimately carried him to El Alamein, until 26 May. But the air assault had so weakened Malta's offensive power that there was now a dramatic improvement in the quantity of supplies reaching the enemy in Libya. The ability of this island fortress to interfere with Rommel's supplies had to be restored.

In April 1942, the fortitude and bravery of the Malta people were recognized with the collective award of the George Cross to the island by King George VI. The citation read:

<blockquote>

To honour her brave people
I award the George Cross
to the Island Fortress of Malta
to bear witness to a heroism and devotion
that will long be famous in history.

— GEORGE R.I.*

</blockquote>

After a seven-hour flight, the squadron detachment reached familiar, cratered Luqa airfield without incident on 20 April. Not until 22 April would five of our Wimpys be able to take off for the attack on the enemy airfield of Comiso on Sicily.

From a take-off at 2215 hours, it took only fifty minutes to cover the seventy miles or so to Comiso, which was heavily defended. Bill and the aircraft were shaken when one Wimpy, carrying an Australian flying officer and crew we knew well from 148 Sqn, blew up in a horrific orange and oily black ball no more than 600 yards to port from our cockpit. Its armed bomb load must have suffered a direct hit.

With a total flight time of only one hour and fifty minutes, the surviving aircraft took turns descending through the smoke of the nightly German raids to tricky landings on the potholed Luqa strip. Junkers 88s followed some of the Wimpys on their landing pattern, dropping bombs behind them and spraying them with a fusillade of 20mm shells. Most of the crews escaped, but on that night and the following days, from air bombardment, we lost all of the aircraft of the detachment from Kabrit.

The detachment crews were marooned on the island until 28 April. They spent much of their time in the air raid shelters, which did not protect the group from further casualties. On 24 April, during an air raid on Valletta, Sgt Alex Balinson and F/S Art Charron joined some civilians in a surface air raid shelter. By tragic chance, a large bomb exploded right outside the steel door of the shelter. Alex and Art, along with all the

---

* Some fifty years later, for actions around Malta and the Mediterranean in 1942, Bill Dixon and the author were awarded the Malta George Cross Fiftieth Anniversary Medal by the President of Malta.

others, were killed instantly by the shattering concussion. Their unmarked bodies were buried in Malta's Capuccini Naval Cemetery.*

The only way our stranded crews were going to get back to Kabrit was to steal aircraft staging through Malta on their way to Middle or Far East bases. Bill was the first captain authorized to grab one of these Wimpys and to escape the island. He owed this honour to the fact that he was the only pilot experienced on the Merlin-powered Mark II Wimpy, the only available aircraft. By an amazing coincidence, the pilot whose Wimpy Bill was confiscating was another Bill Dixon, this one from Aylmer, Quebec.

In the week following 28 April, our remaining crews made their way back to Kabrit in their purloined Wimpys. Despite considerable damage done to the enemy at Comiso, the squadron detachment to Malta had been a disastrous venture.

The squadron had only two days rest from the punishing Malta misadventure when we were called again to a briefing for another Mediterranean operation. This time our target was Leros, one of the Dodecanese Islands in the southeast Aegean Sea. It was a small island, only twenty-one square miles in size with a population of 6,600 citizens of Greece. It lay close to the west coast of Turkey.

The plan for this raid surprised us. Our force of five bombed-up Wimpys was to fly to ALG 106 in the Western Desert early on the morning of 1 May and be prepared to take off on the sortie from there late that evening. What was most unusual was that we were to receive our detailed briefing for the operation at the advanced landing ground. No explanation was given, but we assumed that it had something to do with a critical need to preserve the secrecy of this attack.

When our crew took up our positions in our Wimpy to prepare for take-off, I was handed another surprise. I sat staring in some shock at the wireless set in front of me. I had not been warned by the radio section that this particular aircraft was equipped, not with the familiar Marconi, but with the old 1082/1083 transmitter-receiver that I hadn't seen since Wireless School in Calgary in 1940.

I couldn't very well announce that I might not be able to operate this archaic equipment; it would have cancelled our crew's participation in the operation. By our noon arrival at the advanced base I had figured

---

* With these deaths, and that of Jimmy Chalmers on Christmas Day 1941, Joe Findlay became the only survivor of the four passengers we had taken with us to Egypt from Malta on 7 December 1941.

out the receiver easily enough, but was still pondering some of the idio-syncrasies of the transmitter. Fortunately, I would not have to use it until after we had bombed the target, and I was confident that I could unravel the mysteries of the set before then.

It was dark when we entered a large tent to join the other twenty-four aircrew of our squadron force. Four or five coal-oil lamps lit up the scene, throwing ghostly shadows on the tent walls. Boxes and benches on the sand floor provided makeshift seating for the crews. Two large maps were displayed on easels. The dramatic setting seemed to me to be lifted right out of a Hollywood movie of the thirties.

A squadron leader flight commander and a flight lieutenant intel-ligence officer gave us the details for our raid. Our target was a large cluster of oil storage tanks situated around the only harbour on the small island of Leros. These were being used to refuel German U-boats active in the Mediterranean Sea. The tanks had to be destroyed. We were car-rying a full load of 500-pound explosive bombs for the purpose. We had a clear moonlit night for our run-ins, which would have to be carried out at low level to ensure the accuracy of our drop. Our take-off was to be an unusually late 2315 hours, which meant that we wouldn't be over the target until 0300 hours the following morning. We were to make an early dawn landing back at the ALG.

It was a bright night, and we had almost enough visibility ahead of us on the runway to do without the flare path made up of the oil- and petrol-filled steel drums. It was a smooth and serene flight to the target, and we were almost there before I had the transmitter figured out.

Bill announced to the crew that our target was dead ahead, and we could see the small island sitting in a sea glistening from the moonlight. As Bill banked to port to line up for our bombing run and opened the bomb bay doors, Robbie went forward to arm the bombs and to begin giving the course corrections to Bill for the drop. We watched the first Wimpy dive over the harbour and score direct hits on several of the larger oil tanks. Oily black smoke and flames rose quickly and obscured part of the harbour, making it more difficult for Bill and Robbie to time the bomb release. The first aircraft had stirred up the flak crews so that we were met by a barrage of medium flak as we swooped in at mere hundreds of feet and released our entire lethal load. As Bill took us up and away from the harbour area and out over the sea, we looked back and saw that we, too, had made direct hits on the tanks; we had doubled the fires set by the first Wimpy.

At that moment Bill and Robbie got into one of their rare arguments. As we gained altitude, Robbie suggested, "Let's go back and do another run over the island to get another photo."

Bill retorted, "We already have a good photo, and there are still three crews to go in. I'm not putting all of us in more risk for nothing." Robbie persisted until Bill uncharacteristically shouted, "I'm captain of this aircraft, and I'll make the decisions, thank you!" Will tactfully suggested that we might do a wide sweep just to watch the remaining aircraft on their runs. Bill agreed to this, and as we circled, the bright moonlight gave us a clear look at the other Wimpys making their drops over the harbour. We left behind a satisfying picture of an island totally engulfed in flames.

Robbie gave Bill a course for our return flight to the ALG, and as we droned peacefully along in the still, clear air, I tuned up the forbidding transmitter to pass the "target successfully bombed" message to operations at Kabrit. No reply! I knew that I had an output of only fifteen watts compared to the Marconi's twenty-five watts, not enough power for the distance involved. But I thought my trailing antenna might save me as it had back in England. I reeled out about forty feet of the weighted wire and adjusted the length for maximum signal output on the antenna meter. Eureka! I received a reply on my next transmission, and a receipt for my coded bombing message. I enjoyed the sweetness of the tone of this receiver for my remaining work that night, and couldn't resist having a feeling of pride in having mastered this old radio set.

Three hours later we landed at ALG 106 for a refuelling stop. It was also our last foray into the northern part of the Mediterranean.

Compared to all of our other bombing raids, in Europe and in the Middle East, this strike could almost be called serene. On our return flight, sitting at my desk under its faint red light, the quiet broken only by the steady drone of our Merlin engines, I had had plenty of time to reminisce and to contemplate my lot. My fellow crew members and I had come through a great deal together, and we still had a dangerous way to go. But I knew my job, and with the skill of our captain and the other members of our crew, I felt we had an excellent chance of pulling through. I was proud to be a member of this family — I was a lucky man.

FOUR

ALL
SPENT

23
OUR LAST BOMB RUNS

IN MID-APRIL, FOR THE FIRST TIME my crew went off on a raid without me. Sand-fly fever and a dysentery bug had caught up with me. I suspected that the source of my bug could be the buns of unknown origin served to us along with tea by our *dhoby wallah* (laundry man) in our tent in the early morning. Louie the Rat had obstructed Bill's efforts to organize the little luxury of having a laundry man, but on his departure Bill had quickly hired one.

On my second night in the station sick bay three Heinkel llls bombed our airfield. At the first wail of the air-raid sirens all of the patients were rushed out to the slit trenches near the beach. I joined six other patients and two nurses in one of the trenches. I could see the bombers in the circuit to make their bomb run, and I could also see that after releasing their bombs they would pass at low level right over the beach. I had no doubt that they would strafe the whole area as they overflew our trenches. I quickly briefed my companions, "Listen, the front gunner is going to machine-gun us as they fly over, and then the rear gunner will have a go. I want you to crouch down now and press yourselves against the wall towards the plane approaching, and when I shout 'move,' you have to jump as fast as you can to the other side. That way the bullets will go over our heads."

I had no sooner spoken when the first bombs shook the ground under our feet and thundered in our ears. I peeked over the lip of the trench and watched as the first Heinkel came towards us. I ducked as the first bullets kicked up sand and then thudded into the sandbags on the opposite side of our trench. I screamed "Move!" and everyone scrambled as briefed to the other side. Sure enough, the rear gunner opened fire, and his bullets plowed into the other side of the trench only a foot above our heads. Our strategy was working! The other two Heinkels dropped their bombs on the field and the hangars, and repeated the strafing run of the first aircraft. We lurched from side to side on my command and escaped the fusillades.

Each of the enemy bombers made another strafing run over the base and our beach before leaving. The wing commander CO of 104 Sqn had rushed out to the beach and planted a Lewis machine gun on a tripod into the sand. He was clearly exposed in the moonlight, but fearlessly fired away at the Heinkels as they passed over. The "putt! putt! putt!" of his shots were interposed in almost comical contrast with the heavy crack of the 40mm Bofors guns sited around the airfield. Miraculously, the gallant but foolhardy wing commander escaped injury.

As soon as the Heinkels left the scene and the all-clear sounded, we scrambled out of our trench to see two hangars engulfed in flames. We lost several Wimpys, but the greater loss was one of the six-man gun crews of a Bofors installation, killed by a near-direct hit of a bomb, and three airmen burned to death in a fiery hangar.

I spent sleepless nights worrying about my absent crew. I was anguished about deserting them, even though I had been given no choice. When they returned on the third day I rejoiced, and thanked God for their safe return. If they had not come back, I don't know how I would have managed my feelings of guilt; my place was with them, regardless of what might happen.

Barely a week after my release from sick bay, we were off again to bomb the harbour at Benghazi. Our crew made it back safely; not all were so lucky. On our return, Bill and I discussed the fact that both he and I were at the end of our tour of bombing operations. In fact, counting the raids we had made in Europe, and considering that a total of 200 operational flying hours were required to complete a tour in the Middle East, we were well over our operational requirements. Each one of us had over 300 operational hours, and had spent nearly a year continually on ops on a bomber squadron. The other members of our crew had not completed as many hours, not having had as much operational experience on our previous squadron, 218, in England.

If only in the sense that I had completed my bombing tour, the return of my fever and a much more severe case of dysentery was timely. I took ill again around the beginning of June. I barely had time to pack my gear and say goodbye to Bill and the other crew members when I was packed off quickly to the army's 13th General Hospital in Suez. I fully expected that I would be coming back to the squadron and my crew in a week or so for whatever flying or other disposition was waiting for tour-expired aircrew, but things did not turn out that way at all. Except for Bill Dixon, I was not to see my other crew members again.

On arrival at the hospital in Suez, I was assigned to one of the dozen beds in a large tent. I could scarcely believe my eyes — the bed had a mattress, white sheets, a blanket, and a real pillow! I was feeling extremely ill, so I was grateful to fall onto this pallet of unaccustomed luxury.

The next day I saw the medical officer, and was put on a high dose of sulfa drugs. I then had the opportunity to meet my fellow patients, most of them members of Eighth Army. They had a variety of injuries and ailments. Several of them had interesting stories to tell.

Across the sand-floor aisle from me was an American merchant marine sailor, who said in his distinctive twang that he was from "Joisey." He had come ashore on a day's pass from his oil tanker, and had promptly picked up a case of VD — in his words, the "clap." He was a small, wiry man, blackened from the sun, with an irrepressible sense of humour. He was also unusually enterprising. Somehow he talked the medical officers into allowing him day passes into Suez, on the condition, of course, that he ignore the local women. In town he arranged to have beer smuggled in to our tent, which he hid in the sand under the beds. The beer was warm, and when opened often sprayed the canvas over the beds. On inspection, the medical officers and orderlies sniffed the air suspiciously, but never uncovered the hidden beer.

In the bed on his right was a young corporal of the armoured corps, no more than twenty-three years old, who had suffered dangerous burns to his stomach when a shell penetrated his tank and stopped inches from his belt. He had been awarded the Military Medal for bravery in an incident that is the stuff of legend. In modest understatement, he gave us the details.

He had been placed in command of a tank in an armoured squadron commanded by a major. In one of the battles around Gazala, where Rommel had renewed his offensive, the squadron had been surrounded by German armour, and was being pounded unmercifully. In the heat of the exchange of fire, and the dust clouds thrown up by the melee, the major panicked. He found an escape route and fled in his tank, abandoning his squadron. Faced with crumbling morale among the remaining six tanks of his group, the corporal took over as leader and rallied the surviving NCO tank commanders in a desperate attempt to break out of the encirclement. He found a gap in the converging ring of enemy armoured vehicles and led his comrades out. He suffered his wound during the escape, but kept on going until they were in the clear and on their way to friendly lines. He admitted that he didn't know what possessed him to do what he did; he simply credited it to a reflex action when no one else seemed to be doing anything in the wake of the major's defection.

On his return from one of his day passes into Suez, our American friend from Joisey brought us startling news. In one of his bar hangouts, he eavesdropped on a conversation between two senior officers. He listened as one of the officers described the court martial and execution of a major in the armoured corps for cowardice in the face of the enemy. We needed no more evidence to conclude that this was our corporal friend's squadron commander. The timing fit, and it was standard practice to mete out this kind of military justice in one of the backwater army camps like the depot on the outskirts of Suez. We knew that there had been other executions within the Allied forces for cowardice or desertion but, thankfully, they were isolated incidents.

This sombre news was not greeted with any feeling or show of satisfaction. It affected the corporal much more personally and deeply than it did the rest of us, but he kept his emotions to himself, and we respected his privacy by keeping our own counsel.

The next week, my own condition took a bad turn. My dysentery was of the bacillary type. It travelled to my knees in the form of arthritis. Both knees swelled up to football proportions. The pain was intense, and led the medical officers to encase both legs in splints lined with cotton-batting. This led to two other problems. I had to make over twenty trips to the latrine daily, which was nigh impossible in splints. A martyr-like fellow patient, a warrant officer some forty years of age, took it upon himself to carry me to the latrines whenever my signal alerted him. The other problem was that sand fleas infested the cotton wrapping of my splints. When the bites became too much to bear, I had to call for the orderly to change the batting. I began to feel like a real nuisance.

Over the next few weeks, with drugs and heat lamps on my knees, I progressed to crutches and then to a cane before being pronounced well enough to leave. I had gone from the 155 pounds I weighed on arrival in England to 140 pounds on the squadron at Kabrit, and now to 129 pounds on my departure from the Suez hospital. I did not feel fighting fit.

From Suez, I was sent directly to the RAF unit at Abu Sueir, near the Bitter Lakes, to appear before a medical board for assessment. I was given a temporary lower flying category and told to report to AFHQ Cairo for convalescent leave.

The following day, I was in the sergeants' mess waiting for transport to Cairo to be arranged when I was approached by a warrant officer. He asked if I was a qualified wireless operator. I confirmed that I was, but asked why he wanted to know. "Well," he replied, "I've been asked to look for someone like you. There's a 108 squadron Wellington in here on detachment and their wireless op has gone sick on them. They have some flight they have to make right away and they desperately need an operator. Can you go and talk to them if you're available?"

I had mixed feelings about this. Sensibly, I should have said simply that I was on sick leave and in no condition to fly. But I decided, foolishly, that it wouldn't do any harm to talk to the crew.

I found the crew in a hangar operations room and approached the captain, a flight lieutenant. He greeted me with enthusiasm, and told me that this operation of his was not a bombing raid but simply a visit, for a purpose he didn't disclose, to an advanced base in the desert. He assured me that it would be a short night flight, and that we would return the next morning to his base at Fayid, where I could get transport just as easily to Cairo.

My better judgment told me that taking off with this crew was probably against regulations, given my present status and reduced medical flying category. But I gave in to the flight lieutenant's entreaties, and rationalized that it wouldn't do any harm to help out. Who would know?

After briefing, I was given the parachute and harness of the crew's absent wireless op. We took off just before sundown, and set course almost due west towards the area of our advanced bases that had not been overrun by Rommel.

Two hours into a black night, at 10,000 feet, we were suddenly shaken by the eruption of our starboard engine into a blossom of flame and black smoke. The rear gunner cried out that we had a Junkers 88 on our tail. We could hear the frantic chatter of his Brownings as the captain threw us into a sharp downward turn to port. For some reason there was no further attack. The rear gunner called to the captain that he was certain that he had made good hits on the Junkers. Perhaps this had discouraged the enemy pilot or damaged him enough that he had to break off his attack.

A steep dive didn't diminish the fire in the engine, and the flames quickly spread to the wing. The captain announced that we could not keep flying but that he preferred to try a landing on the desert rather than bail out. The moon had come up to give him enough visibility to make a landing feasible.

The front gunner scrambled back to take up his crash position against the main spar, and the navigator and I folded our arms on our desks to cushion our heads. "Hold on, chaps!" our cool captain cried as we braced ourselves for the crash. The violent contact with the rocky ground crumbled the front turret and compressed the fuselage enough to crush my legs against the radio equipment under my desk. Searing pain shot through my knees as we bounced along the desert floor and came to a shuddering stop. I couldn't pull my legs out from under the radio equipment; I was trapped, and the fire was spreading rapidly down the starboard side of the fuselage! I just had time to curse myself for my poor judgment in taking this flight, when both the navigator and captain arrived at my side. They grabbed me and with desperate strength pulled me clear. Somehow we all got out through the astro dome to the wing and slid off to the ground. I couldn't walk, so the captain hoisted me on his back as everyone ran as fast as possible from the Wimpy, whose fuel tanks were going to blow up at any moment.

We were a good distance away when our aircraft went up in flames like a monstrous candle, shooting sparks out into the darkness and lighting the desert in its garish orange glow. Everyone was shaken up, but thankful that all had escaped, with all the credit belonging to a skilful and composed captain. I was the only one injured, and as the captain continued to carry me on his broad back, I had time to wonder how my condition was going to be received in Cairo. To paraphrase Laurel and Hardy, "Another fine mess I had gotten myself into!"

We had not gone far, fortunately, when we were discovered by a Sikh armoured car patrol, which was reconnoitering a few miles behind the

German lines. We were taken on board and eventually passed on to other transport, and arrived late the next day in Cairo. I was not in great shape, so I was taken straight to the RAF hospital at Heliopolis while the rest of the crew was taken to Air Force Headquarters. I didn't see them again, nor did I find out the purpose of the doomed flight.

After I was given a bed and examined by a medical officer, I had a lot of explaining to do. I simply told the story as it had happened, but for the life of me I could not remember the names of the crew members, or some details of the flight. This was unusual for me; I seldom forgot the name of any person with whom I have had any significant contact. The medical officer's opinion was that this was purely due to the shock I had experienced in the crash. I had more explaining to do to the senior medical officer, who said that he would have to inform AFHQ Cairo of my case. He must have done so with some compassion for I heard no more about my predicament.

The X-rays revealed no breaks in my legs; they were simply badly bruised. I was lucky. Following a week of massage treatments and rest, I was able to limp about quite well.

The first week of July, I was discharged from Heliopolis, and transported to the convalescent depot at El Ballah, where I was to spend the next two weeks. This camp was situated on the banks of the Suez Canal, about fifteen miles north of Ismailia.

The convalescing troops were quartered in small plaster and wood huts, each of which accommodated four men. Our beds were straw palliasses placed on a concrete floor. Rather Spartan conditions, but the huts were clean and kept free of scorpions and centipedes, and the weather was warm and dry.

I shared a hut with three Eighth Army soldiers who had been wounded manning their woefully inadequate two-pounder anti-tank guns in the desert fighting leading to the first battle of El Alamein. It was difficult, if not impossible, to dig into the hard, rock-covered ground of the northern desert to gain any useful cover for their guns. Thus they were cruelly exposed to the 50- and 70-mm guns of the German tanks.

To my great surprise, one of my hut mates was the warrant officer who had carried me to and from the latrines at the Suez hospital. To my relief, he was still on speaking terms with me. My other companions were a Sgt Cutts and a "Geordie" corporal. I was the only air force patient in the camp.

I discovered that many of the patients had been wounded in a raid by one of our own Wimpy squadrons. The story was that the "bomb-line"* established jointly by the air force and army staff at the advanced desert HQ had been overrun by the army units, unknown to the air force squadrons; consequently the troops were bombed by their own aircraft for nearly five hours. My fellow patients were apparently aware that the ensuing casualties were therefore largely their own fault. Putting together the date this occurred with my recollection of our crew's operations during that period, I thought it highly likely that we were one of the culprits. I did not need the wisdom of Solomon to tell me to keep these thoughts to myself.

I found this camp ideally suited to its convalescent purpose. My companions were fine fellows, and we struck an instant rapport. We spent much of our time swimming in the warm waters of the canal, where I taught my warrant officer friend to swim, and had tea and cakes at the native-run tuck-shop on the canal bank. I was rapidly regaining my strength, and even gaining back some of the weight I had lost.

For at least half an hour each day I was engaged in an unusual activity. My Geordie hut-mate had suffered minor wounds from a spray of small pieces of shrapnel. These bits of steel, about the size of small fingernails, travelled about just under his skin, appearing daily in small, irritating lumps on his back. For some reason he selected me as the amateur surgeon to relieve his torment. I reluctantly agreed to perform this minor surgery. I used his sharp penknife to make a small incision over the lump, and then used tweezers to remove the offending bit of shrapnel. I sterilized everything with liberal applications of alcohol, and then covered the small cut with a Band-Aid. We were both quite proud of ourselves.

The only discordant note in our idyllic routine was struck during a performance given in the small camp theatre by a travelling troupe of ENSA, the Entertainments National Service Association. The membership of this association included aspiring young musicians and entertainers, and also some jaded older veterans of the British vaudeville stage, all of whom had banded together to travel in many different groups to all the theatres of war in which British forces were engaged. They deserved accolades for the courage and endurance this demanded, and for the uplifting of spirits that their performances engendered.

---

* Through consultation between army and air force tactical commanders in a forward battlefield headquarters, a bomb line was drawn, beyond which the air force was free to bomb the enemy within specified times, and across which, for their own safety, the troops must not cross.

On this particular occasion, I was seated with nearly a hundred other privates and NCOs in the small theatre for a program of singing and comedy sketches. One comedy act featured a beautiful young woman, and a rather seedy-looking older man. The dialogue startled us. It was vulgar, even disgusting. One sergeant promptly got up and left. He was followed by a growing stream, including me, until the theatre was emptied. It was obvious what the sergeant and the rest of us inferred from the language and gestures used; the performers felt that they had to get down to our level to entertain us. Lowly troops we might have been on the rank scale, but none us had been raised in the gutter. We were insulted. I wondered what effect this had on the ENSA group, who otherwise were doing a commendable job in dangerous places.

■ ■ ■

Before the end of July, I was transferred back to Cairo and given a temporary billet for two days awaiting another medical board at the Heliopolis hospital. How Bill found me there, I didn't know, but he arrived one evening with three other unfamiliar aircrew. They were on their way back to Canada, and would be flown by transport aircraft to Khartoum, in the Sudan, and then to Accra on the African west coast, and from there through Brazil to Canada.

It was good to see my captain again and to know that he and the rest of our crew were well. It was an emotional, but brief, reunion. Bill advised me not to enter into a second bombing tour; he was not optimistic that I would survive another round of the kind of experiences we had been through together. It was with great reluctance that I said goodbye to the man whose skill and determination had brought us safely home from so many fiercely defended targets.*

My medical board decided that I needed another month of convalescence before I could be considered fit for flying again, and I was transferred to the Hurricane House Hotel on Sharia Solomon Pasha, one of the main streets of Cairo. This small, well-appointed hotel with a nice backyard garden had been appropriated for convalescing aircrew.

On my arrival, the flight sergeant manning the front desk gave me a warm welcome. He had some sort of file on my case. He then rang a

---

* Bill Dixon was commissioned soon after his arrival in Canada, and instructed at Pennfield Ridge, New Brunswick, on Lockheed Venturas. He ended the war a flight lieutenant. We were reunited in Ottawa before the war's end, and have kept in close touch since.

bell, and a small, dusky man wearing a red fez appeared as if by magic. This was Mahmoud, a Sudanese, and he was to be my batman. I was even more astounded when he led me to the second floor and into my room, which was furnished with a sumptuous bed with white sheets and pillow, a dressing table, and an armoire for my clothes. A large window looked out upon the main street. Mahmoud then showed me the bathroom, which featured one of the largest bathtubs I had ever seen. He said he would draw my bath for me whenever I wished. Breakfast, lunch, and dinner were served in a pleasant dining room looking out French doors onto the garden.

I stood there in disbelief. Surely they had me mixed up with some air commodore! This was luxury I hadn't been accustomed to since enlistment. I had nothing to do but keep quiet and hope it wasn't all a dream.

I was free to come and go at will, and soon discovered the many service clubs in the city. The Salvation Army was there, of course, but my favourite club, as it was with so many of the troops, was the Kiwi Club, staffed by attractive ladies of the New Zealand forces Women's Auxiliary. This is where I met Tony Jenkins, of Bristol, England, an RAF wireless op who had been burned in a Blenheim crash and was convalescing on the Nile on a houseboat, which was owned and operated by Imperial Airways. Tony and I became good friends, and toured the attractions of Cairo together.

In the light of increasing successes by Rommel's Afrika Korps, the local Egyptians were becoming bolder. Signs reading "Welcome to the victorious German Army" began to appear in some of the shop windows. With the arrival of Rommel's forces at El Alamein, only sixty-five miles from Alexandria, the general feeling against the British mounted. There were even street demonstrations by crowds chanting, "Advance Rommel." In his book, *In Search of Identity*, Anwar El-Sadat recounts an astonishing story of intrigue by officers of the Egyptian Army, ostensibly an ally. In July 1942, the twenty-two-year-old future president of Egypt was a junior officer in the Signals Corps of the Egyptian Army, stationed near Cairo, and a member, along with the senior Abdel Nasser, of the subversive Free Officers' Association. To paraphrase his account:

> *I called a meeting with my friends in the Free Officer's Association,*
> *and said that something must be done to inform Rommel that we were*
> *an organization within the army dedicated, as he is, to defeating the*
> *British. Our message, in the form of a treaty, will confirm that we are*

prepared to recruit forces that will join with him on his approach to Cairo to ensure that the British forces do not escape. We will also provide him with photographs showing the lines and positions of the British forces. In return we ask for assurances that Egypt will remain independent, and free of German or Italian interference in her affairs. The "treaty," dictated by me, was to be flown to Rommel at El Alamein by a pilot friend, who would borrow a Gladiator from an Egyptian airfield. The film, and a draft of the treaty, were put into a bag and given to the pilot. My friend flew the aircraft as if on a regular patrol, but then diverted to the German lines at El Alamein. He quickly came to grief. The aircraft had British markings, and although he tried to give friendly signals, the German gunners shot him down and he was killed. The documents were lost.

This did not end the subversive scheming of the Egyptian officers, but it was the end of that kind of covert activity.

I settled in to the restful routine at Hurricane House, but little did I suspect the bizarre course my convalescent period was to take.

24
MISSION BEHIND ENEMY LINES

ON 5 AUGUST, I HAD BEEN TAKEN on the supernumerary strength of Air Force Headquarters, Cairo. I was in a backwater of the war, and nobody seemed the least bit interested in how I was spending my time.

August brought temperatures to Cairo above the hundred-degree mark, but with numerous fans and the usual evening breezes that coursed through the large, open windows and French doors of Hurricane House, our small group of convalescent aircrew had little cause for complaint.

I was into the second week of my stay at this cozy hotel when our idyllic routine was interrupted by a surprise visitor; we were stunned when we found out who our visitor was.

In the company of three other sergeants, I was about to sit down to lunch in the pleasant dining room overlooking the backyard garden when I turned my head to follow their wide-eyed stares and open mouths. Coming through the doorway was an RAF air marshal, resplendent in summer uniform, the whole left side of which was covered in medal ribbons.

"My name is Tedder," he said as he approached each one of us with outstretched hand. We returned his vigorous handshake like mute automatons; none of us could think of a thing to say. "May I join you for lunch?" he asked. Surely he could not have supposed that he would get an objection from us. We mumbled something to the effect that we would be honoured, and he took his place at the head of our small table. I had not recognized him, not having seen photos of him in any of the newspapers, but I now knew he was Air Marshal Sir Arthur Tedder, commander-in-chief of all North African and Mediterranean air forces.

This fine man engaged us in talk about the desert air forces, and wanted to know about our experiences. He was even kind enough to ask for our humble opinions about the state of our bomber and fighter squadrons. He had a personality of such genuine warmth that he quickly put us at ease. I thought it remarkable that this man, with his awesome responsibilities, could find time to make contact with airmen as low on the rank scale as we were.*

As we talked, one of the Sudanese waiters approached with a bowl of soup to serve to our guest. In his nervousness, he stumbled on a fold in the rug, and tipped the soup bowl so that the entire contents splashed over the shoulder and arm of the air marshal's splendid uniform! Our guest bolted upwards from his chair as the poor waiter stood shaking in horror and shame. The dismal plight of the unfortunate fellow calmed down the good air marshal almost immediately. He tried to ease the obvious suffering of the waiter, and asked that someone bring a wet cloth to clean as much as possible of the soup from his uniform.

The Sudanese fled to the kitchen and didn't return. In his place, a flight sergeant appeared to offer his abject apologies to Sir Arthur, and took the soiled tunic away to get it cleaned up as best he could.

The air marshal quickly regained his composure, and we finished our meal, brought by a different waiter, in pleasant conversation, before our commander-in-chief took his leave of us.**

Two days later we were introduced to the other half of this august family. Lady Tedder arrived to preside over and chaperone an evening

---

* In his book *The Right of the Line*, John Terraine wrote that "Tedder had a common touch, a nice informality that helped him greatly in an informal Service to keep contact with his air and ground crews — broad vision, long sight, complete professionalism — such were the ingredients of Tedder's undoubted greatness."

** In 1949, when the author was a flight lieutenant adjutant at the RCAF Staff College in Toronto, Sir Arthur, by then Air Chief Marshal Lord Tedder, was guest of honour at a reception given for the Imperial War College. In the bar, this illustrious man noticed my Africa Star medal ribbon and singled me out to ask on which of his desert squadrons I had served. When I found voice to reply, I became bold enough to mention the incident of the spilled dance, held in a large room on the second floor. Our partners were ladies from the numerous auxiliary units who supported the canteens in the city. Two teenage daughters of the Tedder family were pursued about the garden by our two intrepid Aussie convalescents. It was a pleasant affair.

At one point, Lady Tedder persuaded me to get on my feet and join the dancers. This matronly lady was a most kind and gracious person.

■ ■ ■

Although General Auchinleck had stopped Rommel's advance at El Alamein, barely sixty miles from Alexandria, a sense of defeatism poisoned the atmosphere of the city. Smoke seen rising from the roof of Air Force Headquarters was widely rumoured to be from the burning of military documents in preparation for a quick retreat from Egypt to Palestine. The expectation of a victory by Rommel and the entry of his Afrika Korps troops into Cairo was lending a new boldness to the locals of the city. Their pro-German demonstrations were becoming more frequent, and lent speed to the failing confidence of the British forces in the city.

A day or so after the dance at Hurricane House, as I walked along one of the city's main avenues, I paused in mid-step as I suddenly sensed a change in the air. There was something different in the hustle and bustle of the people and traffic about me. What had happened? I soon found out — "Monty" had arrived!

"Monty," of course, was Lieutenant-General Bernard Law Montgomery. On 12 August, he had arrived to take over command of Eighth Army from the beleaguered General Auchinleck.[†]

I felt increasing discomfort about the idle life I was leading at Hurricane House. The cause of my uneasiness was my awareness of what was going on at the El Alamein front, and the fact that I had been away from operational flying for nearly two months. A nagging voice over my left shoulder told me that I deserved a rest, but I could not shake off a feeling of guilt. I knew that I was not yet in any condition to

---

soup. He did not remember me, of course, but he readily recalled the mishap, and therefore carried on our conversation too long for the comfort of senior officers of the college, who waited to draw his attention. They were not pleased with me.

[†] Winston Churchill and his chief of the Imperial general staff, General Sir Alan Brooke, had come to the conclusion that Eighth Army had lost confidence in its commander. They arrived in Cairo on 4 August to assess the situation, and soon decided that Auchinleck had to be replaced. His troops had suffered too many defeats to sustain a high morale, or to retain confidence in their commander. Rommel, in his diaries, was more generous to his opponent.

fly, but I began to feel that I ought to be making some kind of a contri-
bution. I made another foolhardy decision, similar to the one that only a
few weeks before had almost cost me my life. I decided to go looking for
something useful to do.

Just four or five blocks from the hotel, off on a side street from
Sharia Soliman Pasha, I had noticed an RAF transport facility, and
thought I might as well look in there to see if there was any job that I
might take on.

Without challenge, I crossed a large yard filled with an assortment of
vehicles, and entered the despatch office, where I found an Australian
flying officer in charge of the section. He seemed unimpressed with my
story, but handed me over to a flight sergeant who made up the sched-
ules for all the transport runs for which the section was responsible. He
was an affable individual, who said that they could always do with
another driver, if that was all right with me. I quickly affirmed that it
was. I concealed my surprise that neither he nor the officer had thought
to ask if I could drive. *In fact, I had never driven a car in my life!* No
matter; I had watched people drive often enough to believe that I knew
the procedures, and I felt confident that I could bluff my way through
until I learned how to drive.

The flight sergeant explained that this section reported to Air Force
Headquarters, and took care of the various transportation needs of the
staff of that HQ in and around the city. He then took me to a lounge to
meet the other drivers. What a surprise this was. At least ten of the drivers
were Canadian aircrew sergeants: pilots, navigators, and wireless air gunners, all unhappily driving Hillmans and Bedfords about the city on all
sorts of jobs. The story they had to tell me was indeed an unusual one.

During the series of defeats suffered by Eighth Army leading to the
retreat to the El Alamein line, the RAF began to suffer a critical shortage
of Wellington "airscrews," RAF nomenclature for "propellers."* A
cyphered message was despatched to England urgently requesting the
immediate shipment of a hundred or so airscrews for Wellington bombers.
The message had to pass through the cypher centres at Malta and
Gibraltar, and at one of these centres, someone with the proverbial "digit"

---

* The British navy has always referred to ships' propellers as "screws"; with the formation
of the RNAS, the Royal Naval Air Service, in WWI, it seemed only natural to call an aircraft's propeller an "airscrew." With the absorption of the RNAS and the RFC, the Royal
Flying Corps, into the new Royal Air Force in 1918, the term persisted. To this day, veterans
of the Fleet Air Arm refer to an aircraft's propellers as "screws."

trouble omitted the first "s" from the word "airscrews" when relaying the coded message. Thus it arrived in England as a critical plea for a hundred *aircrews*! The brass wasted no time. Faced with a great shortage of experienced bomber aircrew at that moment, they had to resort to a draft of Canadian aircrew at Bournemouth waiting for their OTU training. These unfortunates were promptly shipped out to Cairo, mostly by transitting Wimpys through Gibraltar and Malta, only to find that it was a proper "balls-up," and that they couldn't be used on ops until they had undergone some operational training. Some were lucky, and were sent to an OTU set up in Palestine, but most became dogsbodies like my companions in the transport section.

This incident prompted the RAF to change its nomenclature for "airscrews" to "propellers."

These misplaced aircrew were trying to get a message through the RCAF liaison officer at Air Force Headquarters, Cairo, to Charles "Chubby" Power, the Canadian minister of national defence for air, in Ottawa, to explain their plight. They finally succeeded, and the minister had them flown home to Canada via the West Africa and South America ferry routes.

■ ■ ■

The next morning I arrived early at the transport unit, and my adventures in driving began. I was surprised to be given an immediate assignment by the despatcher. I was to take a small, four-door Hillman sedan to Air Force Headquarters, pick up a Wing Commander "X," and take him to the main Middle East Headquarters, which was almost across the city from AHQ.

I got into the Hillman and surveyed the controls. The steering wheel was on the right, of course, in this British car, with the gear shift on the left. This didn't bother me as I had no experience with an alternative, and I am largely ambidextrous in any case. I cautiously engaged first gear and jerked my way forward as I hesitantly let out the clutch. Luckily, I looked up just in time to avoid running over a corporal. Although the Hillman was blessed with synchromesh gears, I nevertheless managed to clash the gears as I changed them upward — no mean feat. The resultant screech turned heads. I was relieved when I succeeded in jolting my way through the gate and onto the street, escaping the startled stares of the airmen in the yard.

I familiarized myself with the controls over the next few blocks, trying not to stare downwards as I changed gears. It was a miracle that I missed pedestrians and other cars. In Cairo, all local drivers considered that they had the right of way so long as they leaned on their horns. This made for some dramatic pile-ups at intersections.

I had become reasonably familiar with the layout of the city, and with much luck, and what I thought must be divine guidance, I reached Air Force Headquarters. Waiting for me, looking at his watch irritably (I was not on time), was the wing commander. With what seemed to me greatly misplaced trust, he entered the back seat, and we were off.

By another miracle, we reached Middle East HQ, my passenger by now exhibiting considerable nervousness. I pointed the Hillman at the curb, and felt for the brake pedal to slow our approach. Unfortunately, my foot slipped off that pedal onto the accelerator! We mounted the wide curb before the engine stalled, bringing us to an abrupt stop. The rear door flew open, and my passenger jumped out to recover his brief case, which had been ejected from the floor of the car and had landed in the dust of the sidewalk.

When I faced the wing commander, he was sputtering in anger, his face turning slightly purple, with veins at the temple swelling alarmingly. He almost screamed, "You bloody idiot. One would think you had never driven a car in your life!" He demanded my name and number, which I gave him, not thinking to fudge both. To my great relief, he stormed off. How fortunate I was never to hear from him again.

With the help of an understanding corporal driver, my driving improved quite rapidly, and I progressed to other types of vehicles. Other adventures awaited me. One assignment took me through a narrow street near the local market. Ahead of me were stalls of produce crowding the lane, and an interesting musical "hurdy-gurdy" being wound by a *fellah*. Sitting on the wooden contraption was a monkey on a leash. As I approached, I had to swerve to miss a child who had run into the street, and the right fender of my Jeep struck the music box, shattering it to pieces. The monkey flew into the air. I knew enough not to stop, and took off down the laneway as fast as obstructions would permit. In my rear-view mirror, I saw a small crowd of angry people, some with sticks, running after me. I also caught a glimpse of the monkey hanging with one arm from a section of overhead drainpipe. I was lucky to reach a main street and make my escape.

The job I had found for myself was exciting, but none of my assignments shook me up like the run I made to deliver a package to the airfield at Heliopolis in the northeast outskirts of the city. As I approached the exit gate, I stopped to watch a Hudson aircraft on its landing approach, struck by the fact that it was trailing a great deal of smoke. Just before touchdown, the right wing dipped in what appeared to me to be a stall, and hit the runway. Immediately, the aircraft cartwheeled and exploded in a ball of fire and black oily smoke. As I sat in shock, firetrucks and ambulances rushed out to the blazing wreck. There could be no survivors. There was nothing I could do. After I had calmed down, I left.

I received a greater shock the next morning when I was told that one of the ill-fated passengers on that Hudson had been Lady Tedder. For some time after the tragedy, I was tormented by images of that gracious lady mingling with us at Hurricane House, and by what I had witnessed at the airfield. I never learned what had caused the crash.

Several days later, I had just arrived in the drivers' lounge when the Australian CO entered the room followed by a tall, well-built army captain. He called the assembled drivers to order, and introduced his companion.

"This is Captain 'S,' and he is looking for a driver for a special run. I'm going to let him give you the details."

The captain looked us over and addressed us: "Well, chaps, as your commanding officer has said, I am looking for a driver. I am not at liberty to give you all the details. I can only tell you now that we will be gone for about two weeks, and the whole drive will be spent in desert areas. Whoever comes with me and my batman driver will have to drive a truck, which I need to accompany my vehicle with supplies of petrol and oil. I have to tell you that there may be some risk involved, and driving in the desert is never the most comfortable of experiences. I will say that I have some experience in the kind of excursion we will be undertaking, so I don't expect that we are going to get into much trouble. Well, there it is, chaps. It's a volunteer job all the way, and we leave very early tomorrow morning. What do you say?"

There was an embarrassingly long silence in the room. No one was anxious to respond to the captain's appeal. As he and our CO exchanged rather disappointed glances, it became obvious that there were no takers to the invitation. I decided to ignore the little voice of caution nagging at me again and take the plunge into what seemed to me a new adventure, and a welcome change from the daily routine runs I had been making throughout the city. I stuck up my hand. "I'll go along, sir, if it's all right with the CO."

I was beckoned to the front of the room, and as I made my way through the chairs, I was well aware of many glances that clearly said, "You must be an idiot to volunteer for such a pig-in-a-poke job."

I was introduced to the captain, who shook my hand and thanked me for volunteering, and proceeded to give me my instructions. He also outlined to the CO how many "jerry cans" of petrol and oil would be needed in the truck. He informed me that he would supply me with a rifle, the standard British .303 Enfield, and a supply of ammunition. I didn't ask why he thought I might need that weapon. My loaded truck, a quarter-ton Ford, would be waiting for me at the section at 0500 hours the next morning. He cautioned me to bring some warm clothing and sunglasses. I was to meet him at 0600 hours at Mena House hotel, which was near the pyramids at Giza. The CO didn't comment on my being a novice driver — perhaps he was just relieved that someone had responded to the captain's appeal. I left for Hurricane House to gather my gear for the expedition the following morning.

One interesting thing I had noticed about the captain — he wore an RAF pilot's wing. I could only guess that he had been grounded for medical reasons and had transferred to the army. Being air force, I took some comfort and confidence from this.

After dinner that night, I informed the flight sergeant manager that I would be absent for about two weeks on a special drive. He knew I was working at the transport section, so he wasn't too surprised at this news.

Mahmoud awakened me early, and I took off for the section to pick up the truck. I found it loaded with petrol and oil cans. The rifle and pouches of bullets were on the seat. I was wearing my holstered Enfield .38 revolver that I had not turned in when I left the squadron, so I felt well armed. I drove back to the hotel and parked at the front curb while Mahmoud brought out my duffle bag. I had saved up quite a few pounds because of my hospital stays, and I entrusted this money to Mahmoud, who vowed to protect it for me. He was in tears as I departed. Dramatically, I had told him that I was going away to fight the Germans, and he wailed that he feared I was going to be killed. He yelled after me *"Nemchou Iallah!"* (Go by the grace of God!). Somehow, I knew my money would be safe with my trusty servant.

I made my way in the powerful Ford V8 through the teeming streets towards the pyramids west of the city. Unfortunately, making a right turn about ten streets from Mena House, I found myself in the middle of a long army truck convoy proceeding in the opposite direction. With large trucks in front and behind me, and a stream of traffic in the other lane, it was miles before I could extricate myself and turn around. As a result, I was nearly forty minutes late arriving at Mena House.

In spite of my excuse, the captain was quite furious. When he calmed down, he introduced me to his batman and driver, a corporal about thirty years old. "Well, let's get going. We have already wasted an hour. Hewer, you follow us and keep us in sight at all times. It's too easy to lose your way in the dust of the desert."

The captain had a British Humber station wagon loaded with all sorts of desert gear, from water containers to canvas bags for washing. I followed him as we made our way past the towering pyramids of Giza, and took off westwards on a rocky path that made small pretence of being a road. The sun rose swiftly, and I was beginning to feel the heat that would punish us for the rest of our journey into "The Blue," which was the common term for the desert used by all British forces. It probably derived from an easy metaphor for the almost unfailingly blue desert sky.

We had been travelling for nearly five hours before we made our first stop. In that time, I had learned to keep enough distance behind the Humber so that I didn't eat too much of the dust it threw up. We had long since left the "road" behind, and were driving on the brown, rock-strewn crust that made up the Western Desert surface for some seventy-five miles south from the Mediterranean coast. Periodically, we would strike soft patches of loose sand, and I would frantically double clutch and shift to low gear to avoid getting bogged down.

As the corporal brewed up some tea, and we tackled tinned bully beef and biscuits, the captain apparently decided that it was safe to take me into his confidence. "Let me tell you what this trip is all about, Hewer. For some time, the Germans and the Italians have been carrying out sporadic bombing raids on the oil storage tanks at Suez. To do this, they've been flying from Benghazi on a course that takes them fairly close to Siwa Oasis, which we happen to hold with a battalion. Now, the powers that be decided to investigate whether it might be feasible to station one or two Hurricanes or Spitfires at Siwa to intercept and shoot down these aircraft. I was selected because I have an air force background, and also because I have been over some of this ground before on various army patrols. My job is to survey the ground at Siwa, and assess the practicability of utilizing an airstrip there for the fighters.

"You may not know that Siwa Oasis is near the Libyan border, some 400 miles from Cairo, so we have a long, hot drive ahead of us. We also have to go through what is called the Qattara Depression. This is a deep salt marsh, and there are only one or two passable tracks through it. It's quite a hellhole, actually. Well, there it is. We'll have to press on for a few more hours before we camp for the night."

I did know where Siwa Oasis was; I was quite familiar with the geography of the Western Desert from our navigation maps. I told the captain this, and that I had done considerable flying over the area not too far north of the Depression. I added, "It seems to me that from the eastern edge of the Depression, we will be travelling behind the German lines at Alamein, and I know that Siwa is almost 200 miles west of the enemy lines."

The captain seemed surprised at this. "You know the geography. I didn't know we had a veteran with us. Good show. You're quite right, we will be going a long way behind the German lines, but you probably know that the southern end of the battlefront ends at the northern edge of the Qattara Depression, and that's the one place we'll be close to Rommel's forces on our track through that valley. The only forces we may run into are their recce patrols."

It was hard driving for the next few hours. The temperature had risen to well above 100 degrees Farenheit. The desert humidity is near zero, so low that not enough water vapour exists to form clouds. The sun's rays beat down through cloudless skies like a blowtorch baking the land. The ground heats the atmosphere so much that air rises in waves that can be seen plainly. The shimmering waves confuse the eye, causing the traveller to see mirages. At night, desert areas cool quickly because they lack the insulation provided by humidity and clouds. Temperatures can drop to 40 degrees Farenheit or lower. Without shelter, in winter months, one can die from exposure.

The corporal had gotten some sand in his eyes, which became inflamed and irritated. He had not brought adequate sunglasses with him, so I gave him my Ray-Bans. This eased the pain in his eyes, but it meant that I had to squint from then on through the dust and shimmering heatwaves that blurred the horizon and made it difficult to keep the Humber in sight. The captain was not pleased that he had to take over the driving from the corporal.

The captain finally called a halt for the night as the sun was lowering towards the horizon. We had a welcome wash in the canvas bags, which were part of the captain's desert gear, and brewed up the all-healing tea. The corporal heated up some tinned sausages, which seemed to have the barest suggestion of meat in them. But even they and the ubiquitous hardtack biscuits were more than acceptable at this stage.

By the time we had finished eating the air was becoming quite cool, and we took blankets from the Humber to wrap around our shoulders. We also had thin, straw-filled mattresses to lay out beside our trucks. The captain then said that the three of us were to alternate on watch for two hours, which meant that two of us would have four hours sleep. I drew the first watch.

By the time we had settled down, the stars were out in their millions. I sat wrapped in my blanket where the trucks would not obscure my view of the terrain about us. I kept my rifle close by my side. The silence was eerie, but it was broken by slight cracking sounds and faint groans. I was alarmed by these noises, but I eventually traced them to superheated rocks now shrinking as they cooled in the desert night air. What really caused the hairs on the back of my neck to rise were the shadows born from the light of the stars. As I stared intently at the shadows, I could almost swear that they were moving. Was it some Arab or commando creeping up on us? Moving as silently as I could, I forced myself to investigate some of the ghostly apparitions. I found nothing. It was a spooky night.

My little voice of caution intruded on my thoughts to ask, "What in hell are you doing out here when you're supposed to be on convalescent leave in Cairo?" I had no logical answer, of course, but I was not unhappy with my decision, despite the rigours of our venture. Even so, I was thankful to be relieved by the corporal and to retreat to my pallet on the rocky ground for what remained of the night.

Some four hours after we resumed our trek we arrived at the eastern edge of the near-impassable Qattara Depression. We had barely begun our descent into this forbidding valley when we met a small convoy of trucks climbing out of the Depression towards Cairo. Several of the trucks mounted heavy-calibre Lewis machine guns. The captain seemed to be acquainted with several of the officers in the lead vehicles. When we got underway again, he told me that the convoy was part of the LRDG, the Long-Range Desert Group, which operated behind the German lines gathering intelligence for Eighth Army. Some time later I learned more about this intrepid force.*

---

* R.A. Bagnold, a distinguished British scholar, originated the idea for the force, which was accepted by General Wavell in summer 1940. After the First World War, Bagnold, a fellow of the Royal Society, had explored most of the desert from the Sudan to the Mediterranean Sea. His main object was to research material for his book *The Physics of Blown Sand and Desert Dunes*. He made many expeditions from Cairo to Siwa Oasis, in the process establishing tracks from Cairo through the Qattara Depression (it was his tracks, *trighs* in Arabic, that the

On a stop to top up our oil and petrol from the cans I carried in my truck, the captain cautioned me to keep close behind him, and strictly on the same path. He explained that most of the Depression floor was a salt marsh that could swallow a ten-ton truck in a few minutes. This threat limited the width of the battle front at Alamein to less than seventy miles. The depression, called a *deir* by Arabs, was impassable by heavy trucks and armoured vehicles, which would lose their caterpillar tracks in the soft sand or marsh. The Qattara formed a flank that could not be turned.

We had turned south from our course very close to the right flank of the Afrika Korps battle line and were following the better of only two passable trighs crossing the valley. I needed no further warning as I pursued the Humber into a cauldron of dry, scorching heat, down a twisting route towards the bottom of this brutal aberration in the desert landscape, 150 miles in length and seventy-five miles across at its widest point.

On our track we came close to the floor of the Depression, almost 400 feet below sea level. We were flanked by miles of cracked salt crust, and leered at by grinning gargoyles carved out of the limestone cliffs by centuries of wind erosion. In some places we were hemmed in by cliffs reaching 800 feet in height, and by towering escarpments called *djbels*. I clung to the steering wheel, almost dizzy in the blistering heat. It took effort to breathe with anything other than shallow intakes of the stifling air. Twice we drove into attacking swarms of murderous flies and narrowly escaped before panic set in. Between some rock formations, the dead air would come suddenly to life, powerful gusts of wind that blew fine sand into the truck cab and into eyes and nostrils. I knew that the captain and the corporal, thirty feet in front of me, would not be faring any better than I was.

Late in the day we climbed out of the western edge of this hellish bowl, and gained the flat, firmer ground of a track that led to the small cluster of scrub bushes — the tiny oasis of Qara, our objective for the night.

---

captain was following). In 1940, as a major, Bagnold became the first commander of the LRDG, whose primary job was reconnaissance and intelligence gathering. Most of Eighth Army's information about enemy supply lines and movements came from these elite groups. All members were specialists in radio, guns and explosives, or navigation. For desert navigation, they used sun compasses for "dead-reckoning," and thedolites for sun or moon true bearings, techniques pioneered by Bagnold. Their main vehicle was the one-and-a-half ton truck with Lewis guns on compressed-air mountings. Another important job of this force was to give logistic and intelligence support to SAS, the Special Air Service.

We had driven only a few miles when the fading light was further darkened by fog. This was not a rare phenomenon in the desert, where quick changes in temperature produced condensation, which turned to fog. The captain slowed his vehicle, and I tried vainly to keep his rear bumper in sight. When he disappeared from my view, I could only keep to the track we had been following and hope that I wouldn't lose him.

I was peering intently out my side window when a ghostly form appeared out of the mist. As I crept forward, the figure became a man in Arab headdress. He was wearing a military shirt and shorts. His face was almost obscured by a heavy black beard. He carried a Sten gun, or was it a Schmeisser? He looked menacing, and I pondered what to do. I held my revolver in my right hand as I steered slowly forward with my left, but I held no hope that I could do much with this small weapon. My anxious dilemma was relieved when a decidedly English voice called out, "Your captain is over here in the wadi. Follow me and join us for a brew."

At the wadi, I found my captain standing by a brazier in conversation with a tall, slim officer who looked to be in command of the small group of motley-garbed soldiers squatting about with cups of chai in their hands. I was introduced to Captain Stirling, commander of SAS, the Special Air Service force, which was carrying out a kind of guerilla warfare against German airfields and transport, ranging far and wide behind enemy lines. I was not to find out until much later just what this force was accomplishing, and how famous Captain David Stirling had already become as we shared tea in that wadi.*

---

* SAS was born in July 1941, and was largely the brainchild of then Lieutenant David Stirling. He approached a receptive Major-General Neil Ritchie, Eighth Army deputy chief of staff, who recommended the idea to his chief, General Auchinleck. With approval in hand, Stirling fell prey to a Brigadier Dudley Clarke, who was devising schemes to deceive Rommel, at Middle East Headquarters, Cairo. He wanted to form a bogus parachute unit called the 1st Special Air Service Brigade. To humour the brigadier, Stirling agreed to name his new force, L Detachment, Special Air Service Brigade. From carefully recruited and skilled volunteers, he formed his force into four-man specialist modules and set about to conduct raids in depth behind enemy lines, and to attack airfields and enemy tactical headquarters. He also recruited and armed local Arab guerilla elements. He often operated out of Siwa Oasis, a main headquarters of the LRDG that supported SAS with supplies and intelligence. SAS made much use of jeeps, specially fitted with four Vickers machine guns capable of firing almost 1,000 rounds per minute. In raids against aircraft parked on enemy airfields, the jeep firepower was devastating. Stirling was likely an acting major when we met him, and his fame had spread enough to gain entry into Rommel's diaries, in which he was described as a serious scourge and labelled "the phantom major." Just before our meeting with him, Stirling's group had returned from raiding the German airfield at Sidi Haneish in the Fuka area near the coast. Four jeeps and 14 men had followed the track to Qara. One man was killed; he was buried among the scrub bushes in the wadi.

It was strange (and lucky for us) that throughout the whole of the African campaign neither the Germans nor the Italians copied the British guerilla patrols. Both feared and disliked the inhospitable, uninhabited desert regions. The British were fascinated by deserts, just as they had been for a century.*

We bedded down for the night in the cold air. When we awoke in the morning, Captain Stirling and his men had gone like the phantoms Rommel had called them.

■ ■ ■

We set out at the first sign of the sun's rays, with the captain setting as fast a pace as he dared over the treacherous ground. We had a good hundred miles of hard driving ahead of us across the hard, rocky scrub ground and patches of hazardous sand before we would reach Siwa Oasis.

We stopped to refuel, and to have a light meal. After that, it was over three hours before we sighted the scraggly palm trees and bush that identified an oasis. I was following the captain as he took us forward into a narrow laneway bordered by walls of mud brick when it happened.

It felt as if the side of my head had been slammed by a rock, and I heard a loud crack. I turned my head. There was a large hole in my back window, unmistakably a bullet hole. I put my hand to my head, and it came away covered in blood. What kind of reception was this?

I had little time to ponder our plight; the captain pulled in quickly to stop against the wall, and I followed directly behind him. By now we faced a fusillade of rifle shots; bullets were whizzing over our heads. I grabbed my rifle and cartridge pouch and jumped out my right door to press myself against the mud wall. The captain yelled, "Keep your head down!"

He added, "This isn't Siwa Oasis."

My head was throbbing, and I stuck a rag from my pocket on my skull to slow the bleeding. I could still see, and I didn't think I was

---

* The Englishman's apparent love of the desert always puzzled the Arabs. From my experience, Arabs have no affection for the desert whatsoever. They see it for what it is: a dry, barren, and harsh place, either too cold or scorching hot. They live there because they were born there, and make their living there; they have no other choice. They know, as so many of our downed airmen discovered, that the desert, when challenged, is a pitiless adversary.

wounded too badly. In any case, I didn't have time to think about that. Just a foot from where I was pressing my face, several bricks had fallen away, leaving a narrow aperture that I could peer through. I could see where the rifle fire was coming from — the commotion disturbed a large clump of bushes nearly a hundred yards from our wall. Taking my cue from the captain and corporal, I shoved a clip into the Enfield and began firing back into the bushes.

Our enemies' bullets whined above and thudded into the mud wall. I couldn't help wondering why they didn't throw a grenade at us. The thought also crossed my mind that I was perilously close to the petrol and oil cans on my truck, and if a grenade or incendiary bullet hit them I would most likely go up with the explosion.

Our little battle had been going on for only twenty minutes or so when I heard screams coming from the bushes. For a moment I thought our bullets must have struck one or more of our assailants, but a great commotion and the rapid fire of a heavy machine gun told us somebody else had joined the fray. The firing ceased, followed by a great deal of shouting and the gunning of several truck engines.

The captain came over to me in a crouch, "What happened to your head? Have you been hit?" He was very concerned.

I told him what had happened, and that I was all right. "I probably look much worse than I am."

At that moment a truck rolled around the corner and came towards us. The captain recognized it with great relief as an LRDG vehicle, and stood out in the road to raise his arms in welcome. The lieutenant driver jumped down to shake hands with the captain, who exclaimed, "We're sure glad to see you. Who in hell was firing at us?"

"You ran into a patrol from the Italian battalion that holds the town of Jarabub just across the Libyan border. There were about twenty-five of them. These chaps are not really anxious to mix it up with anybody their size, so they took off in a hurry as soon as we opened up on them with our Lewis guns. We hit a couple, or you chaps did, but they took their wounded with them, fortunately. We don't want them."

A second LRDG truck pulled up behind the lieutenant's vehicle as our captain explained, "We're headed for Siwa Oasis, but we seem to have overshot. Where have we landed up?"

The lieutenant replied with a grin, "This area is very close to the border. It's actually the far eastern outskirts of Jarabub, so you've come too far north and west. You may know that Eighth Army has a battalion of Sudanese troops stationed at Siwa, and they have a kind of half-hearted mini-war going on with the Jarabub Italians, who are only sixty miles away. The battalion is staffed with British officers and NCOs, of course. We use Siwa as one of our main bases, and we were out on a recce patrol from there when we heard the firing. We're going back there now so you can follow us in. It isn't far."

The captain readily agreed to follow, but said that my head needed a little attention before we took off. One of the LRDG sergeants, who was obviously used to this sort of thing, took a look at me and pronounced that it was nothing serious. With a first-aid kit, he cleaned up my face and the cut on my head, applying a dressing and an oversize bandage, which wrapped around my head. We then fell in behind our rescuers' trucks and took off for Siwa Oasis.

I was surprised by the size of the oasis. We entered through a large gap in what looked like the remains of a high wall that encircled the whole village. There was an abundance of beautiful palm trees, and many substantial buildings. We passed groups of smiling children, who waved at us as if we were familiar visitors. This was an ancient village that had been fought over in the First World War; it was famous for its dates, which were exported all over the world. Like Jarabub, Siwa lay on the edge of the great Libyan Sand Sea, about 150 miles south of the coast. It had long been a stronghold of the Senussi Arabs, who had resisted the Italian conquest, and allied themselves with the British.

At the western outskirts of the village, our LRDG friends took us to the battalion headquarters, and introduced us to the lieutenant-colonel commanding officer before leaving on other business.

While the captain discussed his mission with the CO, a sergeant took the corporal and me to separate tents where we were to be billeted during our stay. I was to share a tent occupied by an Australian sergeant, who greeted me with more warmth than I imagined was genuine. After all, I was invading his comfortable quarters.

My new Aussie friend showed me around the battalion grounds, and told me about the troops he had helped to train and discipline. The Sudanese were all over six feet tall. They were an impressive sight in their red fez headdresses, khaki tunics and shorts, and puttees wrapped to their knees.

The Aussie explained, "These fellows love the army, the discipline and order, and would drill all day if we let them. I think, for them, their acceptance as soldiers in the British army is a high point in their lives not attainable in their own country. They are excellent, courageous fighting men, who will follow their officer and NCO leaders unquestionably. They have two oddities. They demand spit and polish, and absolute cleanliness, and it can be a bloody nuisance. It means that we have to shave and shower daily, and keep our uniforms impeccably clean and pressed, otherwise we couldn't lead them to water. The stranger quirk is that they don't appear to miss their women at all. They walk about hand in hand, and can be seen embracing. We don't ask any questions, but neither do we ever walk about in the nude. They have their own mess, and we share a mess with the officers, their table being separate at the end of the mess hall tent. Altogether, except for the occasional raid on the Italians, at Jarabub, who are all over forty or otherwise misfits, we lead a cushy life compared to our cobbers up at Alamein." Needless to say, we had no untoward incidents with our Sudanese allies.

For the next three days, the captain and corporal set about surveying a large tract of level ground north of the battalion camp that looked like an unused airstrip, possibly suitable for a runway for the Spitfires or Hurricanes. They had brought with them an engineer's level, a tripod-mounted telescope with a spirit bubble and a crosswire. They also had a transit, or theodolite, another tripod with telescope and crosswires that indicated angles in degrees, minutes, and seconds. The corporal seemed to know more about using this equipment than the captain, which is likely why he had been chosen for the venture. I knew how to "swing the compass" on our aircraft, but little or nothing about these procedures. I moved the tripods to designated positions, and called out readings from the instruments.

On the fourth day, the captain summed up the results of our work: "Well, I'm satisfied that this strip will do very well for our gambit. It's not perfect, but I'd have no trouble getting a Hurry or Spit off this ground once it's been cleared of some of the rocks. The colonel tells me his Sudanese will take care of that, and they'll lay out markers along each side of the strip as we have indicated. They'll need some smoke for wind direction too, but the small advance party that Group will send out here will take care of that, and provide a radio van as well. Looks like we've done our job, chaps. I think we deserve a day or so's rest here."

The corporal and I had no argument with this. For the next two days, we were shown around the splendid oasis, and introduced to some of the resident Senussis. We were treated to lunch by one Arab host. This was probably not a new experience for the captain, but it was for the corporal and me. We sat in a circle, and a large bowl of couscous was passed from one to the other, each person in turn licking the communal spoon clean. This dish was made up of millet, large chunks of lamb or mutton (or camel?), which I had grown to hate back at Kabrit, and other bits I didn't care to know about. As the bowl emptied, I was horrified to stare into the remains and see an eye staring back at me! Somehow, I managed to keep a straight face. I had heard that this was considered a delicacy reserved for the most important guest. The captain was the victim, of course, for which I was greatly thankful. I marvelled at the aplomb and feigned pleasure with which he accepted and swallowed what seemed to me a gastronomical horror.

Following the meal, we were given bowls of water to rinse our greasy hands in. Also, to satisfy Arab custom, we all belched loudly to show that we had enjoyed our meal. We then sat through an elaborate coffee ceremony before thanking and leaving our gracious hosts. It was an experience I wasn't anxious to repeat.

On our last night at Siwa, I had an experience of another kind. A bright moon cast enough light on the tent wall so that I could make out the form of my companion sleeping on his canvas cot a mere five feet away. Before going to bed I had followed my habit, acquired at our advanced landing bases, of placing my revolver under whatever served as my pillow. As I lay there, trying to clear my mind of its frequent parade of disturbing memories, I turned my head and stared into two beady yellow eyes not twenty-four inches from my face! I froze in horror; I knew what it was — a sand viper! I knew from a trip to the Cairo museum that their bite was deadly. I have always been repelled by snakes of any kind, and this one wasn't any grass snake.

I knew that I couldn't make any sudden movement, but I had to do something. Very slowly and deliberately, I slid my hand under my pillow to feel for my pistol. I drew it out very carefully and raised it, all the while fixed on those deadly viper eyes. I didn't dare blink. Aiming between the yellow orbs, I slowly squeezed the trigger. The shot shattered the quiet of the camp, and was followed instantly by another shot from my companion. I felt his bullet pass through my hair! He had also seen the snake between our beds and took action. We didn't wait to see if we had hit the thing. We both plunged out of the tent, taking part of it with us in our panic.

As the Aussie and I stood outside in the moonlight, a crowd soon formed around us. We felt a little sheepish, but we didn't know what else we could have done. There was no sign of the snake; obviously, we hadn't hit it.

Everyone went back to bed, but my companion and I had difficulty getting to sleep, seeing snakes in every shadow. I felt lucky to have escaped the viper's fangs, but I knew that we had most likely come closer to disaster from each other's bullets than from our intruder's bite. If we had been found, each drilled through the head, how could it have been explained? A double murder? A stupid accident? What would our next of kin be told? It would have been a bizarre mystery.

The next morning we thanked our battalion hosts for their help and hospitality, and topped up our water bottles and food supplies for the trip back to Cairo. My Aussie friend and I had bonded over the snake episode. We even shared a laugh over a parcel he had received from home. His mother had carefully packed several delicacies that she knew her son would like, including a package of dates from Siwa Oasis!

The LRDG officers at Siwa told us they knew of no change in conditions that should cause us to change our route back to Cairo from the tracks we had followed on the way out. With that assurance, we set off on our return journey, planning to reach Qara for our first night stop.

We spent that night at the Qara oasis, doing our watchkeeping shifts, and made our entry to the forbidding Qattara Depression in the first light of a long day that saw temperatures above 120 degrees Fahrenheit.

Close to noon on the fourth day of our return drive we saw the tips of the Giza pyramids poking above the shimmering horizon. What a welcome sight! The Humber ahead of me picked up a little speed — the captain was as anxious as I was to get back. I wondered if our vehicles would hold out until we reached the city. They had stood up unbelievably well through a pounding that should have destroyed them. What had been a deep tread on my new desert tires was now fabric. The only rubber left was on the sidewalls. It would be a miracle if they didn't blow before I reached the transport section.

Forty minutes later we hit the road past the pyramids, and stopped at the first bar the captain could find. We fell into the nearest chairs, and the captain ordered three cold beers. As we gulped down the heavenly nectar, I felt a great sense of relief that our ordeal was over, as exciting as it had been.

The captain asked me how my head was feeling, and although it was still throbbing on and off I told him it was okay. He told me to see a medical officer as soon as I could. Then he raised his beer glass, his second one, and said, "Look, chaps, I think both of you did a great job out there. Our little dust-up with the Italians was unexpected, and it was my fault for getting us off our track, but you both kept your cool and handled it well. As for you, Sgt Hewer, my young fellow airman, it was obvious, when we started out, that you didn't have much of a clue about desert driving or much about cars in general. But for someone who was out of his element I think it was bloody marvellous how quickly you learned. You did well in that little firefight we had, especially after being hit on the head. Well, we have to part company and get on our way. I wish you the best of luck in the rest of your war. Thank you for sticking your neck out and helping us with this little caper."

I told him I was glad to have been able to cope, and in spite of everything, I was glad I didn't miss the trip. He was a good officer.

We shook hands firmly, and I took off in my ailing Ford through the teeming streets towards the transport section. I felt completely drained. How could I have known this bizarre experience awaited me when I impulsively stuck up my hand to volunteer for this excursion? How many people knew where I had been these last two weeks, most of it spent miles behind the German lines? Not many. The air force had no reason to believe I was anywhere but convalescing at Hurricane House.*

As I made my way through the mid-day pandemonium of the Cairo traffic, I muttered, "I have to stop putting myself into these crazy situations!"

---

* I never did discover whether the airstrip we had surveyed was ever used for its speculated purpose, or whether events overcame the need. Apparently, it was much improved after our visit. In his diaries, Field Marshal Lord Alanbrooke describes his visit, by air, to Siwa Oasis on 28 January 1943 from Cairo where he was staying with Winston Churchill after the Casablanca Conference. Strangely, he mentions Siwa changing hands between the Italians, British, and Germans during the Libyan fighting (couldn't have occurred in 1941–42 SAS-LRDG days!), and that Rommel visited the oasis on 21 September 1942.

25
EXIT FROM
EGYPT

Y RETURN TO THE TRANSPORT section stirred little interest or curiosity. The staff were more concerned with the sad condition of the truck. I told the Australian CO that a posting was coming up, and it was unlikely that I would be returning to the section. He thanked me for helping them out, wished me the best of luck, and shook my hand. Then, with sudden concern, he exclaimed, "What have you done to your head?" I was a sorry sight. The blood had seeped through the old bandage. I told him, very briefly, what had happened, and he hustled me quickly to the section first-aid clinic. The medical assistant on staff took a look at the wound on my head. He didn't think it needed any stitches, but he cleaned it up and put a fresh dressing on it to guard against infection.

Since I hadn't been taken on strength officially, there was no paper work of any kind involved in my departure.

I walked wearily the few blocks to Hurricane House. The flight sergeant greeted me warmly, but asked no questions. Mahmoud was beaming with relief and delight, and proudly produced the money he had been keeping for me. Not a piastre was missing. When I pressed a few pounds into his hand he recoiled. "La, la," he cried, "That is far too much for such a lowly person as me!" I told him he was not a lowly person, and that I would be unhappy if he didn't take the money, which he had truly earned. At this, he gave in and accepted his reward.

Mahmoud had kept my room undisturbed for me. In my exhausted state, I just wanted to fall into bed, but I was too dirty. I climbed gratefully into the warm bath my faithful servant quickly prepared for me, and lay soaking up to my neck in blissful relief. The cool sheets of my bed were sheer luxury after my desert pallet. Although it was before dinner time, I did not open my eyes until 0700 hours the next morning, feeling blessedly rested and restored.

After I had devoured a large breakfast, the flight sergeant informed me that he had instructions from Air Force Headquarters that I was to report that day to the personnel officer.

At 0900 hours, I reported to a flight lieutenant at AHQ who informed me that I was posted to No. 5 ADU, the Aircraft Delivery Unit, headquartered at Abu Sueir, and that I was to report back in two days for a date of transfer.

I had been told quite a bit about this unit by my convalescing companions at Hurricane House. I wanted no part of it. It was a ferry operation, delivering aircraft and supplies on a route from Takoradi on the western gold coast of Africa, across the continent to Khartoum in the Sudan, and then northward to Abu Sueir. Once on that unit, I could be buried in Africa for years.*

Somehow, I had to get out of this posting, and find a way to get back to England. I struggled for a solution for hours before it came to me. I remembered that the flight lieutenant who had curtly informed me of the 5 ADU sentence was the type who prided himself on perfection. I devised a plan, and decided to give it a try.

Reporting as instructed, I saluted the personnel officer smartly and stood at attention in front of his desk. As soon as he mentioned a date for reporting to 5 ADU I feigned great surprise and fibbed shamelessly,

---

* It took seventy days for supplies and reinforcements via the Cape and Red Sea route to reach Egypt, which was entirely insufficient. In July–August 1940, construction began to turn the existing airfield at Takoradi into the much larger base required for reception and transit of aircraft and all sorts of material. The passenger and mail route established in the thirties, running from Takoradi to Khartoum, was greatly expanded, with staging bases at Lagos, Kano, Maiduguri, and Fort Lamy. It was a six-day, 3,697-mile journey. The last leg, from Khartoum to Abu Sueir, Egypt, was 1,026 miles. Altogether, this was a punishing and monotonous route in the backwater of the war.

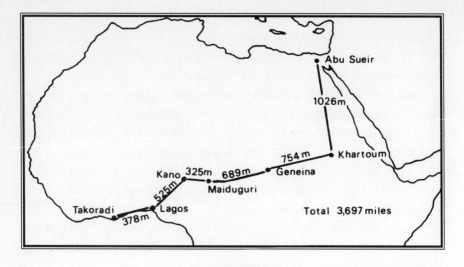

THE TAKORADI ROUTE

"But you must have made some mistake, sir. You told me on Thursday that I was posted to the United Kingdom!"

At this, the flight lieutenant's face turned red, and he bristled, "What do you mean, I made a mistake? I'll have none of your impertinence! We do not make mistakes in this department. If I said you're going to the U.K., then that's precisely where you are going."

"Yes, sir. Sorry, sir," I said with a suitably chastised look on my face.

He shuffled some files on his desk, opened one, and looked up at me in some little triumph. "You are to report to No. 23 Personnel Transit Centre at Helwan in one week's time to await embarkation to return to the U.K. by ship for further disposition. Make sure you are on time. That's all!"

I couldn't wait to escape the office. I could hardly believe my ruse had worked, and I congratulated myself on my thespian skills and amateur psychology.

I said goodbye to my friends at Hurricane House, and to my faithful Mahmoud, who was again in tears, and reported to the transit camp at Helwan, which was a short electric train ride to the city's far outskirts. What I found was a far cry from my luxury room at the convalescent hotel. I was shown to a tent that had no extra cover to help as a heat shield. A thin, straw mattress pallet lay on the sand floor. There were no other furnishings! This was even more Spartan than my quarters on the squadron at Kabrit. A wooden building housed the sergeants' mess.

A few days after my arrival at Helwan, I was walking towards the sergeants' mess when I saw a tall, familiar-looking airman approaching me. As he came closer, I saw that he was a flight sergeant pilot, and then exclaimed out loud, "My God, it's Jack Kelly!"

Jack was a high school friend from Toronto. I had not even known that he was in the air force. Jack's eyes widened as he recognized me, and echoed my surprise. "It can't be Howard Hewer! What in hell are you doing out here?" A good question for both of us, I guess, but it was a remarkable coincidence that we should meet in this remote area of the world.

We shook hands warmly, and sat down in the mess to tell each other our stories. Jack had been flying Hurricane fighter-bombers on No. 33 RAF Sqn in the Libyan desert until they had to make a hurried escape from Rommel's tanks as they swept eastwards towards Alamein. He also was now posted back to the U.K. for reallocation. This was a happy reunion. We celebrated with many trips into Cairo on the electric railway, sometimes returning from Groppi's cabaret a little the worse for wear.

Our remarkable meeting followed another that was even more unlikely. Earlier in the year, on visits to Cairo, Jack and I had separately met another high school friend, Bill Galer, on one of the main Cairo avenues. At Parkdale Collegiate, Bill had been a sports star, winning honours on the gymnastic team. Now he was an RCAF observer, and had flown with 9 Sqn RAF in England. He was passing through Cairo to India, where he flew on Wellingtons of 215 Sqn bombing the Japanese in Burma. It did indeed seem a small world.

On 5 November, everyone was celebrating the news of General Montgomery's great victory at El Alamein. Rommel's Afrika Korps was in a headlong retreat that would end with final defeat in Tunisia in 1943.

On 17 November, our group of about eighty aircrew was instructed to report to the supply section to be kitted out for the return to the U.K. We were to leave that week, and it was a poorly kept secret that our destination was the port of Suez, for embarkation.

At the supply section, we were completely dumbfounded by the items we were given. The kit included desert water bottles, khaki shorts and shirt, straw topi (we already had one), cartridge bandoliers, and canvas pack-sacks. We protested that this was all desert equipment, and we weren't going to the desert — we had just come from there! Most of the equipment we had never been issued when in the desert, and we certainly had no use for it now. We protested in vain, and were ordered to board buses with all this gear. Someone was slavishly following standard orders for desert kit.

We arrived at Suez and immediately boarded a magnificent liner, Holland-America Lines' *Nieuw Amsterdam*, which had been completed just prior to the outbreak of war and converted immediately to trooping. There was no band to play us aboard. The only sound, other than groans, was the clanking of tin cups and water bottles as we clambered awkwardly up the gangplank under the weight of our duffle bags and useless desert kit. From childhood, I had been a fan of the comedy team Laurel and Hardy, and to me, our ascent up the gangplank, with all our paraphernalia, was a scene right out of their movie *Beau Hunks*, when they boarded a ship to Morocco as Foreign Legionnaires.

This was the end of my year on the desert squadron. I was leaving behind the Land of the Pharaohs, with memories of experiences that, even in my wildest dreams, I could never have imagined.

26
SOUTH AFRICA — UNCLE PERCY'S BOERS

OUR DEPARTURE FROM SUEZ was swift, and we left Egypt and its port of Suez to head south into the 1,200 mile-long Red Sea. It was going to take us at least two days to reach the Gulf of Aden and the Indian Ocean.

Despite the size of this liner, we were crammed like sardines into cabins fitted with three-tier wooden bunks. With other members of our aircrew group, we took our turn descending long escalators to the ship's kitchen to bring up large containers of food to our dining hall. It was far better food than we had been used to on the squadron. The ship seemed uncrowded, with its mixture of military and civilian passengers. On the upper sun deck where we spent most of our time, everyone's interest was drawn to a group of twelve attractive young women, who were dressed almost identically in flowing dark robes and hooded headpieces. They were presided over by a matriarchal figure who sat in their midst like a watchful queen. Apparently, they were refugees from the bombing of Malta, but a rumour that they were nuns was soon to be scotched.

It wasn't long before the troops uncovered the true profession of the "nuns." The queen mother was actually the "madam" in charge of her brood of prostitutes. These women began a brisk trade in any secluded corner of the deck they could find, until the ship's captain intervened to remove the enterprising little group and confine them to an area below decks for the duration of the voyage.

Early on the second day, Jack and I took a look at the pile of useless desert kit with which we had been burdened and decided it would have to go. When the path looked clear, we gathered the gear and carried it to the railing where we were sure we wouldn't be observed. We heaved our bundles over the side, and with great satisfaction and relief watched the bubbles rising to the surface as the kit plunged downwards to the bottom of the sea, where it probably lies to this day.

By the end of the third day we were out into the Indian Ocean. We were not "On the road to Mandalay, where the Flyin'-fishes play," but nevertheless we were fascinated by scores of flying fish planing down from the wavetops.

We were now in waters patrolled by German and Japanese submarines. At nearly thirty knots, our ship sped southwards, and began to zigzag on course, making small degree changes in heading, port and then starboard, every twelve minutes. The ship's officers told us that this was on Royal Navy advice, based on their experience that it took a minimum of thirteen minutes for a U-boat to sight its target, get into position for attack, calculate the torpedoes' run, and fire. We all hoped that the navy was right.

Three days out of sight of land took us to an unexpected berth at Diégo-Suarez, the most northerly port of Madagascar. Here we took on a battalion of South African troops who were heading home after hard garrison duty in the jungles of that tropical island. Once underway, most joined us on the sun deck, and occupied themselves by digging out with their knives little white slug-like creatures called "chiggers," which had infested their toenails.

It took us nearly three days to sail the 1,500 miles from Madagascar to Durban, South Africa. Anchored in this port, we marvelled at the expanse of greenery and foliage covering the surrounding hills, which was in marked contrast to the desert scenery we had become accustomed to in the past year. As I looked at the waters of the bay, I suddenly recalled one of my Uncle Percy's Boer War stories. He had arrived in this same port, and had dived from the deck into the waters of the harbour for a cooling swim. And here I was, forty-three years later, in the same place.

■ ■ ■

Although we were billeted in tents again on the outskirts of this fine-looking city, the whole experience was a delight. The tables in the mess tent groaned with the weight of a variety of foods: eggs, milk, fresh whole wheat bread, and salads, which we had almost forgotten existed. We were greeted by all the locals as brave veterans from the front up north, and the city's school teachers organized a dance and managed to find enough partners for our large group.

On 1 December we left our gracious hosts and boarded a train to take us to Cape Town, at the southernmost tip of the African continent. We had a long trip ahead of us. The railway first tracked northwest to Johannesburg before turning south to pass through Bloemfontein and De Aar.

At each of the main stations we were greeted on the platform by the ladies of the Imperial Order of Daughters of the Empire, who were resplendent in their white dresses with sashes that carried the letters IODE in gold letters. We were plied with cigarettes and sandwiches, and greeted again as veterans from the front.

Midway on the three-day journey, we made an eight-hour stop at the small rail-junction town of De Aar to await a change of engine. This was Boer sheep farm country, and because of the long-lingering hostility of the Boers towards the British, the RAF were instructed to remain on the train. With "Canada" badges on our shoulders, Jack and I decided that this order didn't apply to us, so we jumped train and headed for a good-looking white stucco hotel facing us across the tracks.

We entered the beverage room and took our seats with a little apprehension. In a few moments, a waiter arrived at our table with two huge steins of beer. He wouldn't take our money, telling us that they had been paid for by the three gentlemen sitting across the room from us. We went over to thank them, and we were invited to join their table (it is doubtful that this courtesy would have been extended to our RAF comrades). We soon discovered that they were rich Boer sheep farmers, all over eighty years of age and veterans of the Boer War.

After an exchange of war experiences, and a few more beers, I felt bold enough to confess to our hosts that my uncle had been stationed right here with the Canadian Mounted Infantry during the Boer War. I added that he had arrived early on in the war, and had taken part not only in the relief of Mafeking, but even in the capture of their General Cronje. My revelation was greeted enthusiastically, and with more beer! One of our Afrikaner hosts became quite animated talking about the

Canadian troops. "We weren't too worried about the Englanders, but when the Canadians were about we didn't dare show ourselves against the sky. The Canadians could shoot us off our horses at over 400 yards, even in the poor evening light. The Englanders never came close to them."*

After much shaking of hands, our generous hosts left to look after their sheep. When they had gone, our waiter informed us that our friends had set up lunch for us in the dining room, and had also reserved a room for us upstairs so that we could take a shower. I had to wonder whether our need had been that noticeable.

Before we had finished our last beer, we had a new companion at our table, a British major in the South African Army who had asked if he could join us. He surprised us by openly discussing his assignment. His task was to visit the Boer farmers in a large area centred on De Aar to inspect their cellars and storage sheds for guns and ammunition, which they were suspected of stockpiling for a planned uprising against the British. Apparently, it had become a good-natured game. The Boers knew of the major's visits well beforehand, and simply moved their guns to other farmhouses ahead of his arrival. This was well understood and accepted by the major, who knew that there was no serious plan for rebellion; it simply pleased the Boers to carry on the facade.

On the major's departure, we hastened to the hotel dining room. On a white tablecloth, we feasted royally on long-denied chicken, salad, and fruit before climbing the stairs to our bright, sun-filled room to shower in blissful luxury.

With a full stomach, wonderfully refreshed from our showers, we rejoined our comrades, who were diffidently picking over the remains of their box lunches. Our story was not well received.

Our new engine finally arrived, and for the remainder of that day and most of the next we crossed the rolling hills and flat livestock farms of the South African veldt, to be received by British troops at Cape Town and whisked away to Camp Retreat on the northern outskirts of the city.

We spent over two weeks in this camp, and were well fed and reasonably comfortable in concrete huts. Jack and I had ample time to look about this strategic port city with its extensive artificial harbour. The

---

* This contradicts an observation by Air Chief Marshal "Bomber" Harris in his book *Bomber Offensive* that "dominion and colonial troops are on the average . . . damned bad shots . . . until they have been put through the standard musketry drill, after which they are no better and no worse than the British themselves."

capital of South Africa, Cape Town lies on the southwest side of Table Bay, along the base of 3,500-foot Table Mountain, which dominates the city and port. We were intrigued by the phenomenon of the perpetual white cloud that flowed over the flat escarpment top of the mountain, to dissipate almost halfway down the vertical slab face of the rock. It looked like a waterfall.

Our restful sojourn ended one morning when our large group was transported to the docks to board a ship for the U.K. Everyone had an instant sense of foreboding when we saw the ship we were to board for the long, perilous voyage. It was a small, one-funnelled ship, with a bridge separated by open deck from the passenger superstructure. Another open deck space separated the poop deck. This fragile-looking vessel seemed more suited for lake service than the vast, open seas. It bore the grand name of HMS *Almanzora*. It had been a supply ship in the Battle of Jutland in 1916, which explained its royal title and aged state.

A large number of our group rebelled at the prospect of setting out to sea in this unlikely vessel, until a British army senior warrant officer had all our kit placed on board. We had no choice but to obey orders and follow our gear aboard.

Our dismay deepened when we found that we were to eat and sleep in a mess deck. Hammocks were slung over the long tables, but most of our large group would have to sleep on the table top or on the floor. Old, thin mattresses were piled in a corner for us to sleep on. We suffered another setback when Italian prisoners, who were to be our shipmates, passed through our quarters on their way to a brig in the forward part of the ship and pocketed the knives and forks that were laid out on our tables. We were left with only spoons; our protests were ignored. We were to sail early the next morning, and would join a large convoy of ships with mixed cargoes.

We were leaving behind our African adventures, but Jack and I shared in the apprehension of our aircrew comrades about our long voyage through U-boat–infested waters.

27
CHRISTMAS CONVOY

AT FIRST LIGHT THE NEXT MORNING, we sailed out of the harbour. All of our group gathered on the poop deck to watch Table Mountain recede slowly from view. The white cloud cascading over the flat top of the mountain was our last sight of South Africa. It was 20 December 1942, exactly one year and thirteen days since our Wimpy had touched down outside Cairo, Egypt, from Malta. It seemed much longer than that.

In the next two hours we took our place on the starboard side of a convoy of twelve ships of all shapes and sizes. The distance between ships was about 300 yards. The Dutch "banana boat" trailing us off our starboard quarter was even smaller than our ship. Two corvettes escorted us on our side of this formation. Their ensigns identified one as British and the other as Free French. We didn't know what other escorts the convoy had been given, or who was in charge. We just had to have faith that we were in good hands.

The good weather we had enjoyed almost every day since sailing from Suez now deserted us. Heavy grey clouds hung low over equally grey seas. Our small ship rose and fell with monotonous regularity on the long, six-foot high swells that persisted for days. Like most of our

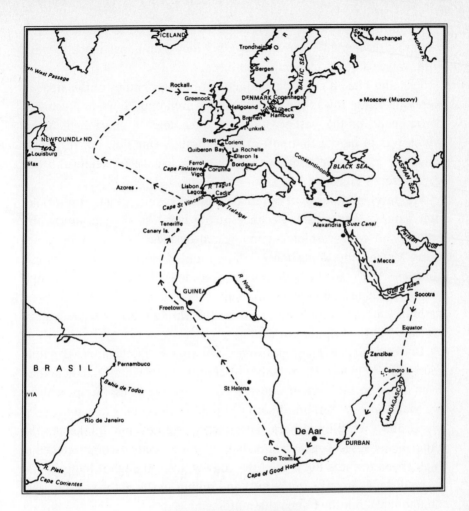

THE ROUTE FROM SUEZ TO GREENOCK

group, Jack and I spent the days in a small, thirty-foot-wide upper deck salon playing cards. On either side, the wide doors were open to give us views of the endless grey seas, and of our companions in the convoy.

On our fourth day at sea, in cloying, oppressive heat and humidity, we had to be reminded that it was Christmas Eve. Few of us had been thinking of Christmas, but now nostalgia and homesickness invaded our thoughts. This was my third Christmas away from home since joining up, and here I was ploughing through grey seas in the South Atlantic. We weren't allowed to give details of our movements in letters home, of course, so my family had no idea where I was; perhaps it was just as well, I thought.

On Christmas Day, the cooks made a valiant effort to produce something that resembled a festive dinner, but they didn't have much to work with. It was a quiet, contemplative day.

Jack and I had a good mental picture of the geography of the area we were traversing. It was almost 3,000 miles from Cape Town to Freetown, Sierra Leone, on the west coast of Africa, ten degrees above the equator, which was to be our first port of call en route. Our slow convoy could not quite make nine knots, so it was going to take us nearly thirteen days to reach Freetown.

We developed our own covert method of keeping track of our position, course, and speed. Because of the wireless-silence policy, the escorts and convoy ships communicated by means of the Aldis lamp, using Morse code to exchange information on position and on course changes. As I read the code, Jack copied down the latitude and longitude coordinates, and other information about our course. We had to be careful that we weren't observed by the ship's crew. We could have ended up in the brig for our actions.

On the sixth day, Jack and I were discussing the fact that we were little more than 100 miles from the island of St. Helena, where Napoleon had been exiled in 1815, when we were shaken by an explosion. Speechless, we watched our "banana boat" companion burst upwards out of the water and then plunge back, spewing out flames and smoke. As the unfortunate vessel began to sink, both of our corvette escorts steamed at high speed towards the rear of the convoy. Even though it happened at some distance from us in the mist and rolling swells of the sea, we were able to make out the drama that unfolded.

The plumes of water that soared skywards told us that both corvettes were dropping depth charges. This went on for some minutes as our distance from the scene widened. Suddenly, the water's surface boiled as first a conning tower, and then the long, grey hull of a U-boat breached the surface. We could dimly make out figures clambering from the conning tower onto the deck. The corvette captains must have believed that the submarine's crew was attempting to reach their deck gun because the whole upper surface of the U-boat erupted in smoke and flame as both escorts opened up with 20-mm Oerlikon cannons and 50-calibre machine guns. It was a shocking sight, even from our distance.

The U-boat crew was shown no mercy. We watched the corvettes use their 4-inch guns to sink the damaged U-boat. We doubted that there would be many survivors.

■ ■ ■

On New Year's Eve we entered the port of Freetown. When we came to a stop at our berth at one of the dock extensions, the evening light was fading, and we thought we had come alongside a mountain. Completely dominating us was the huge, dull-grey bulk of the liner *Queen Elizabeth*. We felt our diminutive size more than ever in the shadow of this monster ship. Like the *Queen Mary*, it had been converted to a troop transport, and just some months previous had carried a phenomenal 15,000 troops from England to Egypt to bolster General Montgomery's force before Alamein.

We stayed only long enough to refuel our convoy's ships, and were off again towards the North Atlantic.

A week later, the seas began to rise in the beginnings of what grew to be the worst storm experienced off Gibraltar since 1918. Even in daylight, the heavy rain obscured the other ships from our view. As our tiny vessel pitched down into the troughs of what were becoming mountainous waves, the propellers came out of the water to shake the whole superstructure so severely that we feared the hull might come apart. Keeping station in the convoy became impossible.

At the height of the storm, someone in authority decided that gunners would be placed on the forward bridge to guard against any break-out by the Italian prisoners during the storm. We knew the Italians didn't have plans to revolt in this storm. The poor creatures in the violent-pitching bow devoted all of their energy holding on for dear life.

A Royal Navy officer of the ship's crew came to our quarters to identify the gunners in our ranks. I was selected, along with several others, and placed on a shift of two hours on, and six hours off, manning a Lewis machine gun that had been mounted on the starboard side of the open bridge. Another gun had been placed on the port side. We were given rubber boots, and oversized, hooded oilskin parkas that were so stiff that we had to walk with arms partially outstretched. We looked like Frankenstein monsters jerkily stalking the deck.

To reach my post, I had to follow a taut rope that had been strung from the centre superstructure across the open deck to the foot of the ladder leading to the bridge. Hand over hand, I made my way forward through the blackness, trying not to be hurled over the side by the wind and water that swept across the open, pitching deck. I was relieved to reach the ladder and climb upwards to clasp the machine-gun mount on the forward railing. For the next two hours, all I could do was hold on to the gun handles, and peer forward to the rising and falling bow, bracing myself against the wind and spray. How I envied the ship's officers whom I could see through the porthole on my left, snug and warm in the enclosed cabin of the bridge. The whole affair was ludicrous.

I welcomed relief from this duty, but I found the arrival of my replacement unnerving. Out of the mist and the screaming wind would appear this ghostly robot in the yellow oilskins and hood like some menacing creature from another world. Fortunately, I endured only three shifts before this pointless exercise was called off.

Days later, we emerged from the storm, and the scattered ships reformed into the comparative safety of the convoy formation. We began to experience the increasing cold of the more northern latitudes. Jack and I had carried our thin mattresses up to the open deck to escape the heat of the crowded cabin, but had to return inside to sleep because of the storm and cold.

Still furtively reading the Aldis lamp exchange of messages, we knew that our convoy had been rerouted westwards to avoid the Western Approaches to the English Channel, where there was a reported concentration of a U-boat wolf pack. At one point, we came within 900 miles of the Newfoundland coast.

Just when we despaired of ever seeing land again, the welcome green hills of Scotland came into view through the mist and drizzle. We had been twenty-eight days at sea.

We slipped past the submarine booms and anchored off the same familiar docks of Greenock. I had the feeling that I was coming "home."

With our blood thinned out from our year in the desert heat, we felt the penetrating, damp cold more severely than before. We were thankful to get into the heat of a train to begin our journey south. It was a long, tiring trip, and I had ample time to reflect on the events of the past year.

As I sat looking out of the window at the dark, blacked-out countryside passing by, my mind was occupied mostly by thoughts of my fellow crew members. I was relieved that Bill was safely back in Canada. Robbie, Will, Doug, and Tony would have arrived back in Britain some months before I left Egypt, and would likely be employed in Training Command on a screen tour. But what weighed upon me most heavily was concern for the members of my first crew — Ted Crosswell, George Fuller, Willy Poirier, and Len Mayer. I had no idea at the time what had happened to them on operations over Germany after Bill and I left with our new crew, and the worry nagged at me.

Our journey ended at RAF Uxbridge where, for the second time, I would be assessed for "disposal." It had been almost two eventful and hazard-filled years since I had first left Uxbridge for my operational training. Through what had to be some combination of divine guidance and luck, I had come full circle.

28
A "SCREEN TOUR" AND TRAGIC NEWS

IT WAS TWO WEEKS BEFORE I WAS GIVEN a posting from Uxbridge to an RAF unit. This gave me ample time to renew my acquaintance with London, and especially to visit the Whites, and Ted Crosswell's wife, Lily. I would find out Ted's whereabouts, and hopefully get some information on the rest of my first crew.

We were given nearly every day off, and could remain away overnight if we wished. I took the first opportunity to board the Northern Line tube for the Burnt Oak station, which was the nearest to the White home at No. 8 Dean Walk.

Mrs. White opened the door to my knock, and when she recovered from the shock of seeing me standing there, let out a happy shriek that brought Lily and Mr. White running to the door. I was treated like a long-lost son, and plied with questions about what I had been doing in the past year. I was surprised to find that Ted, as captain of his own crew, and George Fuller had departed for India soon after I had left for the Middle East. A recent letter relieved Lily that Ted and George were in good health on their Indian RAF squadron. I was disappointed, however, that Lily had no news about Len Mayer or Willy Poirier, except that they did not leave England with Ted, but apparently had left 218 Squadron and Marham.

I was also introduced to Lily and Ted's daughter, Patricia, who was then about eight months old.

The Whites insisted that I stay the night. I was given the double bed in the front living room that their aircraftman son, Chris, used on his leaves at home.

Mr. White had the night off from his air raid warden duties, so I took the family to the local pub to celebrate our reunion while a neighbour minded Patricia. I spent several days with the Whites, and their home was to become my second home for most of my leaves for the remainder of my time in England.

The next evening, Lily and I decided to go to Covent Garden to dance. At intermission we left for a drink at the White Lion pub, which was just across the road from the Opera House. It was a fateful visit.

The pub was wall to wall with people, but we were lucky enough to find a free table near the door. I had just returned with Lily's gin and orange and my ale when my glance across the crowded, smoke-filled room fell upon a young woman who was standing rigidly, staring at me as if she had seen a ghost. I peered more intently. My God, it was Maureen! Lily was surprised when I asked, "Would you excuse me for a moment? There is someone over there I just have to talk to."

When I pushed my way through to Maureen and took her hand, her tone was anguished as she cried out, "When did you get back?"

I replied, "Just three days ago." Then added, "Where is Bessie? Is she here with you?"

Maureen's voice was accusatory. "After you left, without a word, Bessie found out where you had gone. A few months later, she left the hospital, and applied for a nurse's commission in the army, on condition that she would be posted to Egypt. She told me that she was going to find you out there. Maybe you didn't know this, but Bessie was very much in love with you. I hoped she would find you, but I knew from her letters that she hadn't. I don't know what she will do now."

I was stunned, and for a few moments speechless. I had to admit that I had not known how serious Bessie's feelings for me had been. I tried to explain away my failure to contact Bessie before I left, and said that I expected Willy would tell her that my departure was too sudden to contact anyone.

"You don't know then that Willy was killed?" I stood there in shock.

"Willy and Len Mayer were both killed last year, on 12 February. I found out from some airmen friends that they were on one of the raids against the German battleships going through the Channel.* Willy and I were very close, and it isn't easy to get over."

Her words became an ice-cold hand that gripped my chest so that I could hardly breathe. Although it was happening every day to so many thousands, I had not let myself believe that it would happen to them.

We stood in silence for some moments before I could gather myself enough to speak. I wanted to continue speaking to Maureen about Bessie and Willy, but we couldn't do it there. I asked, "Will you meet me here tomorrow night about seven? We have to talk again." Maureen looked sombre and undecided, but after a moment looking away from me and then back, agreed to meet me at the pub.

I made my way unsteadily back to our table, and sat down to face Lily. "You've had a shock," she exclaimed. "There's no colour in your face. What happened?" When I told her my tragic news, Lily grabbed my hand in sympathy, and immediately declared that we were leaving for home.

I have little recollection of our journey back to Burnt Oak, and "home." After the Whites and Lily had tried to console me, they left me to my grief.

I lay in the darkness, staring at the ceiling, as a jumble of recollections and images of Len and Willy paraded in front of me. I felt angry at the war, and at whoever had sent them out on such a suicidal operation. Above all, I felt wrung out and empty. It was hours before sleep mercifully blotted out my waking nightmare. The loss of these friends, especially of Len, to whom I had felt so close, left a permanent scar that, mostly in these late years, flares up intermittently to dampen my mood.

I arrived at the White Lion the following evening, anxious to be on time. There was no sign of Maureen. I waited for nearly two hours before I finally left. The next morning, I called the staff at the Northern

---

* On 12 February 1942, the German battlecruisers *Gneisenau*, *Scharnhorst*, and *Prinz Eugen*, with forward destroyer screen, made a successful dash from Brest westwards through the English Channel. They were aided by a cover of fog and rain. Attacks by British motor torpedo boats, Swordfish aircraft of the Fleet Air Arm, and Wellingtons of Bomber Command all failed. All six Swordfish, the slow biplane "stringbags," were shot down. Their commander, Lt. Cdr. Eugene Esmonde, was awarded a posthumous Victoria Cross. Willy and Len were lost with their Wellington from the Canadian 419 (Moose) Squadron.

Hospital, only to be informed that Maureen had left the nursing staff there many months ago. They could not give me her new location or phone number. I did not see Bessie or Maureen again.*

On 31 January 1943 I was informed of my posting to the RAF Operational Training Unit at Pershore, Worcestershire. I was to be an instructor, but I was given few other details. I left Jack Kelly behind at Uxbridge where he was to spend quite a few more weeks, and where he met Elsa, a member of the WAAF and his future wife. Jack and I were not to meet again until a reunion in Toronto before the war ended.

On arrival at Pershore, I was assigned a small room to myself at the end of a barrack block. It was furnished with a cot, a chest of drawers, and an armoire. The corner held a small pot-bellied coal stove. Compared to what I had been used to, this was manorial.

At the GIS, or Ground Instructional Section, I was welcomed warmly by the two senior NCO instructors, Flight Sergeant Fred Rose, from Wales, and Flight Sergeant Al White. These men were operationally experienced and well versed in their instructional roles. I was non-plussed to learn that I was expected to give daily lectures as part of my instructional duties, something I had never done before. I needn't have worried. My two new friends were wonderfully supportive, and intro-duced me to lesson plans and other techniques to ease me into my classroom debut. I had considerable swotting up to do before I felt ready to face classes of twenty or more trainees, on subjects as varied as oper-ational procedures, wireless set operation, and even navigation exercises peculiar to some types of operations.

I was surprised to find that more than forty percent of my students were Canadians, most of whom, by this stage of the war, were commis-sioned in rank from flying officer to squadron leader. At the end of a month, I had become comfortable in my new role, and began to enjoy this new-found skill. I did little flying, but one flight, in a Lysander, reunited me with Warrant Officer Ian Vinall, a sergeant pilot I had known well on 148 Squadron at Kabrit.

My experience at Pershore was a happy one. There were frequent bus trips to dances at the Shakespeare Memorial Theatre in Stratford-on-Avon, and evening get-togethers at the Coach and Horses pub a mile from the station. On our time off, my instructor friends and I often rode

---

* Four months later I learned that Bessie had married a British Army medical officer with whom she had been working in Egypt. I was happy for her.

our issue station bicycles to nearby villages with the improbable names of Upton Snodsbury, Inken Drypot, and Piddle on the Wee. At Snodsbury we discovered a small pub that served a lunch of cooked ham, peas, and mash, along with the finest ales. The publican implored us to keep our find a secret; we kept our promise.

Letters from home told me of my cousin Harvey Ireland's arrival in England, and his location in Sussex. I visited Harvey at his Canadian army base, and brought him back for a short stay at Pershore before his signals unit left for the Sicily invasion.

On 23 March I was sent down to London to 1 CMB (Central Medical Board). My chest was X-rayed, and two medical officers of air commodore rank tapped every inch of my chest, frequently muttering ominous "hmms."

In the middle of May, I had just finished my last lecture when I was called into the office of Squadron Leader Jambles, the station signals officer. He greeted me warmly, and after a few pleasantries and congratulations on the work I was doing, asked, "Why haven't you been commissioned?"

I couldn't answer his question. It wasn't something I had dwelled upon, although the arrival of so many inexperienced Canadian officers in my classes had given me pause for thought. I had been a sergeant for two years and six months, and had completed a tour of ops. I had to respond, "Well, sir, one of the reasons, I suppose, is that I have been on RAF units ever since my arrival from Canada, and the RCAF has had no idea of my whereabouts. I certainly haven't had any communication with them. I must say that none of the RAF aircrew I was flying with on ops seemed to be getting any promotions either, so it never really became anything we thought much about."

"Well," the squadron leader exclaimed, "that's not good enough. If the Canadian Air Force isn't going to commission you, we bloody well are!"

I was pleasantly stunned by all this, and couldn't think of much to say except that I appreciated the compliment. I was to go through tests and interviews; the squadron leader would arrange everything. I left with the good feeling that the job I had been trying to do to the best of my ability was appreciated.

I was given challenging examinations in wireless theory and procedures, general air force administration, and even on operational navigation, material Canadians were not subjected to for commissioning.

They were generally commissioned automatically off course. Somehow, I managed to pass everything.*

Interviews followed with the chief instructor, Wing Commander Roncoroni, and with the station commander, Group Captain Combe**.

On 17 May, for a final interview with the air-vice-marshal group commander, a Flight Lieutenant Petts flew me down to group headquarters at Abingdon in a small two-seater Hornet Moth, a forty-minute flight. I was given the royal treatment.

After waiting thirty minutes on a bench in the hallway of the headquarters building, I was ushered into the office of the A/V/M. I saluted and stood at attention about ten feet from his desk. He ignored me for a few moments while he perused some documents in front of him. He was a fine-looking man, with slightly greying hair. Finally, he looked up, and asked a question I should have been better prepared to answer: "Why do you want a commission?"

My mind raced. I had thought that it would be a blessed relief to exchange the abrasive, itchy cloth of the airman's trousers for that of the officer's smooth barathea, but I couldn't very well say that. I mustered up a more appropriate reply: "Well, sir, I believe I have had quite a bit of operational experience, and that I have learned a fair amount about the air force along the way. I think I'm ready to take on more responsibility, and to lead others, perhaps."

I remained at attention while the group commander took another look at the papers on his desk. "I see that on one of your ops over Germany you were to bomb Karlsruhe. You returned to base without dropping your bombs. Why didn't you drop them?"

This totally unexpected question stunned me. "On that night, sir, the bomb doors of our aircraft were hit by flak, and we were unable to open them to release the bombs. We had no alternative but to return with them to base."

----

* Copies of my complete service documents, which I obtained later from Ottawa, include the RAF form recording the results of my interviews at Pershore, 11 May 1943: "A bright and intelligent instructor, suitable for commissioning" — E.A. Jambles, Sqn Ldr, Station Signals Officer; "An efficient instructor, and NCO. Recommended for a commission" — J.A. Roncoroni, Wing Cdr, Chief Instructor; "I concur — strongly recommended for a commission" — A.R. Combe, Grp Capt, Station Commander.

** In 1938, A.R. Combe, then a pre-war officer, participated in a successful attempt of the world non-stop distance record. Positioned at Ismailia, Egypt, and flying single-engined Wellesley aircraft (the predecessor to the Wellington), S/L Kellett, flying L2638, F/L Hogan (L2639), and F/L Combe (L2680) took off 5 November 1938 for Australia. Forty-eight hours later, Kellett and Combe landed at Darwin, having flown a distance of 7,157.7 miles, a record that would stand until 1946.

There was a disconcerting "hmm" from my inquisitor, and some less uncomfortable questions before I was dismissed, with an unexpected smile, from the interview. I had no idea how the interview had gone. I wasn't confident that I had made a good enough impression.

In June, I began to think about the end of my "screen" tour at Pershore, and to wonder where my next posting would be. I assumed it would be to another operational bomber squadron, for a second tour. By this time, the four-engined Lancaster and Halifax bombers were taking over as the main aircraft of Bomber Command's force, so I would have to go to a conversion unit to upgrade my knowledge.

I would be reluctant to leave. I enjoyed my instructional duties, and the company of good friends. Many weekends were free, and I spent several weeks on leave, mostly in London, where I stayed at my second home with Mr. and Mrs. White, and Ted's wife Lily and her daughter. Lily and I enjoyed each other's company, and frequently danced at Covent Garden or Hammersmith Palais. With her parents, we had many pub nights. Although we had grown very fond of one another, our relationship remained strictly a platonic one; after all, Lily was married to Ted, my friend and former second pilot.

One day in the second week of June, I was called to the adjutant's office and informed that I had been appointed to commissioned rank as pilot officer, in effect from 17 May. I had obviously made a better impression on the group commander than I thought I had. I knew that there was nothing automatic about my appointment; the RAF went by their own rules, unlike the more liberal practices of the RCAF. I have always taken a measure of pride in the manner of my commissioning. I was given a week's leave and a liberal clothing allowance, more than enough to outfit myself in uniform, cap, raincoat, and accessories.

Two days before my departure on leave, the phone rang in our instructors' office. An unhappy, almost-sobbing voice informed me that I was posted to an RAF station at Warrington. The distressed voice belonged to Mabel, a WAAF orderly room clerk. Mabel and I had met only a few days before at one of the dances held at the Shakespeare Memorial Theatre in Stratford. It had been an eventful evening. An obnoxious administrative warrant officer, the fourth Neanderthal of his type I had encountered, challenged me to a swimming race across the Avon River. He had been to the bar more often than I, but I was sufficiently peed off with him to accept the duel. Mabel held my tunic and trousers as the WO and I stripped and dove into the frigid waters.

We were cheered on by the large group of airmen and WAAFs, but the river was not very wide, and the race was over quickly. My adversary was overweight, and a clumsy swimmer. I was a good swimmer, so it was no contest. His acceptance of defeat was less than gracious. In any case, it was a foolish caper, and I am not proud to admit that we dried off on the drapes at the rear of the stage, and returned to the dance floor. Mabel and I returned on the bus together, and made arrangements to meet again a few days later. Mabel was young and attractive, and had only recently enlisted in the service. We got along quite well.

I pressed Mabel for more details about my new posting. What squadron was at Warrington? Her answer left me speechless. There was no squadron at Warrington; it was a repatriation depot outside the major port city of Liverpool. I was going home to Canada!

I hurried down to the orderly room to ask Mabel why I was being sent home. I was referred to the adjutant who informed me that the medical board I had attended in London in March had lowered my aircrew medical category and judged me unfit for further operational flying. I was not to do a second tour of ops.

This news came as a great surprise to me. I had taken it for granted that I would remain overseas for the duration of the war. I was also prepared (resigned may be a more honest word) to embark on a second tour, although I laboured under no delusion about my chances of surviving another round. Getting used to a new crew would be part of the challenge. It couldn't be the same again. My two crews had gone their separate ways. Len and Willy were dead, along with so many other friends and comrades; and something had gone out of me. Was I simply too tired in mind and body? My reaction was ambivalent; I had been overseas for two years and four months, over a year of that time flying continuously on an operational bomber squadron, so it would be dishonest to pretend that feelings of relief and joy did not crowd out twinges of guilt pricking my conscience over abandoning the fight.

This new development meant that, after my leave, I would report directly to Warrington where, for the first time, I would be entering the officers' mess. After a small goodbye party in the mess, I had to say goodbye to my superior officers, and to Fred Rose, Al White, and other friends, before boarding the train to London. The Pershore experience had been a great one. I had gained strength and some of my weight back, and had found a new assurance from meeting the challenges of the broad instructional responsibilities I had been given. I believe it played a large part in my future career development.

In London, my first visit was to RCAF headquarters at Lincoln's Inn Fields, where I found out that the RCAF had promulgated my commissioning and appointment to pilot officer rank upon receiving the recommendation from the RAF. I was an RCAF officer now. A flight sergeant in the HQ orderly room informed me that I was entitled to an RCAF clothing allowance upon commissioning. He wouldn't listen to my artless confession that I had already been given a kit allowance by the RAF, and insisted that he had to follow orders and give the money to me. I capitulated then with a clear conscience, and also picked up the balance in my escrow account, which had accrued from the difference between the RCAF rates and the RAF rates we were paid. I had more money in my pocket than I had ever had before.

According to this same flight sergeant, my records indicated that I had been promoted to flight sergeant and then to warrant officer 2nd class over a year before, but he could not confirm the dates, or that the promotions had been promulgated in orders.* Nothing could be done now about that, so I picked up a railway warrant to Warrington and departed.

My officer superiors at Pershore had recommended Gieves and Company in London as the best place to order my uniform. This popular outfitter was commonly known as "Gieves the thieves." Nevertheless, they took good care of me, measured me for my uniform, and gave me a date within the week to pick up my complete officer's kit.

I was sad to leave Mr. and Mrs. White, who had welcomed me almost as one of the family. It was a debt I couldn't repay.

Lily accompanied me to Waterloo station, where I was to depart for Warrington. I wasn't sure if I'd see her or her parents again. It was a poignant farewell.

The train rattled across switches until we were clear of greater London. I was trying to adjust to my new uniform and status; it would take me a few days to feel comfortable in it, and to stop feeling that people were staring at me. I had mixed emotions. London and its brave people had become familiar to me, so leaving the city was almost like

---

* Strangely, it wasn't until 25 September 1944, when I was stationed at No. 6 B&G School, Mountain View, Ontario, that a letter to the station CO from Ottawa confirmed that my promotions to F/S and WO2 were effective 1 Dec 1941 and 1 May 1943, respectively, and had been promulgated in Overseas Orders 24 December 1943. The WO promotion had been deferred for six months because of a severe reprimand — the mutiny! No wonder these promotions never caught up with me. I never wore the insignia for them on my sleeve.

leaving home. But the warm feeling in the pit of my stomach over the prospects of returning to home and family overrode any other feelings. I was on my way home!

29
THE END OF MY ODYSSEY
— GOING HOME

ON ARRIVAL AT NO. 2 REPATRIATION DEPOT, RAF Station Warrington, Lancashire, I was allocated quarters in an officers' barrack block. There were rows of beds, like in any barrack block, but the beds were better than I had been accustomed to.

The officers' mess opened my eyes. For the first time, I was entering one as a member. In the dining room, we were treated to white table cloths, elegant dishes, silver tableware, side tables with coffee and other sundries, and were served by airmen stewards. I thought about how these officers had enjoyed these luxuries while I and my squadron sergeant comrades had been living and eating in tents, and sleeping on straw pallets on the ground. I imagined how much better it must be to return to this from an op instead of to my former primitive quarters.

At breakfast, I had just rejected a smoked kipper that lay on the plate, its one eye staring accusingly at me, and eaten some cold toast and resurrected, desiccated eggs when the Tannoy blared out that all officers were to report to the parade square.

On the square, I joined a mixed group of junior officers, sergeants, corporals, and airmen, all under the supervision of an RAF warrant officer (another one of those!). He brought our little parade to attention, and called out in a pompous manner, "Fall out the sick, the halt, and the lame. Move to it smartly now." After a roll call we were curtly dismissed.

I had not been looking for a hero's welcome, but this treatment was demeaning; for my remaining days at the depot, I ignored the calls to morning parade.

Our small group put in our time with daily visits to the town of Warrington, to attend afternoon flicks and evening dances at the local "palais."

On our fourth day we were summoned to buses, which transported our officer group, and another group of NCOs and airmen, to the historic city of Chester. There we were formed up by a squadron leader into flights, and marched for over a mile to a soccer field. At the start of our march, rain had begun to fall, and by the time we were formed up on the soccer field, facing a covered band shell, the cold, light downpour was soaking through our uniforms. We had been told that the commanding officer of our station and the mayor of Chester were involved in some sort of ceremony, and we were there to lend atmosphere to the proceedings. A small air force band was also in attendance.

We stood there, at ease, wet and shivering, for a good half-hour before staff cars arrived bearing our commanding officer, whom none of us had met, and the mayor with his councillors. We were brought to attention, the band played a suitable tune, and the ceremony, shielded from the rain by the band shell roof, began. Our CO, in a long speech, accepted silver candlestick holders from the mayor.

As I peered through the light drizzle towards the bandstand, I recognized the group captain making the speech. It was Denton Massey, who had been the commanding officer of No. 1 Manning Depot, Toronto, when I was sent there on enlistment. He was the officer who had given us a long send-off speech when we left that basic training course for Initial Training School in July 1940, over three years before, and he was still at it.

The next morning, I was called to the CO's quarters. He greeted me warmly, while I took in the sumptuous furnishings of his suite and the boxes of Laura Secord chocolates sitting on the end tables, all topped by the startling leopard-skin pattern of his dressing gown.

He offered me a chocolate, said he had noticed from the roll-call lists that I was from Toronto, and wondered if I would do him a small favour. His wife did volunteer work at the Red Cross canteen on Adelaide Street, and since I would be going home on leave, he thought I might deliver a package to her. Then he gave me a large, brown envelope and his profuse thanks.

The first week of August our group of repats was transported to the docks of Liverpool to board the imposing liner the *Empress of Scotland*. This ship had been the *Empress of Japan*, and had been renamed following Japan's attack on Pearl Harbor and entry into the now-global war.

Our departure from Liverpool was routine. We were not part of a convoy, nor would we have an escort. The speed of this vessel was considered enough to evade the U-boats.

I was allocated a small, comfortable cabin on the top passenger deck that I was to share with an RCAF squadron leader accounts officer. He was friendly enough, but uncommunicative, so we did little fraternizing. We didn't even keep company at meal hours in the dining room. Perhaps I was too junior in rank for his company.

On the second day, I began the habit of spending many daytime hours at the stern railing, watching the ship's frothing wake as it gradually flattened to leave a white streak in the blue sea, which seemed to stretch all the way to the horizon. Suddenly, I was hit with the emotional impact of leaving behind all the bittersweet events that had so filled my days in the past two years. Images of names, faces, and places paraded in front of me across the endless expanse of water. In spite of my many operational hours, I had the feeling that I was deserting the team. At that moment, I was not as happy or satisfied with myself as I ought to have been. I felt a great let-down.

The crossing was uneventful. We had thought that our port of destination was Halifax, so we were surprised when we entered and berthed at the harbour of Norfolk, Virginia.

First down the gangplanks were some hundred German prisoners of war we hadn't even known were aboard. We watched as they were received on the dock by armed American soldiers, who booted them brutally from table to table as they were documented. The behaviour of the Americans was not that of battle-seasoned troops.

Our transport to a waiting train was swift and memorable. As our train pulled out of the station, a left and a right side window shattered as a bullet passed through the coach, grazing and blooding the cheek of an airman sitting across the aisle from me. The train proceeded; apparently no one else was aware of the incident. We could only guess that an excited guard had fired at or over the head of an unruly German.

Our three-day rail journey ended at the central station in Ottawa, where our group of about thirty aircrew officers boarded a bus for the reception unit at RCAF Station Rockcliffe on the outskirts of the capital. There, our documents were examined and I was surprised to be sent directly to the Ottawa Civic Hospital for a two-week stay, during which I was given several tests for intestinal parasites, stomach ulcers, and spinal meningitis, and X-rays of my knees. My medical documents must have alarmed somebody.

When I was given a reasonably clear bill of health, I made my way to the home of Bill Dixon's parents in Ottawa. They knew of me from Bill, who had been home on his leaves from instructing duties at No. 34 OTU, Pennfield Ridge, New Brunswick.

I was greeted warmly by Mr. and Mrs. Dixon, but Mr. Dixon was shocked to hear that I had not told my parents that I had arrived home. For some strange reason, I didn't know how to greet them after my long absence, and had been procrastinating. Bill's father solved my dilemma by immediately calling my parents in Toronto. My father answered the phone, and his cry of surprise and joy brought my mother running from the kitchen to grab the phone from father. It was an emotional moment.

I was soon given three weeks "disembarkation leave" and headed for home. When the taxi approached the house, I needed a few moments to compose myself, and asked the driver to circle the block slowly.

The family had been watching from the front door all morning, and when my taxi door opened, father fairly flew down the walk to grasp me with both arms. Mother and sister Marjorie followed, and I was smothered in embraces. Everyone's face was streaked with tears. I was home; I had survived. As father confided to me, mother's years of fitful nights and nightmares were over. My family was relieved that my legs were intact — when the message arrived that I had been wounded, they feared that I had lost a leg.

At this stage of the war, campaign medals and ribbons had not been issued, so there was nothing on my uniform to indicate that I was anything but a new graduate of aircrew training about to go overseas. I remember well the Toronto barber who said to me, "Well, you're all dolled up and ready to go overseas, eh?" This disturbed me; I looked into the barber's mirror. Surely, I thought, my face reflected some of the trials and tribulations I had undergone. Apparently not!

As promised, I delivered the package Group Captain Massey had entrusted to me. Mrs. Massey was effusive in her thanks. I didn't reveal that, while aboard ship, I had not resisted the temptation to peek at the contents of the large envelope. Inside was a brief covering note, and twenty or thirty large, professional-quality photographs, each one showing the group captain as the principal at ceremonies and parades (including the presentation of the candlestick holders).

My leave over, it was several weeks before I was posted to instruct at the RCAF wireless training base at Burtch, south of Brantford, Ontario. It was a short stay, as I was transferred to No. 6 Bombing and Gunnery School at Mountain View, on the near-island south of Belleville, Ontario.

After a brief introduction to administrative duties, I was appointed station signals officer, my main task to improve the state of communications between ground and air for flying exercises.

On my first pay day on that station one of my earlier follies caught up with me. I was shocked to find my pay $80.00 short. I had to reimburse the British Army Service Corps for the desert kit that I had failed to turn in on leaving Great Britain. I couldn't, of course — it was at the bottom of the Red Sea!

I was one of the few officers on the station with overseas operational experience, but this was not something that we discussed. It therefore came as a surprise to the station personnel, as it was to me, when I was called to the front of the morning's parade by the commanding officer, Group Captain R.F. Gibb, nicknamed "Smiler" because of an old football injury that had paralyzed his face muscles.

As I stood at attention in front of him, the CO read from a document he held:

This is to certify that, on the authority of the chief of the Air Staff, Flying Officer Thomas William Howard Hewer has been awarded the Operational Wings of the Royal Canadian Air Force in recognition of gallant service, in that he has completed a tour of operational duty in action against the enemy.

— Signed this 12th day of September, 1944

E. MacKell, Air Commodore

After the CO handed me the award and shook my hand, I saluted and returned to my place in formation. This award entitled me to wear the gold, winged "O" badge of the operationally experienced on the left breast pocket of my uniform. Thereafter, I became something of a celebrity, and was embarrassed by the exaggerated respect I received from some of the other ranks and from fellow officers in the mess. Soon afterwards, campaign medals were awarded, and the ribbons on our uniforms clearly labelled those who had served overseas.

■ ■ ■

One incident that summer defined the rest of my life. An officer friend invited me on a Sunday picnic that his girlfriend had organized with another couple and a young woman who was to be my blind date. I had nothing better to do, so I accepted.

When I was introduced to my date, I looked at this beautiful young woman and was instantly overcome with feelings I had never experienced before. It was love at first sight! Luckily, Doris Pigden of Madoc, just north of Belleville, was soon similarly smitten, and we were married on 4 January 1945, having waited impatiently until then to satisfy the propriety of both families. Doris located a small flat for rent in Belleville, and we happily set up our first housekeeping nest.

In February 1945, I was posted to No. 1 Air Command Headquarters, at RCAF Station Trenton, just eight miles west of Belleville. Predated only by the airfield at Camp Borden, Ontario, Trenton became known as the home of the RCAF. I was soon immersed in personnel work related to postings and the release from the service of aircrew returning from overseas. I was also appointed to staff and liaison duties with the growing number of air cadet squadrons in Ontario and Quebec. This was a valuable introduction to air force staff work, which was to stand me in good stead when being considered later for retention in the post-war regular air force.

By March, dramatic events signalled the end of the war in Europe. The great airborne crossing of the Rhine at Wesel was successfully completed, RCAF bombers and fighters sharing in the assaults that prepared the way for the operation; in the last heavy bomber attack carried out by the RCAF's No. 6 Group, 192 Lancasters and Halifaxes dropped over 902 tons of bombs on coastal defences; on 4 May, the German forces opposing Field Marshal Montgomery's 21st Army Group surrendered at Luneburg Heath; on 7 May, all German land, air, and sea forces surrendered unconditionally, the cease-fire to be effective at 2300 hours on 8 May; the final instrument of surrender was signed at Berlin late on V-E Day.

Everyone at Trenton joined the rest of Canada, and most of the world, in the celebrations of V-E Day, on 8 May.

Canada, like all the Allied nations, paid a heavy price for victory. Of the million who served, 40,042 died, and 54,414 were wounded. Air force casualties were disproportionately high. From 10 September 1939 to the end of hostilities in 1945, RCAF aircrew fatalities totalled 16,953, more than half of them in the Allied Bomber Offensive, in which 44,573 British and Commonwealth airmen lost their lives.

■ ■ ■

Although the European war was over, the war with Japan in the Pacific was not. Plans were made to form a "Tiger Force" of eight RCAF heavy bomber squadrons for participation in the Pacific campaign. Accordingly, eight Canadian squadrons flew home across the Atlantic with 165 Canadian-built Lancaster X bombers.

For Tiger Force recruitment, the Air Force issued a memorandum calling upon trained aircrew to volunteer for the Pacific campaign. For those of us who had recently returned from a long period of operations in Europe, this request posed a dilemma. We knew there were enough trained aircrew in Canada who had not seen operational service to satisfy the demand, and most of us thought that they ought to be the ones to volunteer.

In my own case, when the issue arose I felt that I had to make some kind of statement to clear the air. My immediate superior was Group Captain Walter Kennedy, the senior personnel staff officer, and I made my case to him, pointing out that I was recently married, that I had served two-and-a-half years overseas, one year of which was on Bomber Command squadrons, and I would find it hard to tell my wife that I was now volunteering to take off for the Pacific war. Not, I added, that I would refuse the duty if ordered. At the same time, I felt it was someone else's turn.

The group captain agreed, and explained that the request was directed more to the trained but untried aircrew in Canada than to the veterans.

The war in the Pacific ended before the squadrons could be re-equipped with new Lincoln bombers, as had been intended. All eight squadrons were disbanded in September.

On 14 August, Japan accepted the terms of the Potsdam Declaration of 26 July, agreeing to unconditional surrender. On 2 September, V-J Day, Japan officially signed the terms of surrender.

I had been promoted to flight lieutenant, and it was in this rank that I celebrated the end of hostilities.

My six-year Odyssey was over!

EPILOGUE

We few, we happy few,
we band of brothers.
— SHAKESPEARE, *KING HENRY THE FIFTH*

THE TORONTO BRANCH OF THE AIRCREW ASSOCIATION of Great Britain has a membership of 300, and our meetings rarely see less than 160. But being in the twilight of our years, each month at least one member is called to his "last posting." If we do not recruit younger, post-war aircrew members, in the near future the last member will turn out the lights.

Most members are veteran pilots, navigators, wireless operators, or air gunners of the Second World War air operations with RCAF or RAF squadrons. A great many are survivors of Bomber Command.

Our meetings begin with a minute's silence while the chairman recites Lawrence Binyon's poem:

They shall grow not old, as we that are left grow old:
Age shall not weary them, nor the years condemn.
At the going down of the sun and in the morning
We will remember them.

As I stand there, my thoughts are of those comrades I knew so well who did not come home. I know that the solemn figures around me have the same thoughts, and are wondering, as I am, why we were spared. We are grateful, but there is a trace of guilt; we have no answers. Our survival cannot be attributed to any divine guidance; to do so would be to imply that we were more worthy of saving.

Those of us who stayed on in the service were not as able as those veterans who returned to civilian life to put wartime memories behind us. We were still surrounded by uniforms and aircraft, and it wasn't long before we were again flying armed aircraft, this time in the Cold War as part of the North Atlantic Treaty Organization.

Like other veterans, I have tried to make the most of the time given to me, and life has been bountiful. Not only did I have a long, rewarding air force career, and a second mini-career with the Ontario government, I have been blessed with a loving partner, and with a son, Robert, and a daughter, Margaret.

Bill Dixon, my former pilot and captain, became a successful businessman after the war. He is well, and living in retirement with his wife, Ruth, in Brampton, Ontario. They have three sons. It is a joy to be able to meet frequently with this man with whom I share so many memories.

We have lost touch with our former crew members, except for Tony Carroll, our front gunner, who lives in Northampton, England, and with whom we correspond. I have also visited Ted Crosswell of my first crew, and his wife, Lily, in London, England, and they have made one trip to Canada to see us. Peter Mayhew, captain of the "eccentric crew" at Kabrit, also corresponds regularly with Bill Dixon from England.

In 1993, at a reunion of 148 Sqn, held at RAF Marham, seven of us "mutineers" met again, along with "Turkey" Rainsford, our squadron commander at the time of our 1942 rebellion. One of the group was Dudley Egles, the navigator who walked home after two weeks in the desert, and who authored a memoir, *Just One of the Many*.

After the war, during which he was shot down three times, escaped from a prisoner-of-war camp in Romania, and completed two tours of bomber operations, Dudley worked as a teacher in Essex before becoming headmaster of a school in Uganda. He was imprisoned by Idi Amin, but was released. He returned to England to continue teaching. Dudley died in April 1998 and was given a guard of honour with RAF colours in tribute. His wife, Eileen, now lives in Chichester, England, and stays in touch.

Two years ago, I was reunited for the second time with Jack Kelly, my old high school chum and desert companion, and we enjoyed each other's company at our Aircrew Association meetings until his death on 18 February 1999.

■ ■ ■

It is true that war brings out the best and the worst in man, but although we veterans of the air war celebrate the bonds that the challenges of operational flying created, we are deeply conscious of the horrors of war as we have seen it. One writer observed, "The horror of war is absolute. The guilty, although deserving of it, are just as dead as the innocent."

Survivors of Bomber Command, as proud as we are of the part we played, are humbled by words such as those of Marshal of the Royal Air Force Sir John Slessor when he pondered the costly attacks that left such an indelible imprint on the horrors of the two world wars:

> *The compulsions of 1915 and 1940 produced two of the most unbeliev-able manifestations of human courage and endurance in the history of war — the infantry of 1914–1918 and the bomber crews of 1939–1945.*

I have never considered myself a brave man. But I was put into the company of brave men, and I could not very well let them down.

I don't believe I did.

BIBLIOGRAPHY

Bercuson, David J. *Maple Leaf Against the Axis*. Toronto: Stoddart, 1995.

Bishop, Edward. *Wellington Bomber*. New York: Ballantine, 1974.

Bomber Command Association Newsletters. London: RAF Museum, London, quarterly.

The Bomber Harris Trust. *A Battle for Truth*. Toronto: Ramsay Business Systems, 1994.

Bowyer, Chaz. *The Wellington Bomber*. New York: William Kimber, 1986.

Bryant, Arthur. *The Turn of the Tide*. London: Doubleday, 1957.

Deighton, Len. *Battle of Britain*. London: George Rainbird, 1980.

Dunmore, Spencer. *Wings for Victory*. Toronto: McClelland & Stewart, 1994.

Dunmore, Spencer, and William Carter. *Reap the Whirlwind*. Toronto: McClelland & Stewart, l997.

Egles, Dudley. *Just One of the Many: A Navigator's Memoirs*. Durham: Pentland Press, 1996.

Fraser, David. *Alanbrooke*. London: Collins, 1982.

Gilbert, Martin. *Road to Victory: W.S. Churchill 1941–45*. Toronto: Stoddart, 1986.

Hamilton, Nigel. *Monty: The Making of a General, 1887–1942*. London: Hamish Hamilton, 1981.

Harris, Sir Arthur. *Bomber Offensive*. Toronto: Stoddart, 1990.

Hart, B.H. Liddell. *History of the Second World War*. New York: G.P. Putnam's Sons, 1970.

Hastings, Max. *Bomber Command*. New York: The Dial Press, 1979.

Heinl, Robert Debs, Jr. *Dictionary of Military and Naval Quotations*. Annapolis: USNI, 1966.

Hewer, Howard. RCAF Observer's and Air Gunners Flying Logbook, 1940–1966.

Horne, Alistair. *MacMillan 1891–1956*. London: Macmillan, 1988.

Irving, David. *The Trail of the Fox*. New York: Clark, Irwin, 1977.

Jackson, W.G.F. *The Battle for North Africa, 1940–43*. New York: Mason/Charter, 1975.

Judd, Denis. *The Boer War*. London: Granada, 1977.

Kennett, Lee. *The First Air War: 1914–1918*. New York: Collier Macmillan, 1991.

Lacey, Robert. *The Kingdom: Arabia and the House of Sa'ud*. New York: Harcourt Brace, 1981.

Langeste, Tom. *Words on the Wing*. Toronto: CISS, 1995.

Lucas, James. *War in the Desert: The Eighth Army at El Alamein*. New York: Arms, Armour, 1982.

Lucas, Laddie. *Wings of War*. London: Hutchinson, 1983.

Middlebrook, Martin, and Chris Everitt. *The Bomber Command War Diaries*. Harmondsworth: Viking, 1985.

Milner, Marc. *North Atlantic Run*. Toronto: University of Toronto Press, 1985.

Moran, Lord. *The Anatomy of Courage*. Boston: Houghton Mifflin, 1967.

The Official History of the Royal Canadian Air Force, Vols. I–III. Toronto: University of Toronto Press. DND Canada, 1980-86-94.

The Oxford Dictionary of Quotations. London: Oxford University Press, 1955.

Pakenham, Thomas. *The Boer War*. New York: Random House, 1979.

Peden, Murray. *A Thousand Shall Fall*. Stittsville: Canada's Wings, 1981.

Peniakoff, Vladimir, Lt. Col. *Popski's Private Army*. New York: Nelson Doubleday, 1980.

Richards, Denis. *The Hardest Victory: RAF WWII*. London: Hodder, Stoughton, 1994.

Sadat, Anwar el-. *In Search of Identity*. New York: Harper and Row, 1978.

Silver Jubilee (RCAF Logbook) RCAF 1924–1949. Ottawa: Air Historical Section, 1949.

Speer, Albert. *Inside the Third Reich: Memoirs*. New York: Macmillan, 1970.

Stewart, John D. *Gibraltar: The Keystone*. Boston: Houghton Mifflin, 1967.

Strawson, John. *A History of the S.A.S. Regiment*. London: Secker and Warburg, 1984.

Terraine, John. *The Right of the Line: RAF 1939–45*. London: Hodder and Stoughton, 1985.

Tute, Warren. *The North African War*. Toronto: Griffin Press, 1976.

van der Vat, Dan. *The Atlantic Campaign*. New York: Harper & Row, 1988.

Walder, David. *Nelson: A Biography*. New York: The Dial Press, 1978.

World Atlas. New Jersey: Hammond Inc., 1997.

INDEX

Aberdeen, 85
Abu Sueir, 191, 219
accommodations. *See also* billets; hotels
  at ALGs, 145, 147, 177
  civilian, 85–86
  at convalescent depot, 193–94
  in Halifax, 24
  in hospitals, 109, 189–91
  at Kabrit, 135–36, 151–52, 168
  on ships, 24, 223, 227
  at training schools in Canada, 5, 7–8,
    12, 19–20
  at training schools in England, 35,
    39–40, 237
  at Warrington, 244
  in Western Desert, 207–8, 213, 215
ack-ack guns. *See* guns, anti-aircraft
Admiralty, British (Mediterranean HQ),
  116
Admiralty Arch, 32
Advanced Landing Grounds. *See* ALGs
Aegean Sea, 181
Afrika Korps, 137, 179, 207, 209
  defeat of, 221
  victories of, 129, 196
Agedabia, 147, 158
Aircobra (P39), 105
aircraft
  Anson, 40
  Beaufighter, 41, 162–63
  Bell Aircobra (P39), 105
  Blenheim bomber, 48n
  confiscation of, 181
  damage to, 114
  dangers of, 20, 21–22

Fairchild K24, 16
Fairey Battle, 20
Fiat CR42, 121–22
Gloster Gladiator, 122n, 197
Halifax bomber, 41n, 42, 240, 249
Hampden, 90
Heinkel III bomber, 187
Henschel biplane, 93–94
Hornet Moth, 239
Hudson, 201
Hurricane, 214, 221
Junkers 88, 40–41, 54, 64, 139, 180,
  192
Lancaster bomber, 41n, 42, 240, 249,
  250
Lincoln bomber, 250
Lysander bomber, 237
Me 109, 57
Me 110, 54
Norseman, 16
operational problems with, 104,
  164–65, 176
Spitfire, 214
Stirling bomber, 41n
Swordfish, 236n
Whitley, 90
aircraft engines, 42. *See also specific*
  types
Aircrew Association of Great Britain,
  Toronto Branch, 253–54
aircrews. *See also* gunner; navigator;
  pilot; wireless operator
  confusion with propellers of, 201–2
  equipment of, 61, 177
  formation of, 44–45, 56

losses of, 250 (*see also under* losses)
prejudice against by regular NCOs, 46, 151
relationships within, 78, 99, 183, 188
trades in, 22, 41n
air raids, enemy
  on airfields, 123, 187–88
  in London, 26, 29, 32–34
  in Malta, 123, 180–81
  at Suez, 206
air-raid shelters, 87, 88, 123
"airscrews," 201–2
airstrips, desert, 214, 217n. *See also* ALGs; RAF stations
air traffic control, 47–48
Alanbrooke, Lord. *See* Brooke, Gen Sir Alan
Aldis lamp, 13, 47, 230, 232
Algiers, 120
ALGs (Advanced Landing Grounds)
  ALG 09, 160, 162, 164
  ALG 060, 147
  ALG 075, 147, 149
  ALG 106, 177, 181
  poor conditions at, 145, 147, 177
Allied Bomber Offensive, 250
Almanzora, HMS, 227–29
altitude training, 7, 8
Americans, 189, 246. *See also* U.S. Air Force
  accidental shooting down of, 104–5
  approach to cowardice of, 100
  in Britain, 37
  in RCAF, 9, 21, 124
Amiens prison, 31n
Amin, Idi, 254
The Anatomy of Courage (Moran), 99
Anderson shelter, 87
Anson aircraft, 40
apes, Gibraltar, 115–16
Arabs. *See also* Egyptians
  pro-Axis, 162n
  pro-British, 166, 213
armament officer, station, 59, 102
armoured corps, 189–90
armourers, 164, 165
Army, British. *See* British Army; Eighth Army
arrest, military, 154–55, 167
arthritis, 190–91
Astor, Lord and Lady, 109

Athens. *See* Salamis
Atlantic Ocean
  North, 231–33
  South, 228–31
Auchinleck, Gen Claude, 200, 210n
Australian Army, 129
Australians
  in Egypt, 128–30, 213–16
  prejudice against by British, 36
  in RAF, 36, 55, 73, 110, 142, 154, 156–57
  in RCAF, 15–16

B, Sgt, 106–7
  as aircrew member, 56–57, 63–64, 92–94, 103–4
  loss of nerve by, 69–70, 94–96, 97–98
Bagnold, R.A., 208–9n
Baird, Sqn Ldr, 136–37
Balinson, Alec, 124, 139, 180–81
barrage balloons, 59–60, 64
Barton, Jeff, 166
battledress, 37, 135
Battle of Britain, 14, 54
Battle of Jutland, 227
battleships
  Bismarck, 25, 26n
  Gneisenau, 26n, 57, 236n
  HMS *Malaya*, 114
  HMS *Rodney*, 25–26
  Prinz Eugen, 57, 236n
  Scharnhorst, 26n, 236n
BBC, 79
BCATP. *See* British Commonwealth Air Training Plan
beat frequency oscillator (BFO), 13
Beaufighter, 41, 162–63
Beau Hunks, 222
Bedford Basin, 24
Bell Aircobra (P39), 105
Belleville, 248, 249
Benghazi, 138, 160–61, 179, 206
Berlin, 90–94, 95
Bessie (nurse), 88–89, 101, 121, 235–37
BFO (beat frequency oscillator), 13
billets, 54–55, 225. *See also* accommodation; hotels
Binyon, Lawrence, 253
biplanes, 93–94, 121–22
Birka district, 130
Bishop, Billy, 4

Bitter Lakes, 136, 152, 169–70, 191. *See also* Kabrit
Black and Tans, 79n
blackout, 28
Blatz, Dr. William, 29–30n
Blenheim bomber, 48n
Bligh, F/S, 12, 15
Blitz, 87, 91n. *See also* London, air raids in
boats, 168–70. *See also* ships
Boby, Robert, 31
Boers, 225–26
Boer War, 23, 224–26
Bofors 40mm gun, 188
bomb aimer, 22n, 41n, 42, 63. *See also* navigator
bombardier. *See* bomb aimer
Bomber Command, 80, 236n, 240
  Headquarters, 70
  Middle East (*see* Middle East Bomber Command)
  No. 3 Group, 54
  No. 4 Group, 90
  No. 6 RCAF Group, 80n, 99–100, 249
  RCAF squadrons in, 80
  veterans of, 253
Bomber Offensive (Harris), 226n
bombers. *See also specific types*
  German, 187–88
  U.S., 43
bombing
  area, 80, 91n
  bomb loads for, 42, 145, 164n
  low-level, 163
  moral issues of, 77, 91n, 159
  of own troops, 193–94
  photographing, 173–74, 183
  procedures for, 59, 70, 80
  training in, 19–22
bombing raids
  Agedabia, 147–49, 158–59
  Benghazi, 159–60, 163–66, 170–71, 176–77, 188
  Berlin, 90–94, 95
  Brest, 57
  cancellations of, 92, 97
  Cologne, 57, 69
  by Dam Busters, 41n
  Karlsruhe, 102, 239
  Le Havre, 58
  Leros, 181–83

Magdeburg, 91, 94–95
Mannheim, 58, 90
Nickel, 90
over Germany, 249
preparations for, 58–64, 67–68, 101–3
procedures for, 60–64
Ruhr valley, 58, 66, 90
Salamis, 144, 147
Tymbaki, 171, 173–75
bomb-line, 194
bombs
  250-pound, 59, 61, 67
  4,000-pound (cookies), 145, 162, 163–64, 172, 173–74, 176–77
  delayed-action, 163–64, 176
  incendiary, 148, 165
  rodded, 147, 158
Boudreau, Guy, 31
Bournemouth, 27
boxing, 14–15
Brady, Chuck, 31
Brantford, 248
Brest, 26n, 57, 112, 236n
briefing officer, 117
briefings, bombing-raid
  for Mediterranean, 110, 116–17, 182
  for North Africa, 124, 137, 144–45, 163
  for northern Europe, 58–60, 66, 102
  wireless, 57, 60, 117
Brisbane, Alan "Bris," 139
Bristol Pegasus engine, 42, 107
British Army, 178, 189, 248, 249
British Commonwealth Air Training Plan (BCATP), 8, 27
bronchitis, 101–2
Brooke, Gen Sir Alan (Lord Alanbrooke), 200n, 217n
brothels. *See* prostitutes
Browning .50 calibre gun, 20, 43
Browning .303 machine gun, 20, 40, 41, 43, 62–63, 148
bubble sextant, 68
Burma, 221
Burr, F/S, 144
Burtch, 248
Butterfield, Jack, 139
Byron, Joe, 31

cadets, air, 249
Cafe de Paris, 33

Cairo, 127, 130–31, 177–78
Calderwood, Don, 31
Calgary, 13–14, 17–18
call signs, 60
Camp Borden, 249
Camp Retreat, 226–27
Canadian Army. *See also individual corps*
  air force rivalry with, 14–15
  British rivalry with, 116
  hospitals of, 109–10
  soldiers of, 84
Canadian Mounted Infantry, 225–26
Canadian National Exhibition, 4–5
Canadian National Railway, 11
Canadian Pacific Railway, 11
Canadian Red Cross, 109n
Canadians
  in Boer War, 23, 224, 225–26
  Canadianization of forces of, 8n
  prejudice against by British, 36, 116, 137, 167–68
  in RAF, 27, 36, 80, 237
Candia, 171–72
Cape Town, 225, 226–27
Capuccini Naval Cemetery, 181
Carroll, Sgt Tony, 108, 131
  as aircrew member, 148, 158
  as friend, 168, 232, 254
Casablanca Conference, 217n
casualties. *See* injuries; losses
Central Medical Board (1 CMB), 238
Chalmers, Jimmy, 124, 131, 139, 143, 181n
Charron, Art, 124, 139, 180–81
Chester, 245
Chinnery, Sgt Doug, 108, 156, 171
  as aircrew member, 121–22, 148, 158
  as friend, 115–16, 128–30, 168–70, 232
Christmas
  in Calgary, 18
  in Egypt, 140–43
  at sea, 229–30
Churchill, Winston, 116, 200n, 217n
Clarke, Brig Dudley, 210n
climate. *See* weather
Cliveden, 109n
clothing allowance, 240, 242
clubs, service, 83, 195–96
CNE, 4–5

Coach and Horses, 237
Coastal Command, 24n
code, international. *See* Morse code
codes, wireless, 60, 70, 117, 122
Cold War, 254
Cologne, 57, 69
Combe, Grp Capt A.R., 102, 105, 239
Comiso, 123, 180
commission (as officer), 18n, 238–40
communications. *See also* radio; wireless
  in aircraft, 21–22
compasses
  prism, 119–20
  sun, 209n
convalescence, 193, 194–95. *See also* leave, convalescent
convoys, 228–32. *See also* ships
Cook, Frank, 9, 11–12, 16–17, 21, 24
cookies (bombs), 145, 162, 163–64, 172, 173–74, 176–77
corvettes, 228, 230
coupons, ration. *See* rationing
courage, acts of, 165, 188. *See also* medals
Courageous, HMS, 3
courts martial, 190. *See also* LMF
Covent Garden, 29, 89, 109, 235, 240
cowardice. *See* fear; LMF
Cranwell Revolt, 36
crashes, aircraft, 204. *See also* emergency landing; losses
Crete, 171–75
crew. *See* aircrew
cricket, 9
Cronje, Gen, 225
Crossley, P/O, 147, 148–49
Crosswell, Lily, 87, 234–36, 240, 242
Crosswell, Sgt Ted, 49, 63, 98
  as aircrew member, 49, 63, 69–70, 92, 93–94, 103
  family of (*see* Crosswell, Lily; White, Mr. and Mrs.)
  as friend, 232, 234, 254
Currie Airfield, 16
Cutts, Sgt, 193
Cyrenaica, 129

Dam Busters, 41n
Darkie procedure. *See under* radio procedures

Davis, Cpl', 12n
De Aar, 225–26
dead reckoning. *See under* navigation
death. *See also* losses
  accidental, 143, 204
  terms for, 77–78
Debert, 23–24
debriefings, 63, 64, 74, 75, 95, 104, 149,
  165, 174
  radio, 64, 75
Deely, Ty, 14–15
desert. *See also* Western Desert
  English fascination with, 210–11
  equipment for, 221, 224
  survival in, 166, 192–93
Dick, Mr. and Mrs., 85–87
Didcot, 39, 110
Diégo-Suarez, 224
diet. *See* food
Dinant, 69
discipline, military, 105, 137n, 154–55,
  167, 190
  misuse of, 5–6, 99–100, 151–52,
  153–54
Dixon, Bill (Aylmer, Quebec), 181
Dixon, Mr. and Mrs., 247
Dixon, Sgt Bill, 106, 139, 180n
  as aircrew member, 111, 114, 119–23,
  158, 160, 172–75, 182–83
  as friend, 131, 153, 195, 232, 247, 254
djbels, 209
Dodecanese Islands, 181
Dominion Linoleum Company, 14n
Donohue, Carl, 31
Douglas, Howard, 139
drill
  rifle, 153–54
  training, 6–7
drinking
  as cause of accidents, 49, 110, 143
  on leave, 129–30
  in sergeants' mess, 79
driving
  adventures in, 203
  in the desert, 205, 207, 208–11, 216
  learning, 202–3
drogues, 21
duralumin, 41
Durban, 224–25
Dvorak, Ann, 29
dysentery, 187, 189, 190–91

Eder dam, 41n
Edinburgh, 83
Egles, Dudley "Pop," 166, 254
Eglinton Hunt Club, 7
Egypt. *See also specific places*
  alliance with Great Britain of (1936),
  131n
  poor treatment of crews in, 136–37,
  145, 147
Egyptian Army, 196–97
Egyptians, 129–31, 169–70, 187. *See
  also* Mahmoud
  anti-British feeling among, 178–79,
  196–97, 200
Eighth Air Force, U.S., 100
Eighth Army, British, 137, 144, 189,
  193–94, 200, 201, 210n, 212–14. *See
  also* El Alamein
Eisenhower jacket, 37
El Alamein, 179, 196, 197, 207, 221
  first battle of, 193, 200, 201
  second battle of, 156n, 221, 231
El Ballah, 193–94
El Faiyum, 124, 127
Elsan toilet, 42
Elstree Studios, 31
emergency landing. *See also* radio
  procedures, Darkie
  in desert, 192
  in Gibraltar, 114
  procedures for, 43–44, 60
  at West Malling, 72–73
Empire Air Training Scheme. *See* British
  Commonwealth Air Training Plan
Empress of Scotland, 246
Enfant, Pierre-Charles L', 131
Enfield .303 rifle, 205
Enfield .38 calibre revolver, 140, 205
engineer, flight. *See* flight engineer
engines, aircraft, 42
  Bristol Pegasus, 42, 107
  fires in, 103–4
  fuel systems of, 107, 119
  Hercules, 42
  Pratt and Whitney, 42
  Rolls-Royce Merlin, 42, 176
ENSA (Entertainments National Service
  Association), 194–95
entertainment. *See also* drinking;
  prostitutes; sports
  dances, 29, 88, 199–200, 240

films, 29, 31, 131, 132, 150
  radio, 80–81
  theatre, 29
erks, 60n. *See also* ground crew
Esmonde, Lt Cdr Eugene, 236n
Etickulous, Aristides, 178–79
Evans, Len "Wiz," 139
examinations (for commission), 238–39

Fairchild K24, 16
Fairey Battle, 20
Fall, Grp Capt J.S.T., 137, 152, 157, 167
Farouk I, King of Egypt, 131
Farrant, Tony, 166
fear. *See also* courage, acts of
  acts of, 190
  effects of on aircrew, 69–70, 94–96,
    97–98
  managing, 99
Fiat CR42 (aircraft), 121–22
fighters, German, 43. *See also specific*
  aircraft
fights, bar, 83–84, 129–30
films
  entertainment, 29, 31, 131, 132, 150
  training, 6
Findlay, Joe, 31, 38, 40, 124, 139, 181n
fires, engine, 103–4
Fisher, John, 139–40
flak, 63, 69, 112, 114, 148
  evasion techniques for, 70, 94, 158
  short-fused, 160, 164
flare chute, 42, 172–73
fleas, sand, 191
Fleet Air Arm, 201n, 236n
Fliegerabwehrkanonen. *See* flak
flight engineer, 22n, 41n
flying
  personal equipment for, 61
  risks of, 56
  and weather, 60
flying suits, 12, 61
food, 17–18
  Arab, 214–15
  civilian, 86, 238
  in Egypt, 142–43, 187
  in England, 55, 74, 78–79, 244
  in South Africa, 225, 226
Fort Lamy, 219n
Frankland, Noble, 91n
Frazer-Nash gun turret, 41, 42–43

Free Officers' Association, 196–97
Freetown, 231
FTR (failed to return), 70, 74
Fuka, 210n
Fuller, Sgt George, 98, 234
  as aircrew member, 62–65, 93, 105
  as friend, 45, 54–55, 58, 232

Galer, Bill, 221
Gazala, 190
GEE (signal system), 68, 103
Georgic, MV, 24–26
German forces. *See also* Afrika Korps
  attitude towards Italians of, 178–79
  in the Mediterranean, 117, 122, 123,
    124n, 171, 179–80, 182
Gestapo, 174
Gezira Sporting Club, 178
Ghurkas, 152
Giarabub. *See* Jarabub
Gibb, Grp Capt R.F. "Smiler," 248
Gibraltar, 112–14
Gibson, Wing Cdr Guy, 41n
Gieves and Company, 242
Givet, 68–69
Giza, 131, 206, 216
Gloria Hotel, 128, 130
Glorious Summer (Johnson and Lucas),
  88n
Gloster Gladiator, 122n, 197
Gosport tube, 21–22
Graviner switch, 59, 62, 64
Gray, J.B., 31
Green, Bob, 31
Greenhill, F/O Cedric, 40
Greenock, 26, 232
Groppi's, 131, 178, 221
ground crew (erks), 81
  at ALGs, 145, 147, 164
  contributions of, 67–68
Ground Instructional Section (GIS), 237
G-string (safety cable), 21–22
guerilla fighters, 210–11. *See also* LRDG
Guerin, Guy, 31
gunner, 41–42, 177, 231–32
  role of in bombing raid, 62–63
gunnery training, 19–22
guns. *See also specific makes*
  .50 calibre, 20, 43, 230
  20mm, 20, 43, 230
  40mm, 188

anti-aircraft, 32, 63, 117
anti-tank, 193
  hand, 140, 156, 205
  machine, 20, 40, 41, 43, 62–63, 148,
    188, 208, 210n, 231–32
  rifles, 6, 205
  tank, 193
gun turrets, 41, 42–43, 177

Halifax bomber, 41n, 42, 240, 249
Halifax explosion, 24
Hammersmith Palais (London), 29, 88,
    240
Hampden aircraft, 90
Harris, A/M Sir Arthur "Bomber," 80,
    91n, 226n
Harwell RAF station, 39–44, 110,
    111
Heinkel III bomber, 187
Heliopolis, 193
  airfield at, 203–4
  RAF hospital at, 195
Helwan, 220–22
Henchett-Taylor, F/L, 9
Henschel biplane, 93–94
Heraklion, 171
Hercules engine, 42
Hewer family, 3, 4, 11, 19, 23, 247
Hewitt, Ike, 11, 31
Hillman sedan, 202–3
Hispano-Suiza 20mm cannon, 20
hockey, 15–16
Holcombe, Frank "Hokie," 30–31
Holland, 68–69
Holland-America Lines, 222–24
homecoming, 247
Hornet Moth, 239
horseback riding, 16–17
hospitality. See also White, Mr. and Mrs.
  in Calgary, 14, 18
  in Scotland, 85–87
hospitals
  5 CGH (Taplow), 109–10
  13th General Hospital (Suez), 189–91
  Ottawa Civic, 247
  RAF (Heliopolis), 195
hotels
  Gloria, 128, 130
  Hurricane House, 195–96, 198–200,
    218–19, 220
  Regent Palace, 29

  Shepheard's, 131
  Tin Hat, 178–79
Houston, Gord, 11
Howell, Sgt, 20
Hudson aircraft, 201
Humphries, Harry, 11, 31
Hurricane aircraft, 214, 221
Hurricane House. See under hotels
Hyde, Ken, 31
Hyde Park, 89, 101
hysteresis curve, 13

Ian (Australian soldier), 128–30
Ibn Sa'ud, Abdul-Aziz, King of Saudi
    Arabia, 162
Identification Friend or Foe. See radio
    procedures, IFF
IF circuit, 13
illness
  arthritis, 190–91
  bronchitis, 101–2
  dysentery, 187, 189, 190–91
  sand-fly fever, 187, 189
  tuberculosis, 24
  typhoid fever, 109
Imperial Order Daughters of the Empire
    (IODE), 225
Indian Ocean, 224
Initial Training School (ITS), 7
injuries
  accidental, 20, 21, 109, 173–74, 246
  during operations, 70–73, 193, 194,
    211, 218
inoculation, 4–5, 24
In Search of Identity (Sadat), 196–97
insignia, 16, 22, 225, 248
instruction, 237, 240, 241–42. See also
    screen pilots; training
intelligence. See also debriefing; LRDG
  gathering, 174, 208
intelligence officer, 73, 102
Ireland, 48, 79n
Ireland, Harvey, 23, 238
Ireland, Percy, 23, 224, 225
Ismailia, 102n, 152, 169-70, 193
Italian Air Force, 121–22
Italian forces
  in Axis, 124n, 137, 178–79
  in North Africa, 211–12, 214
  as prisoners-of-war, 132–33, 152–53,
    227

Jambles, Sqn Ldr E.A., 238, 239n
Japan in the Second World War, 127,
    129, 221, 246, 250–51
Jarabub, 212, 214
Jarvis, 19
Jenkins, Tony, 196
Johannesburg, 225
Johnson, Johnny, 88n
Johnson, "Snake Hips," 33
Junkers 88, 40–41, 54, 64, 139, 180, 192
justice, military. See discipline, military
Just One of the Many (Egles), 166n, 254

Kabrit RAF station, 127–28, 134–37
    "mutiny" at, 153–57, 167–68
    poor treatment of aircrews at, 136–37,
        150–52
Kano, 219n
Keenan, "Mad Joe," 139
Kelly, Jack, 221, 224, 225–27, 230, 237,
    255
Kennedy, Grp Capt Walter, 250
Khamseen (sand storm), 170
Khartoum, 219
King, Hon. William Lyon Mackenzie, 8n
King's Lynn, 54, 55
Kirkpatrick, Wing Cdr, 58–59
Kiwi Club, 196
Knights of Saint John, 124

Lagos, 219n
lakes
    Bitter, 136, 152, 169–70, 191
    salt, 145
La Linea, 112, 115
Lamb, Major, 4
lamp, Aldis. See Aldis lamp
Lancaster bomber, 41n, 42, 240, 249,
    250
landings, emergency. See emergency
    landings
Langley, P/O, 45, 49, 56
Laurel and Hardy, 222
Lavines, 6
leadership, 150–52, 155
leave
    in Cairo, 128–31, 177–78
    in Calgary, 16–17
    convalescent, 191
    embarkation, 22–23, 247
    in King's Lynn, 81

in London, 28–31, 87–89, 101, 240
in Scotland, 83–87
Le Havre, 58
Leros, 181
letters
    from British Government to Arabs,
        140–41
    to home, 142
Lewis machine gun, 188, 208, 231–32
Libya, 221. See also specific places
Liddell, Alvar, 79
life preservers, 61, 111
Lincoln bomber, 250
liners. See under ships
Lloyd, WO Waitiri, 156
LMF (Lack of Moral Fibre), 99–100
logbook, wireless traffic, 60, 64, 73–74
London. See also Underground, London
    air raids in, 26, 29, 32–34, 87
    wartime, 28–30, 87n, 242–43
Long Range Desert Group. See LRDG
loop bearings, 92–93, 95
losses
    of aircraft, 79, 95, 114, 176, 180–81,
        188, 204
    broadcasting of, 79
    of comrades, 70, 74, 95, 166, 176–77,
        180–81, 188, 235–36, 250, 253–54
    effect on morale of, 79–80
LRDG (Long Range Desert Group), 166,
    208, 212–13
Lucas, Laddie, 88n, 91n
Luftwaffe, 91n
Luneburg Heath, 249
Luqa, 123–24, 180
Lynn, Vera, 81
Lysander bomber, 237

Mabel (WAAF clerk), 240–41
machine guns
    Browning .303, 20, 40, 41, 43, 62–63,
        148
    Lewis, 188, 208, 231–32
    Vickers, 20, 40, 210n
MacKay, Maj-Gen, 129
Madagascar, 224
Madoc, 249
Mae West. See life preservers
Mafeking, 225
Magdeburg, 91, 94–95
magnetic course (QDM) procedure, 46

Mahmoud (batman), 195–96, 205, 218–19, 220
Mahood, John, 164–65
Maiduguri, 219n
"Mail Run." *See* Benghazi
Malta, 117, 180
  German attacks on, 122–24, 179
Mannheim, 58, 90
Maoris, 156
maps, use of
  in briefings, 58–59
  for escapes, 140
  for navigation, 61, 148
Marham RAF station, 53–55, 239, 254
Martin, R.B., 31
Massey, Grp Capt Denton, 7, 245–46, 247–48
Massey, Rt. Hon. Vincent, 7n
Maureen (nurse), 88–89, 101, 235–37
Mayer, Sgt Len, 98, 234–35, 236
  as aircrew member, 61–64, 69–72, 103, 104
  as friend, 44–45, 49, 54–55, 108–9, 232
Mayhew, Sgt Peter, 135–36, 139, 254
  as aircrew member, 139–40
McDonald, Don, 8
medals, 247, 249
  Distinguished Flying Medal, 175
  Distinguished Service Order, 155n
  George Cross, 180
  Malta George Cross Fiftieth Anniversary Medal, 180n
  Military Medal, 189
  Victoria Cross, 236n
medical boards, 191, 238, 241
medical care, 24, 75, 109, 238. *See also* convalescence; hospitals; inoculation
Merlin engine, 42, 176
Mersa Matruh, 124
mess
  officers', 244
  sergeants', 78, 136, 151
Messerschmidts
  Me 109, 57
  Me 110, 54
meteorological officer, 60, 102
Middle East Air Force, 127, 156, 198. *See also* Middle East Bomber Command
  33 Squadron, 221

No. 5 Aircraft Delivery Unit, 219
Middle East Bomber Command, 127–28, 150
  37 and 38 Squadrons, 132, 159
  70 Squadron, 132, 159
  104 Squadron, 188
  108 Squadron, 191
  148 Squadron, 127–28, 163, 237, 254
  205 Group, 128
MID (Mentioned in Despatches), 175
Miller, Andy, 14–15
Miller, Max, 81
Mohne dam, 41n
moles (breakwaters)
  at Benghazi, 160, 163, 177
  at Gibraltar, 114
Montgomery, Lt-Gen Bernard Law "Monty," 131, 200, 221, 231, 249
Moran principle, 99
Morse, Samuel, 12n
Morse code, 12–13
Mountain View, 242n, 248
Munroe, Sgt, 45, 65
Mussolini, Benito, 132
"mutiny," Kabrit, 153–57, 167–68

NAAFI (Navy, Army, and Air Force Institute), 67
Nasser, Gen Gamal Abdel, 131n, 196
navigation. *See also* navigator; wireless operator
  dead reckoning (DR), 71, 209n
  equipment for, 68, 119–20, 209n
  with GEE, 68, 103
  loop bearings in, 92–93, 95, 148
  over desert, 147–48
navigation officer, squadron, 59
navigator, 41–42
  role of in bombing raid, 61, 62–64, 68, 103
  training of, 22
Navy, Army, and Air Force Institute (NAAFI), 67
Netherlands, 68–69
New Zealanders
  in Maori 28th Battalion, 156
  in RAF, 165n
  in RCAF, 15–16
  in Women's Auxiliary forces, 196
Nickel raids, 90
Nieuw Amsterdam, 222–24

Norfolk (UK), 54
Norfolk (USA), 246
Norseman aircraft, 16
North Atlantic Treaty Organization
    (NATO), 254

OBOE (signal system), 68
O'Brien, Grp Capt Geoffrey, 9
observer. See navigator
Oddenino's, 29
Oerlikon cannon, 230
O'Malley, Sgt, 48
operational training units (OTUs),
    37–38, 237–38, 247
Operation Jericho, 31n
operation tour. See tour of operations
Ottawa, 247
OTU. See operational training units

Pacific campaign, 250–51
Pantelleria, 117, 121
parachutes, 21
parasites, 224
Parkdale Collegiate, 3, 4, 221
Pathfinder squadrons, 80
Patton, Gen George, 99
Pavilion theatre, 29, 30
pay, 16, 22
    RAF compared to RCAF, 37, 242
Payne, Sid, 139
Pearl Harbor, 127, 246
Pearson, Sgt Roy, 45, 49
Pegasus engine, 42, 107
Pennfield Ridge, 247
Pershore, 237–38, 241–42
Petts, F/L, 239
photography
    by author, 25, 83, 166
    of bombing raids, 173–74, 183
    studio, 131
The Physics of Blown Sand and Desert
    Dunes (Bagnold), 208–9n
Piccadilly Circus, 29
Piccadilly Commandos. See prostitutes
Pickard, F/L Percy Charles, 31
Pigden, Doris, 249
pilot
    and navigation, 68n, 102
    role of in bombing raid, 60–64
    screen, 43, 55, 144, 147
    training of, 22

Pitrichy, 85–86
plotting, 102–3. See also maps
Poirier, Wilson "Willy," 31, 38, 234–36
    as aircrew member, 92
    as friend, 67, 78, 88–89, 101, 108, 232
    reaction to stress of, 73, 89, 98, 100
Politia, SS, 25
Portman, Eric, 29
Post, Sgt, 21–22
postings, 219–20, 240, 248
Potsdam, 94
Potsdam Declaration, 250–51
Powell, Dick, 38, 40, 123
Power, Charles "Chubby," 202
POWs. See prisoners of war
Pratt and Whitney engine, 42
prejudice
    against aircrew by regular NCOs, 46,
        151
    against Canadians by British, 36, 116,
        137, 167–68
prism compass, 119–20
prisoners of war
    British, 254
    German, 152–53, 246
    Italian, 132–33, 152–53, 227
Pritchard, Sqn Ldr, 171n
promotion. See rank, author's
propaganda leaflets, 90, 171–73
prostitutes, 30, 178, 223–24
Pudney, John, 74

Qara oasis, 209, 216
Qattara Depression, 206–7, 208–9,
    216
QDM procedure, 46, 59
Queen Elizabeth, 231
Queen Mary, 231

radar, 59
radio. See also training, wireless
    use of in navigation, 62–64
radio procedures
    Darkie, 60, 72–73
    IFF (Identification Friend or Foe), 59,
        62, 64, 72
    QDM (magnetic course), 46, 59
    QDR bearings, 59
    ZZ landing approach, 43–44
radio sets
    Marconi R1154/T1155, 36, 61–62

T1082/R1083, 13, 181–82, 183
TR9F, 43–44, 59–60, 72–73
radio stations
  German, 93, 95, 117, 122
  RAF, 72–73
Rainsford, Wing Cdr F.F. "Turkey," 137,
  144, 155, 254
rank, author's
  Aircraftman 2nd class, 5
  Leading Aircraftman, 16
  Pilot Officer, 240
  promotions in, 22, 238–40, 242, 251
  Sergeant, 22
rationing, 78, 85–86
Rawlinson, Wing Cdr, 157, 168, 171
RCAF. See Royal Canadian Air Force
receivers. See radio sets
recreation, 16–17, 168–70. See also
  entertainment; sports
Regent Palace Hotel, 29
repatriation, 241, 244–47, 249
resistance forces
  in Crete, 174
  Dutch, 69
  French, 31n
Rhine River, 249
ribbons, campaign. See medals
The Right of the Line (Terraine), 74,
  124, 199n
Ritchie, Maj-Gen Neil, 210n
Robinson, P/O Trevor "Robbie," 108,
  232
  as aircrew member, 112, 119–22, 124,
  149, 168, 173–75, 182–83
Rockcliffe RCAF station, 247
Rodney, HMS, 25–26
Rolls-Royce Merlin engine, 42, 176
Rommel, Gen Erwin, 129, 147, 158,
  190, 191, 200, 210n, 217n, 221. See
  also Afrika Korps
Roncoroni, Wing Cdr J.A., 239
Rose, F/S Fred, 237
Ross rifle, 6
Royal Air Force (RAF). See also
  aircrews; Bomber Command
  9 Squadron, 221
  10 Squadron, 90
  25 Squadron, 48n
  115 Squadron, 54, 103n
  215 Squadron, 221
  218 Squadron, 54, 57, 239
  419 (Moose) Squadron, 236n
  603 Squadron, 88n
  617 Squadron, 41n
  attitudes to non-British troops in,
  36–37, 116, 137, 167–68
  Cairo transport facility, 201, 203–5
  Canadians in, 27, 236n
  Coastal Command (Mediterranean
  HQ), 116
  Harwell station, 39–44, 110, 111
  Marham station, 53–55, 239, 254
  No. 1 Personnel Reception Centre
  (PRC), 27
  No. 2 Repatriation Depot, 244–46
  No. 15 Operational Training Unit,
  39–44
  pay compared to RCAF, 37, 242
  Shallufa station, 128, 132–33
  Uxbridge station, 26–27, 233
  Warrington station, 240, 241, 244–46
  Yatesbury signals training school,
  35–38
Royal Artillery, 117
Royal Australian Air Force (RAAF), 36
Royal Canadian Air Force (RCAF)
  405 Squadron, 80
  basic training for, 6–7
  enlistment in, 4
  Initial Training School, 7–9
  London headquarters of, 242
  No. 1 Air Command Headquarters,
  249
  No. 1 Bombing and Gunnery School,
  19–22
  No. 1 Manning Depot, 4–5
  No. 2 Wireless School, 9, 12–16, 18
  No. 6 Bombing and Gunnery School,
  242n, 248
  No. 6 Group, 80n, 99–100, 249
  pay as compared to RAF, 37, 242
  postwar career in, 254
  recruiting for, 3–4, 5–6, 7
  Rockcliffe station, 247
  Staff College (Toronto), 29–30n,
  199–200n
  Trenton station, 249
  wireless training schools, 9, 12–16,
  18, 248
Royal Canadian Army Medical Corps,
  109n
Royal Canadian Corps of Engineers, 116

Royal Canadian Mounted Police, 6
Royal Flying Corps, 9, 201n
Royal Naval Air Service (RNAS), 137n,
  201n
Royal Navy, 26n, 224, 231. *See also*
  specific ships and types of ships
  altercations with sailors from, 83–84
  firing on own aircraft, 114
Royal Opera House. *See* Covent Garden
Royal Regiment of Artillery, 115
Royal Service Corps, 248
Ruhr valley, 58, 66, 90
Russell, Grp Capt, 12

S, Capt, 204–5, 206–13, 214, 216–17
Sadat, Anwar El-, 196–97
Salamis, 144
salt lakes, 145
saltpetre, 17–18
Salt's, 131, 178
Salvation Army, 83, 196
sand fleas, 191
sand-fly fever, 187, 189
Sand Sea, Libyan, 213
sand storms, 145, 170
SAS (Special Air Service), 209n, 210
Scarborough, "Marsh," 139
Scotland, 26, 46. *See also specific places*
  hospitality in, 85–87
Scott-Malden-Carter, A/V/M David, 88n
screen pilots, 43, 55, 144, 147
Seaforth Highlanders, 14–15
"Security" (Pudney), 74
Senussi Arabs, 166, 213, 214–15
service clubs, 83, 195–96
Service Police (SP), 6
sextant, bubble, 68
shadow roster, 48
shakedown flight, 57
Shallufa RAF station, 128, 132–33
Shepheard's Hotel, 131
ships. *See also* battleships; travel
  Dutch, 228
  Empress of Scotland, 246
  French, 228, 230
  German, 25, 26n
  HMS *Almanzora*, 227–29
  HMS *Courageous*, 3
  MV *Georgic*, 24–26
  Nieuw Amsterdam, 222–24
  Queen Elizabeth, 231

Queen Mary, 231
SS *Politia*, 25
shooting skills, 226
Sicily, 117, 121–23, 179
Sidi Haneish, 210n
Sidra, Gulf of, 159–60
Sierra Leone, 231
signalling lamps. *See* Aldis lamp
signals officer, 248
Sikhs, 192–93
Siwa Oasis, 206–7, 210n, 213–16
Slessor, Sir John, 255
snakes, 215–16
soldiers. *See specific armies*
songs, aircrew, 81, 138
South Africa, 224–28
South African forces, 224, 226
Spain, 112, 115
Special Air Service (SAS), 209n, 210
Spitfire aircraft, 214
sports
  boxing, 14–15
  cricket, 9
  hockey, 15–16
  horseback riding, 16–17
  swimming, 240–41
  wrestling, 54–55
Squadron Leader X, 29
St. Martin-in-the-Fields, 34
Stirling, Capt David, 210–11
Stirling bomber, 41n
strafing, 187–88
Stratford-on-Avon, 237, 240
Streeter, SWO "Louie the Rat," 151,
  153–54, 157, 187
stress. *See also* drinking; fear; fights
  caused by cancelled raids, 92, 97
  caused by danger, 89, 97, 177
  caused by losses, 79–80, 97, 177
  physical, 177
  relief of, 54–55, 56, 81
  suffered by ground crews, 68
submarines, 224. *See also* U-boats
Sudanese, 212–14
Suez Canal, 128, 136, 193
sulfa drugs, 189
surrender
  German, 249–50
  Japanese, 250–51
surveying, 214
Swordfish aircraft, 236n

Table Mountain, 227, 228
Takoradi, 219
tanks, 189–90
Taplow, 109
Target for Tonight, 31
Tedder, A/M Sir Arthur, 198–99, 199–200n
Tedder, Lady, 199–200, 204
Terraine, John, 74, 124, 199n
theodolite, 209n, 214
Tiger Force, 250
Tin Hat Hotel, 178–79
Tobruk, 128–29
toilet paper as weapon, 139
toilets in Wellington bombers, 42
Toronto Institute of Child Psychology, 29–30n
tour of operations, 80, 188–89
trades, aircrew, 22, 41n
Trafalgar Square, 32, 34
training. *See also specific training schools*
  basic, 6–7
  gunnery, 19–22, 242n, 248
  high altitude, 7, 8
  initial, 7–9
  operational, 39–44, 46, 237
  pilot, 22
  wireless, 9, 12–14, 18, 22, 35–38, 57, 237
trains. *See* travel
transit camp, 220–22
transmitters. *See* radio sets
travel
  by ship, 24–26, 222–24, 227–32
  by train, 11, 19, 82–83
Trenton RCAF station, 249
trighs, 209
Trinder, Tommy, 81
tube. *See* Underground, London
tuberculosis, 24
Tunisia, 221
turrets, gun, 41, 42–43, 177
typhoid fever, 109

U-boats, 3, 13n, 48n, 182
  attack by, 230
Underground, London, 28, 29
uniforms
  in Egypt, 132, 135, 221, 248
  officer, 240, 242
  RAF, 37

RCAF, 5, 6, 12, 14, 16
U.S. Air Force, 100, 104–5
Uxbridge RAF station, 26–27, 233

Valletta, 122–24, 179
V-E Day, 249–50
vehicles
  Ford truck, 205
  Hillman sedan, 202–3
  Humber station wagon, 206
  Jeep, 210n
venereal disease, 6, 189
Very pistol, 60
Vickers Aircraft Company, 41
Vickers machine gun, 20, 40, 210n
Victor Emmanuel II, King of Italy, 132
Vinall, WO Ian, 237
V-J Day, 251
Volunteer Reserve, 155–56

WAAF. *See* Women's Auxiliary Air Force
Wakeham, Sgt Norm, 135
Wallis, Barnes, 41
War Council, British, 90, 91n
Warrington RAF station, 240, 241, 244–46
The Wash, 54
Wavell, Gen Archibald, 129, 208n
weapons. *See* bombs; guns
weather. *See also* meteorological officer
  in Alberta, 15
  in Mediterranean, 120–21, 144–45
  in North Africa, 136, 159, 168, 170, 198, 207–10
  in Scotland, 26, 232
  at sea, 228–29, 231–32
Wellington bomber, 41–42
  flying conditions in, 61–62
  fuel system of, 107, 119
  Mk IC, 110
  Mk II, 42, 176, 181
  Mk X, 42
  structural strength of, 62, 74
Wesel, 249
Western Desert, 137, 140, 206–17. *See also* ALGs
West Malling, 73
White, F/S Al, 237
White, Mr. and Mrs., 87, 234–35, 236, 240, 242
White, Sgt Will, 108, 168

as aircrew member, 120
as friend, 168–69, 172–73, 232
White Lion, 235, 236
Whitley aircraft, 90
Wild, Jimmy, 166
Wilson, Sir Charles (Lord Moran), 99
Wimpy. *See* Wellington bomber
Windmill Theatre, 29
Wings of War (ed. Lucas), 91n
wireless operator, 41. *See also* training,
  wireless
  non-radio role of in navigation,
  119–20
  role of in bombing raid, 41, 60–64
  use of radio by in navigation, 46,
    71–73, 92–93, 95, 112, 122, 124, 148

wireless schools, 9, 12–16, 18, 35–38
Women's Auxiliary Air Force (WAAF),
  78, 240–41
  as ground crew, 67–68
  as wireless operators, 72–73
wrestling, 54–55

Yatesbury RAF training school, 35–38
Yom Kippur War, 136n

Zuider Zee, 69
ZZ landing approach, 43–44

ABOUT THE AUTHOR

Wing Commander T.W.H. (Howard) Hewer, CD, RCAF (retired), flew operations in Bomber Command during the Second World War as a wireless operator in 148 and 218 Squadrons. He has received the Queen's Coronation Medal, the Malta George Cross Fiftieth Anniversary Medal, and the Canadian Special Service Medal. Hewer lives in Toronto with his wife, Doris.